"Should be required reading for anyone who wants to make their second marital go-around work. It is a treasure chest filled with essential and practical information, guidance, instruction, case examples, and tools. I most appreciate how it gives voice to marriage number two's unique challenges, while connecting to the latest social-emotional trends, challenges, and even cultural shifts. Reading the book made me feel like I was getting advice from a best friend who just happened to be an expert in marriage and relationships."

ROSS ROSENBERG, MED, LCPC, CADC, CSAT
author of *The Human Magnet Syndrome: The Codependent Narcissist Trap*

"Second marriages often pose challenges more difficult than first marriages. In this wise and well-written book, therapist Terry Gaspard provides empathy and guidance for those seeking to overcome the predictable but often daunting obstacles that can occur. Save yourself a lot of time, headaches, and heartaches and read *The Remarriage Manual.*"

JOSHUA COLEMAN, PHD
psychologist, senior fellow, Council on Contemporary Families, and author of *When Parents Hurt* and *Making a High-Conflict Marriage Work*

"This practical, well-written manual provides sound advice, and addresses the challenging issues of remarriage. Using examples from interviews, Terry Gaspard identifies common issues for remarried couples. Sure to be helpful to couples planning on remarriage as well as those who are living in remarried families."

CONSTANCE AHRONS, PHD
author of *The Good Divorce* and *We're Still Family*

"If you're remarried, and hoping to stay that way, you and your spouse should make this book your bedtime reading. Drawing on research, clinical expertise, and her personal experience, Terry Gaspard lays out the most common problems vexing remarried couples and presents actionable steps to help them successfully navigate the complex terrain of marriage the second (or third) time around. I will be recommending this reader-friendly manual to all my remarried clients."

VIRGINIA GILBERT, MFT
author of *Transcending High-Conflict Divorce: How to Disengage from Your Ex and Find Your Power*

the Re-marriage manual

ALSO BY TERRY GASPARD

Daughters of Divorce:
Overcome the Legacy of Your Parents' Breakup
and Enjoy a Happy, Long-Lasting Relationship

Terry Gaspard,
MSW, LICSW

the Re-marriage manual

How to Make Everything Work Better the Second Time Around

sounds true
BOULDER, COLORADO

Sounds True
Boulder, CO 80306

Published 2020

Cover design by Jennifer Miles
Book design by Beth Skelley

Printed in Canada

Library of Congress Cataloging-in-Publication Data

Names: Gaspard, Terry, author.
Title: The remarriage manual : how to make everything work better the
    second time around / Terry Gaspard, MSW, LICSW.
Description: Boulder, Colorado : Sounds True, 2020. | Includes
    bibliographical references and index.
Identifiers: LCCN 2019023435 (print) | LCCN 2019023436 (ebook) |
    ISBN 9781683644071 (paperback) | ISBN 9781683644088 (ebook)
Subjects: LCSH: Remarriage.
Classification: LCC HQ1018 .G37 2020 (print) | LCC HQ1018 (ebook) |
    DDC 306.81--dc23
LC record available at https://lccn.loc.gov/2019023435
LC ebook record available at https://lccn.loc.gov/2019023436

10 9 8 7 6 5 4 3 2 1

To my husband, Craig, and my children,
Sean, Tracy, and Catherine,
who have given me the love, courage,
and inspiration to write this book.

Contents

Author's Note

my interest in studying remarriage and stepfamily life began with my own experience, because I was raised in a blended family consisting of three older sisters and a younger stepbrother. My passion for this topic grew after my own divorce in 1995, and my remarriage two years later. After watching my father and stepmother navigate the challenges of a second marriage successfully for over three decades, I assumed that I was well prepared. But after going through a tough period in my own remarriage, it became obvious to me that experience isn't always the best predictor of success in marriage. As a result, I began paying more attention to the issues that the remarried couples in my practice face and looked for books and resources to support them, so they could establish healthy, happy, and long-lasting relationships. Unfortunately, the books I found were either outdated or focused on issues with stepchildren rather than giving remarried couples practical tools to help them thrive.

When I decided to write this book, I supplemented my clinical and personal experience by interviewing dozens of remarried couples who I approached through my practice, website, and referrals from colleagues. Over a period of three years, I interviewed a hundred couples who had been divorced at least once, and at least one partner had been married at least twice. The average age of participants was 43. These interviews formed the basis for *The Remarriage Manual: How to Make Everything Work Better the Second Time Around*.

The couples quoted in the following pages were participants in that study, and the stories told here are profiles and composites based on real people. However, names and details have been changed to protect their privacy. Details about the locations of the interviews were altered in some cases as well, for the participants' protection.

Please note that this book is not meant to replace professional individual or couples therapy. Rather, it is intended to offer an in-depth chronicle of the joys and struggles of remarriage and stepfamily life and to provide concrete ways to improve and strengthen family relationships. For simplicity, the word *stepfamily* is often used in the book to denote both stepfamilies and blended families. In the end, it is my hope that couples reading this book will learn how to be present for each other, so they can heal from past relationships and create a truly loving and intimate bond that will endure the test of time.

Terry Gaspard, MSW, LICSW

Introduction
An Opportunity to Start Fresh

When couples begin a remarriage, the most frequent mistake they make is expecting that everything will fall into place and run on automatic. Love may be sweeter the second or third time around, but once the bliss of a newfound relationship wears off, the reality of joining two distinct worlds sets in. Different routines and parenting styles; financial issues; legal matters; relationships with ex-spouses, children, and stepchildren—all of this can chisel away at the closeness of the remarried couple. If you haven't established a strong connection and are unprepared to deal effectively with conflict and lack the tools to repair daily breakdowns in communication, you may end up pointing fingers at each other rather than being supportive.

For instance, Conner, 49, and Tara, 48, remarried for six years, take seats on opposite ends of the couch during their first counseling session with me. When I ask them about some of the challenges they've faced in their second marriage, Conner clarifies why he feels frustrated with Tara. He also explains that he still loves Tara very much and hopes that our meetings will shed some light on how to get back to feeling good about their marriage.

Conner speaks directly to Tara and puts it like this: "You seem to forget that I have to work long hours to keep us afloat. Since Michael was born three years ago, our budget is really tight. Of course I love all of the kids, but they're expensive. And I wish you'd stop comparing me to your ex. I know he betrayed you financially, but it doesn't seem like you're ever going to get over it."

Tara responds, "That's the problem. Our relationship always comes last. You don't think we have a problem even though I keep telling you how lonely I am. We haven't spent time together in over a month. It seems like you're always working, just like Gary did, and never have time for me and our family."

What is at the heart of this couple's disagreement? Like most remarried couples, they aren't really arguing about how often they have candlelit dinners. They're feeling emotionally disconnected and that has created conflict. Similarly, most of the couples I interviewed for this book were looking to restore intimacy in their relationship but didn't know where to begin. They were longing to rekindle the passion and emotional connection of their early days together, before the stressors of remarried life set in. One thing is certain: you can't return to the glory days. But you can most definitely learn to cherish each other again. This starts with intentionally choosing each other *daily* (more on this as we continue) and letting go of the expectation of a perfect partner who will meet all your needs!

HOW THIS BOOK CAME TO BE

At the age of 42, I endured a high-conflict divorce and two years later married the love of my life. I was hopeful and optimistic about marrying Craig, confident we were more emotionally and sexually compatible than I had been with my ex and better aligned in our values and aspirations. Life had certainly thrown me some curveballs before I met my second husband, but I still believed in marriage. He swept me right off my feet and proposed four months after we started dating. It would be a second marriage for both of us. He had been married and divorced ten years earlier and had no children. I had two children, ages 9 and 11, from my previous marriage. It may sound surprising, but Craig wanted to be a stepparent, and right away we also discussed having a child together. Having a new baby and starting a stepfamily made the first several years of our marriage busy and exciting.

Eight years in, our marriage was on shaky ground. We were dealing with myriad issues common to remarriage, including co-parenting with a former spouse, unresolved emotional baggage from our first marriages, financial stress, and different parenting styles. We were also dealing with jealousy, anger, and resentment around the competing needs of children and stepchildren and the expectations of in-laws. I assumed we would be one big happy family, but Craig still often felt like an "outsider" with my two biological children, and we hadn't truly learned how to nurture our intimate relationship.

We argued frequently, and for many years we were unable to understand the complex dynamics unfolding before us and support each other as loving, devoted partners. We drifted so far apart that we discussed separating. Thankfully we found an excellent marriage counselor and began healing. It took time, but we fell back in love and have learned to accept each other's differences, work through conflict, and repair our relationship after a dispute. We've been remarried twenty-two years and couldn't be happier.

Sadly, we're the exception.

According to experts, even though the majority of divorced people will eventually remarry, most of these marriages will fail due to the difficulties that remarried couples face building a relationship while adjusting to, and combining, existing families and complex relationship histories. Few couples understand at the outset how complicated and demanding remarriage is.

WHAT YOU'LL FIND HERE

If you've been looking for resources on remarriage, you've undoubtedly noticed that conventional books about marriage simply don't address the unique situations remarried couples face, and the current books available on remarriage tend to focus more on stepfamilies than on the remarriage itself. Many also take a religious view.

I wrote this book to fill a major gap in the literature. I can help set you up for a successful remarriage and/or bring back the joy if your remarriage has started to falter. The statistics work against you, but I am here to tell you that with intention and effort, you can make your remarriage work. It will take energy and determination, and I'll be here to support you.

In *The Remarriage Manual*, you'll find all kinds of stories about the problems remarried couples encounter, as well as solutions that work. I feature thirty-one couples who, like Tara and Conner, experience different degrees of emotional disconnection and trust issues. Reading about their struggles and triumphs, you'll be able to examine your own relationship and learn how emotional and sexual intimacy in your marriage is the absolute key to success. It is a means of expressing the profound love you feel for your spouse. When I use the word *intimacy*, I'm talking about a powerful expression of love infused with emotion (caring, empathy, excitement, pleasure), which allows partners to experience a deep sense of connection. This kind of bond cannot be taken for granted, and it doesn't just happen. It takes daily tending, and occasionally it takes some work.

HOW TO USE THIS BOOK

The Remarriage Manual looks at the ten challenges I see most often among remarried couples. Along with poignant real-life stories, I offer exercises with clear action steps specifically designed to be put to use immediately. Ideally this book should be read with your partner. However, you can benefit from reading it alone if you implement strategies and have your partner's support. Throughout the pages of this book, I use the word *remarried* to mean couples who were married to other people and are now married to each other. Sometimes reading the chapters and doing exercises will feel enjoyable and other times it will feel like pulling teeth.

The first chapter in our remarriage journey is about building a culture of respect, appreciation, and tolerance in your family through loving words and actions. The diagnostic tool in this chapter can help you assess your own and your spouse's strengths and weaknesses and points you to other chapters that address your areas of need. In chapter 2, you'll learn the action steps needed to make your remarriage a top priority, so you can beat the odds of divorce. Chapter 3 will offer tools, powerful real-life stories, and proven strategies to help you heal from emotional baggage and begin to love your partner in the here and now.

In chapter 4, we'll focus on the importance of being transparent and not keeping secrets about money, so you can have honesty, integrity, and financial security. Chapter 5 will help you overcome the trust issues that may be stopping you from being vulnerable and intimate with your partner. In chapter 6, you'll learn how to put your inhibitions aside and uncover the pleasures of a dynamic sex life by fostering emotional and sexual intimacy. You'll discover some of the common reasons why couples stop enjoying passionate sex such as the pursuer-distancer dynamic.

Chapters 7 and 8 will illustrate the dos and don'ts you'll need to communicate more effectively, curb defensiveness, and manage and recover from conflict through potent action steps. In chapter 9, you'll learn what you need to do to support each other in your newly created family. You read that right! You can adopt strategies that embody the mind-set of "we're in this together," so your children cannot divide and conquer. Embracing the role of a stepparent is one of the major challenges of remarried couples. The good news is that you can actually begin to create positive family memories and develop a stepfamily legacy right away with some wise planning of enjoyable activities and quality time together.

Finally, chapter 10 will show you the importance of apologizing and granting each other forgiveness so you don't harbor resentments that can pull you apart. Learning the best ways to offer your partner a sincere apology and ways to avoid ruining an apology will help you rid yourself of the toxic hurt feelings that hold you and your partner back from being vulnerable, connected, and emotionally and sexually intimate.

Whether you're thinking of remarrying and concerned about going the distance or you're already remarried and struggling, this book will provide the expert advice, practical tools, hope, and inspiration you need to build—or repair—a strong relationship foundation, avoid the most common mistakes remarrying couples make, and prevent challenges from becoming deal breakers. It will show you why it's so important to focus on cherishing and accepting each other rather than trying to change each other. The steps described in each chapter will help you and your partner create a shared vision for your remarriage, foster emotional closeness, and know how to recover quickly from hurt and miscommunication.

If you show up and do the work, you'll create a deeply trusting, loving, and sustainable relationship.

I

Build a Culture of Appreciation, Respect, and Tolerance

For many remarried individuals, coming out of an unhappy or adversarial marriage and going through a divorce makes them wiser and better able to appreciate a new partner who is cut from a different cloth from their ex-spouse. People will consciously pick a second husband or wife who shares their views of family, values, interests, and even their sense of humor. This intentional action can help set the stage for a culture in which family members appreciate each other for their unique qualities, enabling them to be less critical and defensive when conflicts arise. This is true for me and my husband, Craig. We met in our early forties and felt strongly that we wanted to carve out a marriage based on mutual respect and shared meaning rather than obligation and unrealistic expectations. For example, we share a love of the outdoors and community service and find great pleasure in gardening, hiking, and fundraising for nonprofit organizations. In contrast, my first husband and I realized early on that we were not compatible and didn't share the same interests or vision for the future, so we led separate lives. Our dream to create a loving home for our two children wasn't realistic because our emotional sensitivities, values, and personalities collided. After seventeen years, it became apparent that our attempts to change each other weren't working and that our irreconcilable differences had taken a toll on our once loving marriage.

Making a commitment to trust and appreciate Craig has strengthened my second marriage. My relationship with him is based on the premise that we choose each other every day, and we're dedicated to making time together a priority and treasuring it. No matter how hectic and busy our lives are, we never stop being curious about each other, and we strongly believe that lasting love requires nurturing. We adore our children and families more than words can say, but we love spending time together—to laugh, share, hang out, and cherish each other. We're true partners.

This is also the case for Erin and Ron, a remarried couple in their late forties who agreed to meet with me in their home for an interview. Theirs is an unusual love story filled with passion and longing. Erin cheerfully explains their romantic relationship in both high school and college, their subsequent marriages and divorces to others, and their unlikely, magical reunion.

Erin reflects, "It was amazing to find Ron over social media and to see that he was available after not seeing each other for almost twenty-five years. We were childhood sweethearts who went our separate ways in college, and then I found out online that he had moved home after his divorce. We had been living very different lives, had four kids between us, but the spark was still there."

After connecting over social media, Ron took a leap of faith and asked Erin for her phone number. It didn't take them long to rekindle their passion and realize that their friendship was still strong. After several months of dating, Erin and Ron felt confident that they were ready to make a commitment and say "I do" for a second time. Their seaside wedding took place with all four of their children and a gathering of over one hundred family and friends, there to celebrate Erin and Ron's belief in a remarriage based on acceptance, respect, and a profound understanding of each other.

Erin reflects on the difference between her first and second marriage: "It was a long time coming. I knew in my first marriage, right after having our first child, that we should part. But it took many years for me to convince my then-husband that we should divorce. In my first marriage, almost none of my needs were being met. But in this marriage, almost all of my needs are being met. And if we have an issue, we talk about it. With Ron, we're equals with work, responsibilities, emotional availability, and all other aspects. We are pals."

Many remarrying couples realize that they want a "partnership marriage" that will allow both people to develop and live in a conscious way that's respectful and not bound by traditions or outdated models. Both Erin and Ron describe their first marriages as high conflict, unsupportive, and lacking in acceptance and tolerance. In contrast, Erin and Ron work together as a team to support each other and view their relationship as something that's greater than either one of them.

Taking time to reflect on your first marriage can allow you to go into your second one with your eyes wide open and to appreciate each other for what you bring to the union, including love, passion, emotional baggage, children, relationships with ex-spouses and in-laws, and financial obligations. You no longer have unrealistic expectations of a perfect partner who will meet all of your needs because you realize we all have flaws. Instead, the two of you have each other's back, and rather than throwing each other under the bus when you're faced with difficulties, you face them together. For instance, one of Erin and Ron's biggest challenges has been co-parenting with Erin's ex-husband, Mark, who lives a few blocks away and plays an active role in raising their sons. It would have been easy for Ron to criticize Erin for giving in too much to Mark when he requested that their younger son, Cole, spend more time at his house. However, Ron chose to support Erin and saw her attempts to compromise with Mark as a way to encourage cooperation.

Navigating day-to-day life in their stepfamily was a struggle for Ron and Erin during their first year of marriage. In the beginning, Erin's two sons—Cole, 13, and Tommy, 15—were reluctant to accept a stepfather, a position influenced by their father's complaints about them spending too much time with Ron. Erin and Ron also had financial stress because Ron had difficulty selling his home in another state and they had to wait to purchase a home big enough for all four of them as well as Ron's two children who are in college and visit during the summer and during school vacations. However, Erin and Ron have weathered the storms of raising her two sons in a stepfamily, including communicating effectively with her ex-husband, and their romantic love and friendship have stayed strong.

Erin smiles and explains, "We appreciate each other every day and let each other know it! My appreciation for Ron comes from a place of admiring him for the way he treats [people], and his hobbies revolve around serving others. No one is perfect, and we have our ups and downs. Mark and I had little respect for each other in [our] marriage, and that's not an issue with my [marriage with Ron]. Mark made me feel that he never signed up for the kind of equal marriage that I wanted, so we argued a lot. Ron and I are on the same page and we're growing together."

COMBINING TWO DISTINCT WORLDS

Unlike couples in first-time marriages, or couples who grew up together like Erin and Ron, when people marry for the second time, they usually don't have the luxury of getting to know each other over an extended period of time. A remarried couple's courtship is often speeded up due to factors such as the age of the couple, loneliness, and eagerness to become a stepfamily—with all of its joys and challenges.

One couple I met with, Tamara and Calvin, said their courtship had a good deal of momentum and then they were blindsided by trust issues that surfaced for Tamara after they had been married a few years. Both in their early forties, they met through mutual friends and dated for only one year before getting engaged. Tamara was a single mom with two daughters and a son, and Calvin didn't have children. During their early courtship, Calvin made it clear that he wanted to speed up things so they could do their best to have a child of their own. Tamara was pleased that Calvin was eager to take on the role of stepparent because she found being a single mom daunting.

Tamara is a successful architect and enjoys spending time with her extended family. She was happy to accept the prospect of having another child in her early forties because she loves children and fell hard for Calvin, an accomplished musician and licensed massage therapist. They spent endless hours discussing the prospect of sharing household responsibilities and taking care of the children without considering other potential obstacles, such as the time constraints and the financial pressures of starting a new family and blending a younger child—their "mutual child"—with teenagers.

Tamara explains their mutual attraction and reason for getting married quickly: "It was instant magnetism when we met. Calvin is very strong, yet charming and sensitive. My kids loved him right away, and I could easily envision adding another child to our household. Besides, my kids were teenagers and so a much younger half sibling appealed to them. My son, who was thirteen at the time, hoped for a baby brother, and my girls were in their midteens and loved to babysit."

After dating for a year and being engaged only six months, Tamara and Calvin tied the knot and began the process of forming a new family. Meanwhile, Tamara set her sights on getting pregnant at the age of 42 and surprised everyone when she became pregnant with twins after only four months of marriage.

While most family members settled into a routine after a few months, Tamara experienced a difficult adjustment. She'd been accustomed to being a single parent and now felt the weight of Calvin's expectations for a substantial dinner most nights, the exhaustion of being pregnant with twins, and the complexities of helping her three children adjust to living with a new stepfather. While she loved Calvin, Tamara failed to consider how challenging being pregnant, a parent to three children, and working full-time would be. It wasn't at all like "playing house" with Calvin as she had envisioned. Tamara struggled to be vulnerable and show her disappointment with Calvin because she was fearful of rejection and another breakup.

Tamara reflects, "I actually never envisioned getting married again and was pleasantly surprised by the love I felt for Calvin and his willingness to take on me and my three kids. They're good kids, but like all teens, they can be a handful. Their dad got married and moved away when they were young, so they desperately needed a father figure but balked at a lot of Calvin's attempts to set limits and discipline them. At the same time, I work full-time, so my energy level can take a nosedive in the evening. Sometimes we just have too much going on."

If Tamara and Calvin had had the benefit of time alone to get to know each other's likes, dislikes, personalities, and preferences, it would have been easier for them to adjust to living in a stepfamily. Without a "honeymoon" period to get to know each other, Tamara and Calvin are discovering some things about each other that need to be worked out, such as Calvin's expectation of spending nights out performing music. Tamara is a loving, flexible wife, but she knows that it isn't going to work to have newborns in the house and Calvin out performing. Thankfully she's taken ownership of these issues, and she's spoken to Calvin about modifying his performing schedule so they can still enjoy family time together.

BLENDING YOUR PERSONALITIES AND ADJUSTING TO REMARRIED LIFE

Greg, 58, and Monica, 48, both professionals, have been remarried nine years and are childless. Both are successful in their careers but are dealing with emotional sensitivities from previous marriages. Greg is emotionally distant, and Monica craves more affirmation and closeness than he is comfortable giving. In the therapy biz, we call that a pursuer-distancer dynamic. After being recently divorced from their respective ex-spouses, they dated for two years before getting married.

As Monica puts it, "We were both so happy to have met after getting out of horrible first marriages. We were also aware that we both had flaws and would need to be accepting and work through our issues. Greg says I want too much togetherness; to me, it feels like he's trying to push me away. This creates tension in our relationship. But I love Greg and we both realize I'm usually just looking for reassurance and we won't always see eye to eye."

Truth be told, couples often tie the knot the second time around before they have healed from their first marriages. Statistics back up the fact that marriages entered into on the rebound are more likely to fail than ones where couples gradually get to know each other. People need time to heal from their first marriage or they risk selecting a partner too similar in characteristics to their ex-spouse. Put simply, they need to put these "ghosts from the past" in their proper place so that they can be fully available for a new relationship and the hurdles they'll face.

For example, Monica's first marriage ended abruptly when her ex-husband sent her a text message asking for a divorce. The split was sudden, unwanted, and traumatic. There was infidelity, both sexual and financial, and her feelings of abandonment and shock were severe. In fact, Monica's former spouse not only had a long-term affair but he also cleaned out their bank accounts.

Monica and Greg met just one year after her divorce, and even though she knew she hadn't healed from her prior marriage and sudden divorce, she recognized that he was someone she could be vulnerable with and share her innermost thoughts, feelings, and wishes. They became romantically and sexually involved over a period of many months and they didn't gloss over their differences. Instead, they discussed any concerns that came up fairly soon after they arose. Monica saw in Greg the kind of financial stability she craved, and Greg liked that Monica was a successful entrepreneur. They share many common values such as wanting to own several pets and not desiring to have their own children. However, they are open to adoption.

After a slow courtship and small wedding, they settled into a home that they purchased together. Monica recognized that she had trust issues from her first marriage and was able to talk about them when they arose. For instance, Greg tends to run late when returning home at the end of the day or meeting Monica for dinner or an event. Monica reflects, "I'm glad we took two years to get to know each other so I wasn't blindsided by Greg running late. I'm aware of my trust issues (from being betrayed by my ex) and when they're coming into play. I'm also aware that when Greg runs late, he's not doing it to upset me, and it doesn't mean he's being unfaithful. Since I trust him, I'm able to own my own issues and not make him feel awful or start an argument. We are also dealing with our different needs for intimacy."

Very few people enter a second marriage with the intention of punishing their partner for the mistakes of their former spouse. Nevertheless, if you were cheated on, it's easy to become jealous or controlling. If your ex-spouse spent all of your money and lied repeatedly, it makes sense that you would develop mistrust. It's easy to project the image of a savior onto a person who helps you see light and love again, but a new marriage cannot magically erase all of the pain of divorce.

However, it can give people an opportunity to make their union work in spite of tough terrain if they are aware of their vulnerabilities and hot-button issues.

For instance, ongoing conflict between former spouses can potentially undermine a second marriage if remarried partners do not maintain an open dialogue and set healthy boundaries on that relationship. Likewise, living in a stepfamily can feel like residing in a foreign country for some people. However, once they identify and understand the emotions and threats to their closeness, the remarried couple will be better able to support each other and be resilient, intimate partners who work together as a team. This is true for remarried couples who are childless, like Monica and Greg, as well as those who bring children with them from former marriages.

STEPFAMILY CHALLENGES

Raising children is not easy in any family, but for stepparents it is particularly difficult. Because of the complications that arise, chapter 9 will focus solely on this topic. Throughout this book, when I speak of stepfamilies, I'm referring to a family in which there is an adult couple in the household with at least one of the adults having a child by a previous marriage. Some couples are legally married; some are not. In some stepfamilies, only one parent has children, while in others both have children (a blended family). *Mutual child* is a term used to describe a child born to a remarried couple.

For instance, my daughter Catherine was born less than two years after Craig and I remarried. As an infant and young child, she enjoyed the love and adoration of two parents and two half siblings, but along the way Craig and I experienced stressors related to lack of time to spend with all three children and limited financial resources, especially when my older two children headed off to college. Craig and I both began working two jobs to try to keep up with the expenses, which left us with less time to spend with each other, our children, friends, and extended family members.

Experts agree that stepfamilies are becoming increasingly complex and there are many possible ways for them to handle custody and visitation schedules. This is especially true when both partners bring children from their first marriage and some even decide to have a mutual child. Throughout the following chapters, I will use the terms *remarried, stepfamily,* and *blended family* interchangeably to reflect the diverse experiences of the families in my study. However, the focus of this book is the remarried couple rather than children or stepchildren because adults set the stage for a strong family unit. They are the driving force of building a culture of appreciation, tolerance, and respect in the recoupled family.

BUILDING A CULTURE OF APPRECIATION

How do remarried couples foster appreciation among family members? The first step is to discuss values and expectations. A successful remarriage is not simply about staying together in good times and bad, in sickness and health, for richer and poorer. It's about doing the work of building, enhancing, and repairing the relationship to sustain and deepen it. Remarried couples must construct a foundation for their family identity that includes their past, present, and plans for their future if they hope to achieve a successful relationship that endures the test of time.

In order to foster appreciation in a remarried family, it's crucial to have realistic expectations of each other and of what a remarriage entails. These expectations are not just about appreciating the wonderful personality and unique qualities of your partner. They're also about recognizing that both you and your partner are imperfect. Accepting this is a key aspect of profound love. If you want a good relationship, you must accept your partner and realize that your second marriage can be so much better than your first one. The appreciation you have for your partner, as they are, is a cornerstone for building a culture of appreciation, respect, and tolerance for each other.

Even when we appreciate our spouse and family members, we often neglect to show it, which can lead our family members to feeling unappreciated, drained, and unhappy. We might think it, but we do not remember to say the words "thank you" out loud or give others a reassuring hug or pat on the back.

Forgetting to show appreciation is common in all types of relationships and changing it requires a radical shift in mind-set. Showing your partner appreciation through acts of kindness such as cooking a tasty meal, writing a romantic note, or sharing loving words and gestures might not come naturally, especially if you were raised in a family where people criticized one another. But your efforts to do so will make a world of difference.

Tara, a remarried teacher whom you met in the introduction, puts it like this: "I adore Conner and he's a great dad and husband, but he grew up in a family where praise was reserved for big accomplishments such as straight As in school or a raise at work. And since Conner isn't used to showing praise, I sometimes remind him to give the kids a hug when they do good things."

Partners who create a sense of an emotional safe harbor with each other have more resources to weather the storms of remarried life. They create a culture of unity and are able to face the stressors of a second marriage—complicated by dealing with stepchildren, former spouses, former and current in-laws, mid- and late-life challenges, and so forth. The idea is to express what you cherish about your partner when you catch them doing something thoughtful, such as watering the plants or cooking a meal. It's a good idea to express thankfulness. You might articulate your thankfulness by saying, "It makes my day when you make a home-cooked meal for us."

CREATING A RECOUPLED FAMILY THAT IS TOLERANT, FLEXIBLE, AND RESPECTFUL

One of the joyous aspects of a successful second marriage is that couples are grateful to have a fresh start and so recognize the newness in each day. They know the value of positive intentions, such as deciding to create a loving, resilient marriage. It makes a big difference when love, tolerance, and respect extend to all family members. You might not agree with someone, but it's important to show respect and to demonstrate flexibility and tolerance by your actions. This includes respecting ex-spouses and ex-in-laws who you might not be fond of and being open to entertaining your children's and stepchildren's friends so they feel it's okay to bring friends home. The values that you display to others, in spite of differences, will help create a loving atmosphere for everyone.

If you have loving and caring relationships in your family, you're more likely to have a warm atmosphere in your home. You demonstrate flexibility by sharing roles and responsibilities. A couple with a healthy relationship attempts to achieve a balance between predictable patterns of behavior (eating meals and watching certain TV shows) and the ability to adapt to changes in the schedule. For instance, flexibility is called for when your children or stepchildren arrive early from their other parents' home and are hungry and irritable.

If there's high conflict between family members, the overall atmosphere of your home will suffer. Have you ever gone to someone's house and felt a tension in the air? It's likely that you didn't feel comfortable in this environment. This is a common experience for half siblings and stepsiblings because they may feel like part-time visitors or guests in their own home. It's important to have an open-door policy for all family members and to keep on hand snacks and meals that are quick to heat up when kids and their friends come and go.

If you regularly spend time fostering positive communication, talking or sharing activities, you'll be much happier in your remarriage than if you don't. One area to pay particularly close attention to is technology. It can be vital to our work and help keep us organized and informed, but, as we all know, it can also create emotional distance when it plays too large a role in our free time or communication.

UNPLUG AT MEALTIMES

It may not be possible to do this for every meal but try to turn off the TV and ask all family members to put away their cell phone during mealtimes. Your emails and Facebook feed can wait. Couples use digital technology to manage life, logistics, and emotional intimacy in their relationships, yet, according to the Pew Research Center, 25 percent of cell phone users feel their spouse is distracted by their cell phone when they're together. In fact, when couples and family members unplug from electronic devises, the quality of their conversation and ability to actively listen and support each other goes up.

Although technology has enhanced our society in many ways, it's made it more challenging for all family members to communicate effectively. Most couples report that they have to compete with their kids' smartphones or tablets and often feel they have inadequate face-to-face communication. Alana and Jeffrey, a remarried couple who are both in their early fifties, report that they have difficulty getting their three children to unplug when they are asked to join the family for meals or chores.

Jeffrey and Alana have been remarried three years and each has full custody of their children—Alana's two teenage daughters, Briana and Stella, and Jeffrey's 10-year-old son, Max. They live in an upper middle-class suburb in Massachusetts, and both Alana and Jeffrey work full-time in the finance field and often put in long days.

Jeffrey confides, "It's a struggle in our house to get our kids to join us for meals or to help out with daily chores. I swear if we didn't bribe them with an allowance or ice cream after dinner, we'd rarely see them. Briana and Stella are always on social media—Instagram, Snapchat, or whatever. They get mad at me when I ask them to unplug. Max mostly plays video games, but he does like to text his friends too."

All families are experiencing these downsides of technology, but it can be a greater concern in stepfamilies due to changing custody arrangements, conflicting schedules, and conflicts and rivalries between children and adults. When either biological or step relationships are strained, it can be even more tempting to hide behind screens or overuse technology.

Alana remembered a recent incident where she had asked Stella to get off her smartphone and help out with the dishes. Stella responded by yelling, "I have to check this message or I'll miss out on the plan for later. I'll do the dishes after."

I asked Stella about this (with Alana's permission, of course). She reflects, "I'm on Instagram and Snapchat more at my mom's than my dad's because it gets pretty crazy there with three kids and my stepdad."

Alana puts it like this: "My girls definitely get upset with Max, and they haven't adjusted to having Jeffrey around to impose house rules or take up space in their home. We've only been married three years and I'm sure it will get easier. One thing I want to start is a new unplug rule of no technology at the dinner table and one hour before bed. I read somewhere this might help us all get along better."

During our discussion, it was apparent that Alana and Jeffrey's family was fairly harmonious in spite of their complaints about poor communication and minor conflicts. They seemed ready to tackle the issue of how technology was negatively influencing their lives.

Four Rules to Limit the Use of Technology in a Remarried Family

1. **Turn off your phone!** Adults can set the pace with this one and literally turn off their phones (or, better yet, put them away) for at least one hour each evening. It's also a good idea to have a "tech-free zone" in the most important areas of your home, such as the dining room. Be sure to talk through hard stuff face-to-face and reserve texts for quick check-ins or scheduling issues.

2. **Set mealtime routines and chores.** Family members take turns setting the table and doing dishes; everyone cleans their own plate; and everyone turns off technology during mealtimes.

3. **Spend two to three unplugged hours together on weekends.** Go outside, go somewhere fun, or try a low-key activity such as playing a game of checkers, chess, or cards at home. What you do together is less important than simply connecting.

4. **Turn off technology one hour prior to bedtime when possible.** Younger family members will be more reluctant to do this but will adapt over time by reading and/or listening to music.

Alana and Jeffrey implemented these rules and found that it took their family several weeks to adjust. Max often complained that he was able to play unlimited video games at his mom's house and didn't understand why he had different rules when he was with his dad and Alana. Briana and Stella initially balked about turning off their phones one hour before bedtime but discovered after a while that they were sleeping better and their grades were improving.

In spite of the fact that they are childless, Greg and Monica found that their extensive communication by text messages was wreaking havoc on their second marriage. Greg even tried apologizing by a text and ended up feeling bitter and angry because Monica told him she didn't feel he was being sincere.

Monica reflects, "Since we don't see each other much on weeknights, we were communicating through text and it was creating more distance between us. It got so bad that Greg told me never to call him before sending a text, and I felt insulted. Since we reduced text messages and are devoting at least twenty minutes to talking face-to-face each day, the quality of our marriage has improved dramatically and we're more affectionate and happier to be together."

A 2013 study by Brigham Young University researchers Lori Cluff Schade and Jonathan Sandberg, along with three other colleagues, examined 276 young adults in committed relationships and discovered that couples who communicate constantly through text messages reported lower relationship quality. In fact, the women in the study who received apologies or tried to work out their differences with their partners via texts reported higher levels of unhappiness. For the men in the study, too-frequent texting was associated with lower relationship quality. The solution? Talk face-to-face and reap the rewards of more intimate conversations and more fulfillment in your relationships with family members.

Ten Ways to Increase Tolerance and Respect Within the Remarried or Stepfamily

1. **Adopt realistic expectations about remarriage.** Don't expect your new family to be smooth sailing from the start. Allow your family members time to adjust to a new reality and new people sharing the same space.

2. **Discuss couple and family rules and routines before everyone moves under the same roof.** Meet once a week over pizza or a casual dinner out to set agreements and expectations. Address questions and upsets so no one is surprised by the inevitable areas of confusion that are likely to come up once cohabitation begins.

3. **Be assertive and deal with negative feelings when they arise.** State what you need and expect in a positive way. Find out what others want as well. Create a dialogue that addresses issues as they come up rather than burying emotions and having them turn into resentment and grudges that breed a hostile home environment.

4. **Set personal boundaries or limits.** Step away from issues that are not yours. This means letting your partner deal with their children when you do not own the problem. If you give up the need to be "right," this will be easier. Remember that you can't control other people in your family, only your response to their words and actions. Walk away quietly if you feel a conversation doesn't involve you.

5. **Accept and discuss the fact that you both are completely human.** All your imperfections, weaknesses, and emotional baggage combine with your positive traits to make each of you who you are.

6. **Show gratitude daily for your partner, your children, and stepchildren—just as they are.** Demonstrate your appreciation and love through words and actions, especially during difficult conversations about chores, finances, and problems that arise. Saying things such as "Thanks so much for cleaning up the family room—it looks terrific" can go a long way toward producing positive feelings between family members when people aren't getting along.

7. **Show love and physical affection to your partner.** This holds true even when you're stressed and challenged by the emotional

baggage they bring to the marriage from their past. Remember, you have your baggage too. Make a point to connect physically with a hug or kiss when you reunite after work and ask your partner about their day.

8. **Demonstrate respect to your partner and other family members.** You can do this by showing empathy and kindness when they are having tough times. This can occur on so many different levels, from words—for example, talking to your partner nicely, without "put downs," even when you're upset—to offering to help them with chores or tasks, to avoiding blaming them even when you disagree.

9. **Give your partner, children, and stepchildren room to be unique.** At times, we all can be annoying and difficult. We make mistakes. We parent our children differently. Part of building a culture of tolerance is offering love and understanding during these times, rather than becoming overly frustrated and intolerant. If you pause and consider that your partner probably has good intentions (and try to smile rather than frown), you may learn something and win your partner's and kids' affection in the process!

10. **Have a sense of humor!** Know which battles are worth fighting—and which to shrug off with a grin. Realize that even when someone has hurt you, they need not take away your personal happiness. If a family member has hurt your feelings (even if they do not own it, apologize, or ask for forgiveness), you have the power to forgive them. Try not to take it personally, and lighten up a bit!

APPRECIATION ACTIVITY

Without a doubt, letting your partner know that you understand them and validating their perspective are powerful ways to preserve a marriage. This includes showing appreciation for each other by offering sincere and positive appreciation. In *Why Marriages Succeed or Fail*, psychologist and author John Gottman writes, "With a little effort and empathy, you can replace thoughtless complaints and criticism with thoughtful remarks." While negativity is toxic to any marriage, it's especially damaging to a complicated remarriage because both partners bring baggage and harmful patterns of relating. However, personal growth and love are possible when you're nonjudgmental and express tenderness through words, tone of voice, facial expressions, or actions. Focusing on what you think your partner most wants and deserves to hear from you in any given situation can really help.

Appreciation can be defined as telling your partner what you like about them. In order to do this, you can simply ask yourself, "What do I like about my partner?" or "What are my partner's finer qualities?" and focus on these. In addition, when you go through tough times with your partner, you can draw on this reserve of positive feelings and it will help you be less disappointed and resentful toward them.

The best way to show appreciation to your partner is to offer it in abundance and in front of others. The more you show appreciation, the better you will get at it and the more you'll be helping your partner feel loved and valued. The following action steps will help you show genuine appreciation to your partner and thus improve your feelings of love and belongingness. When you read chapter 7, you'll learn more ways to communicate love and understanding as you turn toward your partner in an effort to be more present and to enhance emotional attunement with them.

Four Action Steps to Show Appreciation to Your Partner

1. **Communicate to your partner what you appreciate about them.** This might include their personality or actions. Even if you don't agree with their viewpoint, praise them for their ability to deal with a challenge or new event in their life. Be sure that your appreciation is specific and detailed. For example, "I love it that you put the dishes away and make sure the kitchen is tidied up before you go to work each day. You're such a thoughtful person."

2. **Show appreciation by doing acts of kindness for your mate.** For instance, arrive home early occasionally, cook for your partner, and set an attractive table with wine or a special beverage. If you don't like to cook, invite your partner out to their favorite restaurant and make it a surprise. You might leave a phone message or a note such as "I'd love you to join me for dinner at Mama Leonie's at 6:00 p.m. on Friday. Please RSVP. Much Love!"

3. **Practice acknowledging and validating your partner's feelings.** Tune in to what they are saying when they have a problem or come home feeling upset. Validate their feelings by saying something such as "That must really feel bad . . ." and "I'm sorry you had to deal with that."

4. **Start an appreciation ritual by sharing two things you appreciate about your partner each day before you go to bed.** The main objective of this ritual is to avoid negativity and to focus on those things that you love about each other. Make this time to emphasize the good and lift each other up every single day!

Before you move on to chapter 2, be sure to fill out the following Remarriage Relationship Checklist. Completing it will increase your awareness and direct you to the chapters that are going to address your hot-button issues!

The Remarriage Relationship Checklist

Read each item on the following pages and check off the ones that are true of you. Each category has five things that might describe your experience or situation. If you have more than three checkmarks in any one category, that's a good indication that that's a trouble spot for you. Be sure to read the corresponding chapter to learn how to cope more effectively with specific concerns. If you check off more than four items in a category, you might want to skip ahead and read that chapter first, rather than starting at the beginning of this book.

1. **Build a Culture of Appreciation, Respect, and Tolerance**
   ___ I often feel unappreciated by my spouse.
   ___ I often feel unappreciated by my children or stepchildren.
   ___ I wish that my family members would show more tolerance for one another.
   ___ In my home, people sometimes yell, call each other names, and argue too much.
   ___ I wish that my family members had more respect for one another.
   ___ **TOTAL SCORE.** If your score is more than 3, go to chapter 1, "Build a Culture of Appreciation, Respect, and Tolerance."

2. **Make Your Remarriage a Top Priority**
   ___ My spouse and I don't spend enough quality time together.
   ___ I can't remember the last time I had fun with my partner.
   ___ I'm not sure my spouse and I have much in common these days.
   ___ I feel that my partner and I have drifted apart and I don't know what to do about it.
   ___ Other people and family members seem to be a priority to my spouse.
   ___ **TOTAL SCORE.** If your score is more than 3, go to chapter 2, "Make Your Remarriage a Top Priority."

3. **Ditch the Baggage from Your First Marriage**
   ___ I sometimes take things too personally when my spouse is upset about work, money, our children/stepchildren, or issues in our relationship.
   ___ I sometimes feel my raw spots or vulnerabilities are easily triggered by things my partner says and does. I overreact when I should listen to their side of the story.
   ___ At times, my partner seems easily triggered by things I say or do and then they overreact.
   ___ At times, I issue ultimatums to my partner when we are having an argument.
   ___ I feel as if my emotional baggage from my first (or second) marriage is weighing me down.
   ___ **TOTAL SCORE.** If your score is more than 3, go chapter 3, "Ditch the Baggage from Your First Marriage."

4. Don't Keep Secrets about Money

____ I'm unsure about whether to combine our money or to keep it separate.

____ When I remarried, I had leftover debt from my first marriage that I kept secret from my spouse.

____ I suffered from financial infidelity in my first marriage.

____ I feel resentful because my partner pays too much child support.

____ Usually, when my spouse and I talk about finances, it doesn't go well.

____ **TOTAL SCORE.** If your score is more than 3, go to chapter 4, "Don't Keep Secrets about Money."

5. Don't Let Mistrust Stop You from Being Vulnerable and Intimate

____ I often feel mistrustful of my spouse when they are running a little late coming home at the end of the day, or if they're meeting me somewhere.

____ I have difficulty being vulnerable and sharing my innermost thoughts and feelings due to fear of rejection or losing my partner's love.

____ When my spouse withholds information from me, I tend to get angry and don't feel as if they love me.

____ When my partner lets me down, I usually assume the worst and lose trust in them.

____ I often mistrust my spouse's intentions and my doubts have a negative impact on my remarriage.

____ **TOTAL SCORE.** If your score is more than 3, go to chapter 5, "Don't Let Mistrust Stop You from Being Vulnerable and Intimate."

6. Get Sexy and Fall in Love All Over Again

____ I feel concerned about the lack of physical affection between me and my spouse.

____ I can't remember the last time my partner expressed sexual desire for me.

____ I often feel disconnected from my partner and worry that we've fallen out of love.

____ I wish my partner and I had sex more often.

____ I'm usually too tired to enjoy sex at the end of the day and want to ignite passion again.

____ **TOTAL SCORE.** If your score is more than 3, go to chapter 6, "Get Sexy and Fall in Love All Over Again."

7. **Don't Make a Big Deal about Nothing . . . But Do Deal with Important Issues**

____ I often feel that my partner and I miscommunicate and are not really able to talk about what's really bothering us.

____ I don't feel that my spouse listens to me when I talk about what's on my mind.

____ I wish that my partner would validate my viewpoint more often.

____ It's hard for me to stay calm when I feel upset about something my partner says or does.

____ Sometimes I feel that my thoughts and opinions don't really matter much to my spouse.

____ **TOTAL SCORE.** If your score is more than 3, go to chapter 7, "Don't Make a Big Deal about Nothing . . . But Do Deal with Important Issues."

8. **Manage the Flames of Conflict**

____ At times, keeping score and winning an argument seem more important to my spouse than keeping the peace or being happy.

____ I get frustrated when my partner and I don't resolve a conflict, and I'm uncomfortable letting go or moving on.

____ I have negative ways of dealing with conflict that make it hard for me to repair hurt feelings after a disagreement.

____ I tend to either withdraw or explode when I get frustrated with my spouse and they aren't listening to me.

____ My partner and I have difficulty compromising when we are having a disagreement.

____ **TOTAL SCORE.** If your score is more than 3, go to chapter 8, "Manage the Flames of Conflict."

9. **Embrace Your Role as a Stepparent and Create Positive Stepfamily Memories**

____ I find that my spouse and I often have opposing styles of parenting.

____ I often feel left out of family decisions, as if I'm an outsider.

____ I feel criticized by my spouse regarding my skills as a parent or stepparent.

____ I often feel that I don't get the love and respect I deserve from my stepchildren.

___ I would like to learn ways to develop a stronger bond with my stepchildren.

___ **TOTAL SCORE.** If your score is more than 3, go to chapter 9, "Embrace Your Role as a Stepparent and Create Positive Stepfamily Memories."

10. Say You're Sorry and Mean It

___ I often feel resentful toward my partner and have a hard time letting go of grievances.

___ It's hard for me to apologize to my partner because I don't like admitting that I'm wrong.

___ It's hard for my spouse to apologize to me because they don't like admitting they're wrong.

___ I tend to take things too personally, let wounds fester, and focus too much on the past.

___ I wish that I could forgive my spouse and move forward to a healthier relationship.

___ **TOTAL SCORE.** If your score is more than 3, go to chapter 10, "Say You're Sorry and Mean It."

Most of all, enjoy showing appreciation for your partner, and give love and acceptance abundantly. As you read the chapters in this book, you will grow in your ability to be present for your partner every day!

Above all else, we prioritize our relationship. It's important to me that Tim is happy and feels good about his life, and I know he cares about my well-being. We make it a point to do small things together, like walking our dog, because we don't want to make the same mistakes as we did with our exes. **NADIA, AGE 48**

2

Make Your Remarriage a Top Priority

nadia, 48, and Tim, 56, happily remarried for five years, were introduced by a mutual friend and they felt instant chemistry toward each other. When they met, Nadia was raising four children as a single parent and Tim was a divorced dad with two grown daughters. When they sat down with me at a seaside café near their large Cape Cod–style home in rural Connecticut, they were happy to share the secrets of their successful second marriage.

Nadia puts it like this: "We leave love notes for each other often in hidden places. We read the paper together on Sunday morning. Tim makes me coffee, even though he doesn't drink it. We make love often—even on weekdays. When my kids go on visitation, we always spend time talking and catching up, walking on the beach, or sitting and reading."

It is clear from Nadia's description that she and Tim make their marriage a priority. Over the course of their interview, Nadia and Tim discussed the positive impact that spending intentional time together, shared activities, and daily rituals of connection have had on their marriage. Their intentional time is planned, sometimes weeks in advance, and is their declaration or assurance to themselves and their children that they place a high value on their relationship. Tim says, "That wasn't the case in my first marriage. We worked different schedules, and when we were home, we went our separate ways. Nadia also led a separate life from her first husband, and we don't want to make the same mistake this time around."

When your marriage is a priority, you and your partner feel a strong physical and emotional closeness. You devote time and attention to each other and your relationship. You spend time alone together regularly. You know the details of your partner's life and their stresses, fears, likes, dislikes, hopes, and dreams. You routinely show attraction, fondness, and esteem for your spouse—even when you disagree. When your marriage is a priority, you and your partner have a strong, intimate relationship and are better able to weather the storms of remarried life.

What does putting your marriage first mean in real-world terms? It doesn't mean that you shut others out or ignore your children's needs. But for your relationship to succeed, you and your partner must let your children, stepchildren, and others know that your marriage is airtight, the bedrock of your family, and sacred to both of you. You can demonstrate your pledge to love, honor, and stay together by making it clear that your marriage is a priority, and that your kids and other family members are not in control. While your children might resent your commitment to your partner at first, it can be immensely reassuring to them in the long run. Kids are smart at figuring out who is in charge and who is on the "inside" versus the "outside" of their inner family circle. If you show them by your actions that your marriage is rock solid, and you are devoting time and effort to each other, this will help clear up any ambiguous feelings they might have about your remarriage and can offer them stability.

For the most part, first-time couples who are securely attached have had time to build trust in the early phase of their marriage. Left to their own devices, newly married couples usually have the ability to establish rituals such as date nights that promote attachment because they are usually younger than remarried couples and childless. When difficulties arise, they can be vulnerable and turn to each other with hurts and complaints and to repair emotional ruptures when they disagree. On the other hand, remarried couples don't always have the time to bond and develop rituals that sustain them because they often get married on the rebound and usually bring children with them. As a result, they might have more difficulty establishing trust and a strong emotional connection early on in the marriage.

In my own remarriage, I struggled with trust issues because I had only been divorced two years when I remarried and I didn't have time to sufficiently heal from my first marriage. Then, one year after we wed, I gave birth to our daughter and we struggled to find time alone without our three children and work responsibilities. My mistrust created a barrier that prevented me, over time, from being intimate with my husband. This barrier grew with the concerns, frustrations, and struggles that we experienced raising three children in a stepfamily.

When marriages fail, increasing conflict isn't necessarily the cause. It's decreasing affection and emotional responsiveness, according to a cutting-edge study by Ted Huston and his colleagues of the University of Texas. Huston's research demonstrates that the demise of marriages begins with a growing absence of responsive intimate interactions. In his sample of 168 couples over a thirteen-year period, Huston found that the spouses in long-term happy marriages often point to each other's admirable qualities and mention the pleasure they find in their relationship and spending time together as significant reasons for the durability of their bond. Even though Huston interviewed first-time married couples, his findings are especially applicable for remarried couples who have countless reasons to decrease affection and emotional closeness due to the complicated nature of blending two distinct worlds and adding children to the mix.

Finding time to strengthen your remarriage is no easy task. It means taking control of your time. More than 70 percent of the remarried individuals that I interviewed for my study stated that they didn't have enough time alone with their partner. Strengthening your remarriage will require an investment in your time. The outcome is likely to be better, more satisfying communication with your mate, a better understanding of your common goals and beliefs, and a more tranquil, well-organized household. There are many pulls, both internal and external, that make it a challenge for a newly remarried couple to adjust to their new living situation. Spending quality time together gives partners time to connect without competing with children, so they can fully attend to each other and not be distracted by other family members.

For instance, the end of the day has always been a hectic time at our house. My husband, Craig, and I both work two jobs and our kids have always had full schedules with sports, dance, and community activities. So after our two older children reached late adolescence, we decided to set our own curfew. We told our kids that we'd be going to bed about 10:00 p.m., barring any emergency, most weeknights. By this time of night, our youngest was sound asleep and the older two were well on their way or occupied. This ritual helped Craig and me connect and catch up. It was also our way of telling our three children that "we were in it together" and that our relationship was important.

Based on his forty years of research in his "Love Lab," John Gottman highlights the value of a couple forming a close emotional bond by spending time alone together. In *The Relationship Cure*, he says, "I believe that failure to connect is a major cause of our culture's high divorce rate." He adds that failure to relate to a partner on an emotional level is a major cause of the 50 percent rate of divorce for first-time marriages and the over 60 percent chance of divorce for second marriages. Spending time with your partner and connecting emotionally may not fill your bank account or land you the perfect job, but it will create an emotional bank account as you respond to each other's bids for connection, affection, and appreciation. Imagine walking down the street with your partner and suddenly they put their arm around your shoulder. This is a bid for connection, and it gives you a chance to put a deposit in your emotional bank account. The simple action of wrapping your arm around your partner's waist is a sign that you're in an affectionate mood. Couples who have a positive balance in their emotional bank account are more resilient when they go through tough times together.

Most likely you and your partner prioritized your relationship while you were dating, but now that you're married you find it difficult to do so. You may be juggling careers, two sets of children, different schedules, ex-spouses, and complex finances. When responsibilities and routines take over, it's not always easy to stay close and connected. As a result, it's imperative for you and your spouse to consciously plan to devote time and attention to each other in order to keep alive the emotional and physical intimacy necessary to sustain a healthy relationship.

Priscilla, 67, and her husband, Dan, 68, have been remarried for over thirty years and understand the importance of prioritizing their relationship in spite of challenges and time constraints. During our recent interview, Priscilla says, "We enjoy being by ourselves. The dinner hour is important for us. When we were first married and our children were young, we enjoyed every weekend that our children were with our ex-spouses. When our own child was born, we still made it a point to get a babysitter once a week or have a late dinner together after she went to sleep a few nights a week."

In fact, Priscilla and Dan blended six children (now grown) and found that their devotion to each other paid off over the years as their children went through rough spots and they endured the deaths of their parents. Now happily retired and enjoying spending time with six grandchildren, Priscilla says, "We eat breakfast together when we can. We play tennis together on weekends. We give each other good-morning kisses, welcome-home kisses, and goodnight kisses every day. These are the little things we do to hold us together and keep us close."

Over ten years in private practice, I have seen many marriages, including my own remarriage, suffer due to lack of attention. Most couples struggle to find the balance between couple time and family time. Some individuals devote so much time to caring for their children or other family members that they neglect their marriage until it's too late.

Over the last several decades, social scientists have seen a trend to put the needs of children first—before a marital partner. Child development experts agree that there are many negative repercussions to this parenting style. Children thrive when they have lots of love, but they also need firm limits. Some parents have become indulgent, placing few demands on their children because they feel they will be more confident and creative if given more freedom. However, developmental psychologist Diana Baumrind's innovative study, published in the journal *Developmental Psychology*, found that children who have parents who are permissive or indulgent are more likely to end up immature, irresponsible, disrespectful, and lacking in self-control. She also discovered that children raised by parents who were nurturing and warm yet who set firm limits, were more likely to be both socially competent and self-reliant.

In remarried families, parent-child relationships have preceded the new couple relationship. Because of this, many parents feel it is a betrayal of the earlier parent-child bond to form a strong relationship with their new partner, and they may not make their marriage a priority, according to stepfamily experts Emily B. Visher and John S. Visher. In *How to Win as a Step-Family*, they explain, "A primary couple relationship, however, is usually crucial for the continuing existence of the stepfamily, and therefore is very important for the children as well as for the adults. A strong parent bond can protect children from another family loss, and it can provide the children with a positive role model for their own eventual marriage relationship. The adults often need to arrange for time alone to help nourish this important couple relationship."

For instance, Jenna, 36, and Kurt, 38, are raising two boys, ages 8 and 10, bringing one each from a prior relationship. They came to a counseling session with me complaining that they were on the brink of divorce because they had drifted apart during their seven years of remarriage. They had lost faith in their love for each other and their ability to repair from repeated arguments. It was apparent to me that they had let their relationship slide and had been putting their two boys before each other for several years. Both working full-time and drained by the demands of parenting, they had fallen into a pattern of neglecting their relationship.

Kurt reflects, "Jenna thinks that I spend too much time with Kevin and Sam, but I feel guilty when I get home after 7:00 p.m. some nights and they are already in their pj's. I see it as a priority to play with them, and then I am totally exhausted after they go to bed. I have to get up early to make it to work, and I have long days."

Jenna responds, "We haven't been out together—without the boys—in months, and when we do go out we usually end up talking about them."

Both Jenna and Kurt were questioning their commitment to each other but were determined to work hard to get back on track because they didn't want to see their remarriage crumble. Kurt enjoyed spending time with his son and stepson but was putting his marriage on the back burner and needed to reprioritize the time that he had available in the evening and on weekends. Otherwise, his marriage would continue to suffer from lack of attention.

In Jenna and Kurt's marriage, they don't devote enough quality time to nurturing their relationship, and the intimacy and trust that they once enjoyed has eroded—leaving them both feeling dissatisfied and unhappy with their second marriage. They must decide that it is a priority to have time alone together and add some daily rituals if their marriage is going to survive. It's natural for remarried couples to devote a lot of time to children and work, but the challenges of stepfamily life will pull them apart if they don't act quickly and practice one or more daily rituals.

Tips for Making Your Remarriage a Priority

Don't buy into the guilt trip that your children and stepchildren will suffer if you don't schedule playtime with them daily. Kids are incredibly resilient, and they will become self-reliant if they have down time to play alone or with siblings or peers.

Let your children and stepchildren know that your relationship with your partner is important. This may sound simplistic, but you can convey this through warmth, affection, and spending time away from them with your partner.

Devoting time to strengthening your relationship isn't selfish. Your strong relationship provides a solid foundation for your whole family's happiness. Also, you don't need time-consuming grand gestures to show love and affection to each other. While dedicated time alone together each week is important, small gestures are the secret to lasting happiness, according to researcher Saeideh Heshmati and her colleagues, who surveyed 495 Americans in a recent Penn State study. Surprisingly, respondents rated small, everyday expressions of love, such as physical affection, as more important to their happiness than over-the-top gestures such as buying an expensive gift.

The task of forming a close marital relationship in the presence of prickly remarriage realities is formidable and can lead to unhappiness or even divorce if you aren't honest about the challenges. If you become disillusioned, stop showing affection, and turn away from each other during times of family turmoil and stress, your marriage will suffer. However, if you learn from your first marriage and nurture your second one, you will be less likely to make the same mistakes the second time around, according to psychologist E. Mavis Hetherington and coauthor John Kelly in *For Better or for Worse: Divorce Reconsidered*. Hetherington, a leading divorce and remarriage researcher, recommends that remarried couples not be intimidated by the high divorce rate for second marriages and the struggles of stepfamily life, and that they stay unified and resilient. In her groundbreaking study of 1,400 divorced families over a thirty-year period, 40 percent were able to build healthy stepfamilies in spite of their myriad of challenges—mostly involving blending children. Hetherington believes that the eventual success of a remarriage hinges on the strength of the couple's relationship. In order to stay strong, you need to adopt an attitude of "we're a united team" *and* attend to your marriage on a daily basis.

INTENTIONAL TIME ALONE TOGETHER

If you want a fighting chance to maintain and even increase your sense of connection and happiness with your partner over the years, you need to become what couples therapist William J. Doherty refers to as an "intentional couple," spending meaningful time alone together on a regular, planned basis. For instance, a year after Craig and I wed, we started taking our kids on an annual summer vacation in early August to Craig's family home in Maine. When we were there, we slept in a private apartment above his parents' garage and our children became accustomed to us having alone time in the evening. During the decade that we made these visits as a stepfamily, our children respected our nightly ritual.

Remarried individuals often have great difficulty sustaining intentional time together due to the complexity of their lives. Over 60 percent of the individuals in my study stated that they rarely spent regular time alone together. However, it's especially important that remarried couples do this in order to solidify their bond. As difficult as it might be, you must not let family turmoil, finances, and challenges with children or ex-spouses disrupt your plans. Of course you need to be flexible enough to change your rituals if they're not working, but come up with a working plan for other rituals as soon as possible.

Create new rituals to celebrate holidays and special events, and to honor the daily activities that bring you closer, such as pizza or game night. In *The Intentional Family*, Doherty coined the term *rituals of connection* to describe the different things families do to be sure they are regularly turning toward each other in ways that are meaningful and satisfying to everyone.

Spending extended periods of quality time doing shared activities alone with your spouse each week is the most important way to deepen physical and emotional intimacy. In fact, the amount of time a couple spends alone with each other, talking or sharing activities, is a key factor in predicting their overall marital happiness, according to psychologist Eli J. Finkel. In T*he All-Or-Nothing Marriage,* he explains that there has been a 40 percent decline in the last three decades in the amount of time that couples who have children spend together. The reasons include busier work schedules and chronic interruptions due to multitasking and technology. In a stepfamily, these interruptions include the activities of your children and stepchildren. Whether you make a standing date to go to the gym, explore your neighborhood, watch a movie, go to a concert, or do another activity you enjoy, you and your partner must make a commitment to time alone each week. I know the demands of daily life seem to leave little time or money left over for such relaxed, fun activities, but alone time together is part of the time and energy investment you are making in your second marriage *and* it will pay off.

Sybil, 37, and Kyle, 38, are childless, work full-time in demanding jobs, and often feel drained at the end of the workday. Over the eight years of their remarriage, they have fallen into the trap of neglecting their relationship. Kyle set up a counseling appointment with me because he had become very discouraged that he rarely spent quality time with Sybil and he felt lonely.

Kyle reflects, "Sybil complains that we don't have time or money to go out, but I need time to recover from work, and I want to spend more quality time with her at home. I spend most nights watching TV alone while Sybil is on the computer and working on her website. I'd like to get back to spending time together, but it seems like she's not interested. Sybil told me this was a problem in her first marriage, but I hoped she would change."

When Kyle expressed his feelings to Sybil after our counseling session, he was relieved to discover that she shared his concerns about their marriage and was interested in spending more time together. She just didn't see how they could do that, given how short on time and money they are. Sybil was also concerned about the impact that cutting back on her work would have on her career. She shared her concerns openly when Kyle invited her to join us for a few sessions.

Sybil puts it like this: "I was hesitant to share my concerns about falling behind in work with Kyle because he thinks I work too much, but I decided to be vulnerable and he really listened this time. He understands that I'm ambitious, and since he respects that, he's going to make more of an effort to show interest in my work and be understanding when I need to work on the weekends or stay late at my office. He knows that I also have debts from my first marriage to pay off and we can work on this together."

After brainstorming for a while, Sybil and Kyle were able to come up with low-cost activities that fit into their budget. They decided to rotate every other Saturday night between a dinner date and a pizza-and-movie night at home. They also spend one weeknight either going for a long walk or bowling, activities they both enjoy. This plan satisfied both Sybil and Kyle and enabled them to give their relationship the attention it needed. After just a few weeks, each felt more contented.

Sybil and Kyle learned an important lesson: you don't have to choose between your career and being a good partner. As a nation, we tend to invest more time in work than we do in our intimate relationships. Working together to find the right balance will pay off in the end for you, your marriage, and your career.

Because many remarried couples are crunched for time, exercising together two or three times a week can help them stay close and healthy at the same time. Nadia and Tim believe that going to the gym or walking together regularly is a good way to recharge their batteries while raising six children and maintaining demanding careers. It's a great way to stay fit and share the joys and frustrations of their day when they are alone together.

Nadia reflects, "We go for a long walk or go to the gym at least twice a week. This allows us to spend time together and stay in good shape. Our kids have gotten used to it and honor it as our special time. Tim and I still have arguments, but they don't last long, and we usually get back on track pretty quickly. Some of the basic things like asking each other questions and listening, and showing interest, helps us stay close."

Ways to Bring More Intentional Time into Your Relationship

Put two to three hours of alone time with your partner on your calendar weekly. This time can be broken into several thirty-minute intervals or spent in longer blocks of time.

Choose activities that are pleasurable to both of you. This will make it more likely that both of you will commit. These can be low- or no-cost activities such as having a picnic or playing a game.

Plan a date night. This can be an enjoyable way for you and your partner to spend time together on a weekly or monthly basis. For instance, you might eat at your favorite restaurant and even call ahead to reserve a preferred table.

Take an annual vacation together without your children or relatives. This doesn't need to be an expensive weeklong extravaganza. An overnight or weekend away at a favorite local spot, such as a campground, is all you need.

Try something new and exciting together. Add a little novelty by learning or doing something new together. Social psychology researcher Arthur Aron and colleagues studied dozens of couples in their laboratory and found that sharing novel and arousing activities with a partner is the antidote for relationship boredom and brings couples closer. For instance, many couples enjoy glassblowing, kayaking, biking, or hiking through an unexplored area.

Tips for Thirty-Minute Alone-Time Activities

- Put on your favorite music, enjoy a glass of wine, and dance and/or listen to music.

- Cuddle. Touch each other, put your arms around each other, and hold hands while talking or watching TV.

- Cook and/or eat a meal together alone. If you have children, choose one night weekly when your children are with their other parent or engaged in an activity in the community.

- Make out. The magical way to spark passion is kissing, and if it leads to making love, even better!

- Do a workout or exercise session, such as walking outdoors, taking a yoga class, jogging, bike riding, swimming, or taking a class together at a gym.

DAILY RITUALS

I am a big fan of daily rituals too. In order to be considered a ritual, the activity has to have meaning and value for both partners. Otherwise it is just a routine. For example, an occasional unplanned hike on a trail in a nearby park would not be a ritual, whereas a daily thirty-minute walk in your neighborhood that you both look forward to would be a ritual.

As William J. Doherty notes, daily rituals can create big changes over time. When they're honored by both partners and practiced regularly, they become part of the glue that holds your marriage together. They become the foundation of your marriage and help you foster the trust and intimacy needed to sustain your bond as you face the inevitable ups and downs of remarried life. Making an agreement with your partner to maintain daily rituals, such as a hug when you reunite at the end of the day, can inject pleasure into your remarriage even if you do not really feel in the mood to connect. Rituals can become habit forming and help you stay connected and count on each other for intimacy and support.

The important thing is to create rituals that have meaning and value for both of you. For instance, some couples appreciate cuddle time in the morning, watching a favorite TV show or a daily check-in time to discuss family issues over a cup of coffee or tea. Throughout their sixty-nine-year marriage, my in-laws enjoyed a nightly ritual of lively conversation and playing bridge while drinking coffee and eating dessert after their evening meal. Prior to moving into assisted living, they would sit together in their living room or on their screened-in patio in warm weather and do this. Recently my husband and I added this nightly ritual (minus the dessert and bridge) and find it helps us stay connected and catch up after a busy day.

What you do for your ritual is entirely up to you, of course. In *The Seven Principles for Making Marriage Work*, John Gottman recommends a ritual of spending at least fifteen to twenty minutes a day having a stress-reducing conversation with your partner. Ideally this conversation needs to focus on whatever is on your mind outside of your relationship. This isn't the time to discuss conflicts between you. It's a golden opportunity to show empathy and support each other emotionally concerning other areas of your life. Your goal isn't to solve your partner's problems but to take your spouse's side, even if their perspective seems unreasonable. The best way to do this is to listen and validate your partner's thoughts and feelings and express a "we against others" attitude.

It's really important to find a time that works for both of you to have these conversations. This often means looking at the schedules of other family members and making sure you pick a time that is least likely to be affected by other people's schedules and can be honored on a daily basis.

You can create other rituals of connection, too, such as a six-second kiss (which John Gottman calls "a kiss with potential") before leaving the house or when coming home, or making sure to text each other throughout the day with positive, loving messages to help you both feel connected.

For instance, Erica, 47, and Rob, 49, who have been happily remarried for ten years and are raising three children in a stepfamily, do the following: "We hug every day when I get home, because physical touch is the way I express love. Rob is not as affectionate as I am, but he's up for it because he knows how important it is to me. So we usually cuddle on the couch for fifteen minutes and catch up about our day." This ritual keeps them physically and emotionally connected.

Many of the remarried couples in my study expressed a strong desire to add more rituals, such as a daily time to cuddle or talk, to their schedule. I suggest that couples try out a few different times a day and locations to see what works for them and their chosen ritual. For instance, my husband, Craig, and I are on different schedules in the morning, but we usually have time in the evening to enjoy a ritual of cooking and eating dinner together to catch up about our day. We've recently added a twenty-minute stress-reducing conversation over coffee during cleanup. Because we have a large kitchen and we enjoy doing dishes together, we find that this routine fits nicely after our mealtime ritual of cooking and eating dinner together. Having a conversation about issues outside of our marriage while doing dishes can help us unburden ourselves after we've eaten dinner, and we aren't distracted by preparing the meal.

Creating a daily ritual can put the spark back in your remarriage, even if you have not connected emotionally, sexually, or physically in some time. Successful couples practice rituals and make sure that intimacy is a priority rather than the last thing on their to-do list. There are three main types of rituals:

1. Rituals of communication: talking face-to-face without distractions

2. Rituals of physical affection: hugging, kissing, touching, or having sex

3. Rituals of kindness and appreciation: doing something nice for your partner

Rituals of Communication

Rituals of communication are one of the most important rituals you can adopt to feel more connected to your partner. Taking time to talk, ask questions, and get to know each other better can make the difference between a happy, meaningful marriage and a so-so, drifting, or declining marriage. This can be a stress-reducing conversation described previously or simply going for a twenty- to thirty-minute walk and talking about your day without distractions.

After seven years of being in a remarriage, Mike, 45, and Elissa, 44, acknowledge that they're drifting apart. In fact, they kept track of how much time they spent with each other for one week and realized it amounted to less than two hours, including meals. Things got even more hectic after Elissa started a more demanding job that involved some travel. Since her two children from her former marriage were already teenagers and somewhat independent, Elissa and Mike had some time together, but it had diminished greatly in recent months. However, they were both feeling committed to working on their second marriage, so they began looking for professional help.

Mike and Elissa were fortunate to find a marriage therapist who assessed that their communication issues were not deep-seated; they were not taking advantage of the opportunities to connect. Their marriage counselor gave them a few articles to read and talked to them about developing at least one daily ritual. Mike and Elissa decided that they would adopt a daily ritual of connecting with each other for fifteen to twenty minutes, without distractions, before going to sleep at night. When they met me for an interview, they were already putting into practice this daily ritual and were beginning to feel more emotionally connected—and happy to report that they were falling in love with each other again.

Elissa reflects, "I love Mike and I know he loves me. We were thrilled when I got the new job, but I just don't always have enough hours in the day. It really feels like our marriage has suffered. Our schedules are so different, and he's usually working when I get home and want to talk. Even though my kids are teens, they still take priority because their bio dad only sees them occasionally and I don't want them to feel neglected. I like to watch TV with them or go shopping with my daughter on the weekends."

Mike responds, "Yeah, I never thought about how much our life changed until Michelle, our therapist, brought it up. I was so happy that Elissa got the amazing job and extra income that I guess I never thought about how we weren't spending much time together anymore. I get that Elissa's kids are important, but they won't complain too much if we go out once in a while by ourselves."

Most couples communicate constantly via text and social media, but they don't have a focused, regular time devoted to talking. A twenty-minute conversation, face-to-face and without distractions, when you and your partner can check in about each other's day and complain and laugh together, makes a meaningful impact. According to John Gottman, one of the nation's leading marital researchers, marriages thrive when couples are intentional about taking time to talk and get to know each other. They are more likely to stay together and are happier because they are always building and repairing friendship, love, and trust.

Rituals of Physical Affection

In their groundbreaking book *The Normal Bar*, Chrisanna Northrup, Pepper Schwartz, and James Witte show that hugging your partner or cuddling increases your intimacy and passion. They studied seventy thousand people in twenty-four countries and found that physical affection, going on a weekly date, and kissing each other passionately are hallmarks of a great sex life. In fact, physical contact releases oxytocin, the bonding hormone, and can improve your mood for days and can keep you calm. Holding hands, hugging, touching, sharing a six-second kiss, and making out can reduce the stress hormone cortisol and increase your sense of relationship satisfaction, according to Julianne Holt-Lunstad, a researcher at the Department of Psychology at Brigham Young University. An added bonus is that oxytocin is also released during sexual orgasm and that the afterglow from sex can last for up to forty-eight hours. When Florida State University researcher Andrea Meltzer examined dozens of newly wed couples, she discovered that those who sustained an afterglow for forty-eight hours, due to having sex, also reported being satisfied with their relationship for months down the road, compared to couples who weren't sexually intimate.

Jonathan, 42, and Sarah, 43, remarried for ten years and raising four children in a stepfamily, find it a challenge to connect with each other at times. Sarah has two daughters, Jenny and Katie, ages 4 and 6, from her first marriage. Jonathan's teenage daughters, Briana and Kayla, live with them almost half of the time. Over the last decade, Jonathan and Sarah have focused on their children and careers and paid little attention to being physically affectionate. As a result, they have lost the passion and intimacy they enjoyed in the early years of their marriage.

When this lively and articulate couple came to my office, they both stated that they were uncertain about whether they could go on any longer—they were in a state of crisis with no resolution in sight. One of my first suggestions, while they were trying to sort things out, was to come up with a daily ritual to see if they could jump-start their sense of connection. It turns out they were sexually intimate about once a month, and arguing and emotionally distant outside of the bedroom.

Sarah reflects on the transition she and Jonathan made to reconnect: "We added a new ritual because we just didn't have enough alone time. Lately we try to cuddle after sharing a ten-minute chat time in bed each morning before joining the family. On Sundays we linger a bit longer and might even make love."

Since Jonathan is more physically affectionate than Sarah, he has been working on being vulnerable and letting her know that even quick kisses satisfy his strong need for physical touch. When Sarah gives him a kiss or a hug, it helps him feel close to her and less annoyed about the irritations he experiences when his two young stepdaughters invade his space when he is trying to relax in the evening. Both agree that making time to be more physically affectionate has helped them feel closer and stay connected in their busy lives.

Rituals of Kindness and Appreciation

Make a habit out of using kind and polite words such as *please, sorry,* and *thank you.* Show your appreciation for the kind and caring actions of your partner by expressing daily gratitude to them in a natural, specific, and spontaneous way, such as "I really appreciate you making dinner even though your day was super busy. You even made my favorite salad with carrots and poured me a glass of iced tea."

These are rituals that give you the opportunity to offer your partner signs of appreciation, such as "I really loved it when you massaged my neck" or "Thanks so much for cleaning the kitchen."

Elissa explains, "We weren't on the verge of divorce but we weren't happy or fulfilled as a couple. It's great to have Mike greet me with a kiss or to stroke my arm when I come in the door at the end of the day and say thanks that I stopped at the store. One night, he even got home early, made my favorite chili, and poured us each a glass of red wine. It was such an uplift for us because we were able to relax together—such a nice surprise. I told him how grateful I was that he made chili the way I like it."

Rituals to Help You and Your Partner Stay Connected

Establish a daily ritual of reunion. This may become one of the most important rituals you develop as a couple. The most crucial moment of your marriage is the moment of reunion—or how you greet each other daily. Be sure to stay positive, avoid criticism, and listen to each other. It might take a while to see any change in your feelings of closeness, but over time this ritual can be a huge boost to your marriage. Open up the lines of communication by validating your partner—even if you don't agree.

Eat meals together without screen time. It may not be possible to do this daily, but if you strive to eat meals together most days, you will probably find you're dining together often. Turn off the TV and cell phones (no texting) and tune in to your partner. This should not be a complaint session but rather an opportunity to discuss things going on in your lives and to show you understand by saying something such as "It sounds like you've had a frustrating day."

Tips for Daily Rituals That Take Less Than a Minute

- Cuddle in the morning.

- Engage in a six-second kiss or hug before you part in the morning and/or upon your reunion in the evening.

- Write your partner a short love note, such as "You're such a great lover—looking forward to making out later." Post it on their briefcase or purse.

- Say "thank you" to your partner for something they did to show love, to comfort you, or to reduce your stress. Be brief but specific, such as "I appreciate you cleaning up the kitchen—it looks great."

Tips for Daily Rituals That Take Twenty Minutes or Less

- Debrief your day when you arrive home.

- Offer your partner a massage and play relaxing music.

- Make your partner a cup of coffee.

- Shower or bathe together.

- Eat a snack and/or favorite dessert together.

- Walk around the block several times and catch up about your day.

DEALING WITH YOUR SPOUSE'S RELUCTANCE TO INTENTIONAL TIME TOGETHER OR DAILY RITUALS

During my interviews, a number of people said that they were unable to gain the cooperation of their partner in planning time together or engaging in daily rituals. The following are ways to encourage a resistant partner to engage in a ritual with you:

- Ask your partner the reasons why it's hard for them to make a pledge to spend more alone-time together (guilt, money, etc.). Some adults avoid rituals because they want to be spontaneous or don't think having a ritual will be easy to implement. Others might resist making a commitment to a ritual because they deny a need for it or use rationalization by saying things such as "We're too busy" or "The kids need us, and we should spend more time with them."

- Once you know the reasons for their resistance or refusal to engage in rituals, reassure your partner that you can be flexible. If it's a money concern, suggest some low-cost outings such as bowling, cooking together, or taking walks. Also, point out that the kids will get a positive message when they see you nurturing your marital bond and that there is no reason to feel guilty.

- Suggest couples counseling if you feel that it would be helpful. Resistance or refusal to spending daily time with you could be a sign of other issues that need your mutual attention.

SMALL GESTURES CREATE SECURE ATTACHMENTS

If you think you need grand gestures to show your spouse love, you are mistaken. One of the secrets to long-lasting love is making small gestures, such as leaving your partner an endearing love note or holding their hand during a conflict. These gestures help couples form a secure attachment and build trust and intimacy.

One of the things that Nadia values about Tim is his ability to show love through his actions. Nadia puts it like this: "I never realized the importance of spending time alone with Tim until he went on a business trip last year. We really missed our time together. My first husband traveled a lot and that was hard in our relationship. It's important that we have our daily rituals like walking our dog and having a glass of wine together and cooking dinner together. Tim and I find meaning in spending time together, even doing the mundane things."

Tim responds, "Just because Nadia works from home doesn't mean she is responsible for all things home related or all of our kids' activities. There are never enough hours in the day. If the kids need something, I'm grateful that Nadia works from home, but I don't see her as a maid. We're a team, and we do things together because we enjoy each other's company."

It would be easy for Nadia and Tim to neglect each other. Nadia's four children, all under age 12, live with them, and Tim's two college-age daughters are often home on weekends and during winter and summer breaks. However, Nadia and Tim embrace the notion that in order for their second marriage to thrive, they need to pay attention to each other on a regular basis.

Nadia shares, "It's kind of like tending to my garden. If I don't pay attention to it, my plants will wither and die. I don't want this marriage to fail like my first one did due to lack of nourishment, because Tim and I have the potential for an amazing long-lasting love."

Many happily remarried couples such as Nadia and Tim find that with a small amount of effort, they can improve their marriage. Much of this effort can be done in five minutes or less and doesn't cost money.

Ways to Make Small Gestures Count in Your Remarriage

Look for ways to lower each other's stress. Problems at work, financial pressures, or family drama can all push a couple apart. Couples who can respond to each other's stress in a way that is soothing rather than exacerbating tend to be able to weather the tenser times. Listen to your partner and express empathy without offering judgments or solutions. Offer to make your partner a cup of coffee or tea.

Use kind and polite words, apologize, and grant forgiveness.
Would you rather go to bed angry, or would you prefer
spooning with your partner after resolving an issue? Studies
show that couples who apologize when they have hurt their
partner's feelings (even if done so accidentally) and practice
forgiveness have a more successful marriage. That may seem
obvious, but it's important to remember. Forgiveness works.

Help each other out. This can include helping your significant
other make plans, run errands, complete tasks, achieve
goals, or manage their time. These positive actions lead
to interdependence, as partners begin to coordinate their
behavior to try to bring their long-term goals to fruition.

NURTURE SHARED DREAMS AND GOALS

Of course, a successful remarriage is about more than raising kids and
paying bills. It is about building a relationship of shared meaning and
purpose. One of the most important lessons I've learned about relationships over the last two decades is that shared meaning is the main
ingredient that can help preserve a marriage. You want to create a
relationship that is full of significance and involves setting goals for
the future while prioritizing time and resources. This is about creating
a legacy—the stories you tell, your beliefs, and the culture you create
to form an identity as a couple and family that has value for you. For
instance, my husband, Craig, and I find shared meaning in participat-
ing in volunteer activities to sustain the environment, such as offering
classes on recycling and gardening, and fundraising for community
organizations. Throughout our marriage, even when under extreme
stress, we've found that these activities bring us closer together and
help us connect with our three children.

A new relationship is often exciting, stimulating, and fun. On the
other hand, having a deep, meaningful connection with your partner
can infuse your relationship with a solid foundation over the long
run. While happiness is an emotion felt in the here and now, it ultimately fades away, just as memories do; positive affect and feelings

of pleasure are temporary. However, developing shared meaning over a longer period will sustain a deep connection in your marriage. In fact, creating shared meaning is the highest level of Gottman's Sound Relationship House, which provides couples with a template for how to have a healthy relationship. In *The Science of Couples and Family Therapy*, John Gottman and Julie Schwartz Gottman explain that shared meaning is the attic of the house where couples can intentionally create a sense of purpose together that will allow them to find long-lasting love.

Intimacy is something not simply arrived at by chance. It's something that is deliberately nurtured over time. Keep in mind that maintaining a deep connection to your partner does not mean you put them on a pedestal or that your relationship is without problems. However, it does mean that you like and respect who they are and how they conduct themselves in the world.

For instance, Sybil and Kyle share a common dream of having a loving, happy home. In fact, their relationship is very different from the ones they observed in their families of origin. Sybil reflects, "I was raised in a dysfunctional home with two parents who argued a lot, and Kyle's parents divorced when he was 2 years old and he rarely saw his dad. Our priority is to be on the same page and not let our differences come between us like my parents did."

Kyle is quick to elaborate on Sybil's points about having a shared purpose in his second marriage. He says, "I respect Sybil because she's a hard worker and a kind and loving wife. When we met, we both worked long hours and had issues from our recent divorces. But we try to be patient with each other and show understanding and empathy. When I get aggravated with Sybil, I try to listen and respect her view. We both avoid issuing ultimatums, shutting down, or being disrespectful."

What is the secret to increasing shared meaning between you and your partner? Getting to know them better and sharing your innermost thoughts, feelings, and wishes. It's discussing how you prioritize your time and resources. It's a lifelong process and takes a strong commitment, but there are steps you can take today to help you and your partner get started.

Ways to Nurture Shared Dreams and Goals

Share a common dream or vision for life. When you and your partner have a shared purpose, the inevitable difficulties of marriage are less bothersome. Creating a larger context of meaning in life can help you avoid focusing on the little stuff that happens and keep your eyes on the big picture.

Talk openly about your vision. Taking time to process your individual objectives and dreams for your future can bring you closer. A crucial goal for remarried couples is to intentionally create an atmosphere that encourages each person to talk honestly about their convictions. When couples talk about their hopes and dreams openly, they are more likely to be happy—and less likely to be headed toward divorce.

Make your weekly date a time to dream and plan together. This time together should include at least one hour for talking and checking in emotionally with each other. The conversation can begin with something such as "How are you doing? What's on your mind?" The focus needs to be on both talking and listening to each other. Look into your future and envision your dreams. Creating a larger context of meaning in life can help you avoid focusing on the little stuff that happens and keep your eyes on the big picture.

Develop a culture of acceptance and respect for your partner. This holds true even when you don't see eye to eye. Your second marriage can work even when your dreams are not in sync. You will probably each have dreams that the other doesn't share but can respect. A successful remarriage is not about sidestepping conflict. The more you can agree about the fundamentals in your life together, the richer and more meaningful your partnership will become.

Implement your shared goals. For instance, your goals might include volunteering in the community, raising your children in a positive way, building your own home, or traveling. Regardless of what your shared vision or goals are, they can strengthen your bond.

USING SHARED ACTIVITIES TO STRENGTHEN YOUR RELATIONSHIP

While intentional time alone together is the bedrock of a strong emotional and physical connection with your partner, spending quality time together with your immediate and extended family members also strengthens your marriage and helps everyone feel nurtured. Ask your children what spending quality time as a family means to them, and consider their answers when you plan activities. Be sure to plan special events and some vacation time with family members on a regular basis so everyone feels nurtured.

Tips for Planning Shared Activities

Make an effort to meet in person. This is important when discussing topics such as planning vacations. Choose a time and location that's convenient for everyone. Skype might work better than a phone call with family members who reside in other locations.

Avoid interruptions or judgments. Someone may want to be the time keeper and another person can write down ideas on a tablet or notepad.

Offer your ideas tentatively and ask for feedback. Use active listening and allow all family members the opportunity to express their desires. Of course, children need to understand the boundaries of your budget and time limitations.

Keep in mind that most family connection rituals need to change. This is especially true as children get older. However, rituals still need to consist of certain activities or events that are repeated and add meaning and significance for all family members.

Relationship Growth Activity

Sometimes in a relationship, it's easy to focus on problems and forget to see our partner as a person. The purpose of a discovery meeting is to help you establish a baseline of knowledge of each other and to enhance a sense of shared meaning in your marriage. It allows each of you to expand your mental space for the relationship and for your partner. Your knowledge of each other will grow by asking open-ended questions. These questions cannot be answered by a simple yes or no response. They're questions such as "Where would you like to see your life in ten years?"

Four Action Steps to Set Up a Discovery Meeting

1. **Decide together.** You need to agree on when to make the twenty-minute conversation happen.

2. **Make a commitment.** For example, try it once a week for at least one month.

3. **Decide the logistics that work for you as a couple.** Some people find that after dinner works well. Couples who are early risers prefer the morning. Be sure to write your questions down.

4. **Sit facing each other.** Take turns answering the questions below. Both people need to feel they can speak without interruption and be listened to. Unplugging from technology will help you pay attention to each other. It is a good idea to check in with your partner to make sure they feel heard. Be gentle with each other and do not make critical or negative comments. Try to focus on two or three questions each time you talk and write new ones for future growth time together.

Discovery Questions to Enhance Shared Meaning

Use questions or prompts from below or write your own:

- Who are your two closest friends?
- Who is your favorite relative?
- Who is your favorite musician or composer?
- What hobby or new interest would you like to pursue?
- What is your favorite thing to do on a date night?
- What is your favorite vacation (location, activities, etc.)?
- What is your preferred way to relax at the end of a long day?
- Describe your day in detail.
- What stresses are you facing in the immediate future?
- What is your dream job or career?
- Describe in detail your preferred way to spend a free day.
- Where do you see your life heading in the next five or ten years?

SHOW YOUR LOVE

Remarried couples committed to success do best when they prioritize their marriage, knowing that their strong relationship acts as the foundation for their whole family's happiness. Never underestimate the power of intentional time alone with your partner. Doing fun things together can bring both of you pleasure, ignite passion, and keep you connected. Spending quality time together is worth every ounce of effort it takes to schedule it regularly. Daily rituals and small gestures of affection are simple, low-effort ways to show your love for your partner. In a successful remarriage, positive interactions outweigh negative ones. These approaches and tools will help you bring more positivity to your remarriage right away and make dealing with any residual baggage from your previous relationships easier.

Key Ways to Preserve and Strengthen Your Remarriage

- Spend intentional time alone together.

- Develop daily rituals of connection.

- Use small gestures of love and attention.

- Nurture shared goals.

- Plan family activities.

Don't forget to make your partner a top priority in your life. If you make your partner's needs equal to your own, you'll create the loving intimate relationship that you desire. It also requires ditching any baggage from your former marriage, which is the topic of chapter 3.

Initially I was wondering if I had it in me to stay in the relationship. After all, I've had two failed marriages. But we've stayed together for ten years and are working things out. One of the most difficult parts of my marriage is trusting that John will be there for me no matter what. **SAMANTHA, AGE 36**

3
Ditch the Baggage from Your First Marriage

We all have assumptions about how relationships work based on prior experiences. These assumptions, which include how we are likely to be treated, can lead to unrealistic expectations, misunderstandings, and disappointment. They can color our view of ourselves and our partner, and affect how we think we need to interact to preserve our sense of self in an intimate relationship. Our assumptions greatly influence how we interpret the behavior of our partner and how we react to them. Unfortunately, this means there will be many misinterpretations, as both partners have their own "lenses" from which they view the relationship and their take on each other's behaviors. For instance, I was at a friend's fiftieth birthday celebration several years ago and was suddenly flooded with feelings of mistrust as my husband, Craig, who enjoys dancing, was swept up in a circle dance with several women—leaving me in the dust (from my perspective). My feelings of vulnerability were so intense that I spent most of the evening in the ladies' room, and I barely spoke to Craig on the way home. Needless to say, he was perplexed, clueless as to why I was so upset. Later that night, in an effort to reassure me, he said, "You're my wife, I love you, there's no cause for alarm."

The next day, after I had time to process what happened, I realized that my emotional sensitivity related to fear of abandonment had been triggered at the dance because I lack confidence in my dancing ability, and Craig is an excellent dancer who takes pride in his flair for folk dancing. In my first marriage, my sensitivity around being rejected was intense because my ex-spouse and I rarely went out together, and when we did, it appeared to me that he paid more attention to others. Once I was able to identify that Craig's outgoing and fun-loving behavior was triggering my fear of abandonment, we were able to discuss ways to deal effectively with going to dances so my triggers wouldn't be provoked and we could enjoy an evening out. For instance, one solution that has worked well for us at circle dances is that Craig now reassures me (between songs) that he simply loves to dance more than I do but can't wait to get me alone later in the evening.

In another situation, Samantha, 35, and John, 36, have been married for a decade, and are raising two children in a stepfamily. During our interview, they discussed having baggage from prior relationships that has an impact on their communication. In fact, Samantha feels that issues she had in her first and second marriages sometimes cloud her view of John so much that she's thought of ending their marriage.

Samantha reflects, "John is very loving and loyal, but sometimes I worry he's going to get tired of all of my complications and just leave. It's as if I'm waiting for the other shoe to drop. We argue about stupid things and both try to prove we're right. This leads to a vicious cycle of bickering and trying to show each other up. There are times that I dig my heels in and lose it rather than responding calmly to his comments."

POWER STRUGGLES

Unfinished business can easily lead to hurt feelings and power struggles, as experienced by both Samantha and John. They are both deeply entrenched in believing they're right. As a result, it's essential to make sure they feel heard by each other and that they respond in a way that seems "acceptable" to both of them.

Samantha puts it like this: "If I can be vulnerable with John and not worry about being alone or rejected, things go a lot better. He knows that I have abandonment issues because I was left by my ex. These issues stop me from telling him what I need from him. Since

John's first wife left him for another man, he has his own trust issues. We both fear intimacy for different reasons and this creates problems."

Many of the remarried couples I interviewed have spoken about the fact that power struggles often surface after romantic love fades and they can actually serve a purpose. After living together for a while, couples naturally come to terms with the reality that they have differences, and the tension of opposites can be a vital aspect of couples healing wounds from their childhood and any previous marriage. In fact, working through power struggles can give you the energy to heal emotional sensitivities from prior relationships if you're aware of them and discuss them. In other words, you can learn to treat your "soft spots" with care and become more accepting of your differences.

In recent years, when I feel that my fear of abandonment is being triggered, I am usually able to let Craig know what's happening, so we can discuss it and our emotional sensitivities don't collide. Since his vulnerability is fear of entrapment, he used to distance himself from me, just at the time when I was seeking reassurance. This created a pursuer-distancer dynamic that prompted me to feel more alone and rejected because Craig would give me the silent treatment when I wanted more intimacy. As you will learn in chapter 6, the pursuer-distancer dynamic is common for couples and a leading cause of divorce. Awareness is the first step in changing this dynamic. When we're dealing with a lot of stress, I tend to talk more, and Craig's propensity is to talk less. Talkers like to share more, and withdrawers need time to recover from stressful situations. However, now that we've identified these patterns, we're more tolerant and accepting of our differences and see the value in both approaches. This is especially important when external stressors such as unexpected bills rear their ugly head and we're scrambling to find resources quickly.

For example, financial pressures triggered both of our emotional sensitivities recently. After discovering that we had a large tax payment due on the same day as our daughter's tuition bill, our vulnerabilities crashed into each other. I told Craig that I wanted to discuss this problem and he turned on the TV to watch his favorite news show. Rather than go into a tailspin, I remembered our differences in dealing with triggers such as financial stress and simply asked that we talk for a while after his show was over. Craig was happy to agree, and we ended up resolving this financial crisis by honoring each other's ways of coping with stress and coming up with a win-win solution.

Power struggles can be exaggerated between partners in a second marriage because couples have usually lived on their own for some time and have taken time to prove their capabilities. But if understood and dealt with in a healthy way, power struggles can give you the energy to work on problems and be a catalyst to building a strong connection and emotional resiliency as a couple. Rather than treating problems in your marriage as "things you do to me," you can view them as "difficulties we have." By putting differences and challenges in a broader context, you'll be better able to see behavior toward each other as a product of many factors and not as a deliberate offense.

However, this can only occur if you see your marriage as a true partnership that helps you grow as a couple and individually. In the beginning of a relationship, we tend to present our best selves and only see the best in our partners. But that honeymoon stage always ends, and disillusionment can set in. A supportive partner helps you navigate the unpredictable, ever-changing aspects of life as your vulnerabilities are exposed and disagreements arise. This type of partnership is only possible if you are compatible with someone. Chemistry can help you weather the storms of life, but compatibility enables you to set goals and find shared meaning in your relationship.

Remarried couples who want to resolve power struggles effectively avoid blaming each other when they have differences of opinion. In fact, when you have a disagreement, it's a good idea to describe what's going on and listen to each other's side of the story rather than try to find fault with each other. In this way, a couple will take each other's side in times of trouble and establish a deeper connection rather than trying to gain power or control. In fact, if they have emotional sensitivities from prior relationships such as fear of abandonment, loving couples will do anything within their power to avoid rewounding each other.

John puts it like this: "I've made many mistakes in my marriage, and I want to stop focusing on what is wrong with Sam and work on our plans to have a great life together. All too often when we start bickering it's because we both have issues from our past that affect how we treat each other."

John describes his hope of having a marriage with Samantha based on love and personal fulfillment. Ultimately, it will enable them to advance their personal relationship and career objectives. For instance, John would like to get a graduate degree in business, and he knows that Samantha would eventually like to open a small private school specializing in supporting children with autism and other childhood disorders. However, achieving these goals will require that they begin to tackle problems together rather than pointing fingers at each other and triggering each other's emotional baggage.

WHAT TO DO WHEN YOUR RELATIONSHIP BAGGAGE IS WEIGHING YOU DOWN

We all have a composite picture of the people who influenced us in the past—their looks, personality, tone of voice, behavior, and so many other factors that help define them. For instance, you might pick some-one as a mate who is emotionally detached because your father was that way and that's what you know. Although you know this person cannot meet your needs, you may have a repetition compulsion—an unconscious tendency to want to fix the past, to recreate it, to make it better. This idea goes back to the early twentieth-century psychoana-lyst Sigmund Freud. In *A General Introduction to Psychoanalysis*, Freud discusses the fact that the repetition compulsion manifested itself in many of his patients who endured problematic relationships by creat-ing toxic relationship dynamics. Breaking this pattern takes insight and great courage for remarried couples who may not be fully aware of it.

Fortunately, a second marriage can provide a chance to gain aware-ness of your vulnerabilities and heal childhood wounds, because you experience them within the safety of a loving partnership. The first step is to be open and feel secure with your spouse. Relationship experts Harville Hendrix and Helen LaKelly Hunt explain that our search for the "imago," the composite picture of those who were most influential in the past, is a desire to heal childhood wounds. In fact, our partner will inevitably reopen vulnerabilities. In *Making Marriage*

Simple, Hendrix and Hunt write, "Marriage gives you this chance to relive memories and feelings from your childhood, but with a different, happier outcome. As a child, you were helpless. As an adult, you have power. You can work with your partner so that each of you gets your needs met."

When we marry the second time around, we might not be aware that our emotional sensitivities may come to the surface and bump into our partner's vulnerabilities. For instance, I was unaware for many years that I brought a backlog of hurt, fears, and ambivalence from my first marriage into interactions with Craig. However, while on vacation with our youngest child one summer, Craig went off fishing and lost track of time. Since he didn't bring his cell phone, he couldn't text or call. Pacing the floor of our cabin, I worked myself into a frenzy, texted several family members, and blasted him when he walked in the door thirty minutes late. This approach caused him to get defensive and yell back at me. Rather than calmly listening to his side of the story, my fear of abandonment was triggered and I wasn't seeing him as the loving, caring husband he really is. As I mentioned earlier, Craig has an emotional sensitivity about entrapment, so he needs to feel more in control of his own schedule and time. In the past, my overreacting to him being late led to arguments and emotional upheaval.

In another situation, Amanda and Erik, remarried for six years and childless, struggle over intimacy issues because Amanda generalizes her fear of being hurt from the past to her present marriage. Amanda, a graphic designer, is articulate and engaging. At 36, she's aware that she sabotages relationships that might be good for her. However, in spite of her on-again, off-again romances, she fell in love with and married Erik, 38. They're working hard on nurturing a second marriage that works for both of them. Amanda knows she's her own saboteur and that Erik plans to stay around—he's faithful and in love with her. They've even discussed having a child, if they can get along better. At times, it's as if Amanda is wired to recreate the past, which casts a dark shadow over her remarriage. She can be self-destructive because she's accustomed to the drama of fights, even though she claims she wants harmony. Unfortunately, Amanda has become addicted to pain and feels uncomfortable when things are calm.

Amanda explains, "It's almost as if I'm hooked on pain. It's as if I'm so familiar with the adrenalin rush that I get from being in a bad relationship, I don't feel comfortable when Erik treats me right. But I'm working on that, and I'm better able to stop myself from threatening to leave him when I feel afraid. Seeing a marriage counselor has helped me work through these feelings and I know it's okay to have disagreements. This doesn't mean things are going to end."

GAIN AWARENESS OF VULNERABILITIES

Couples in second marriages are influenced by their first marriages and by outdated memories of their parents' examples of what it means to be a spouse. For instance, Amanda was raised in a divorced family. Her parents split when she was 6 years old, and she learned early on that when people have difficulty resolving conflicts, it can lead to the demise of a relationship. Amanda saw both of her mother's marriages fail and observed her giving up on love after her second divorce. Her father, who left the family to move in with a coworker, has had many unsuccessful relationships.

Erik reflects, "Suddenly we'll be talking and Amanda's gestures and tone of voice change. It's almost as if she isn't talking to me. She might yell or stomp around the room. That's when her accusations start, and she might threaten to leave or to throw me out. I'm usually feeling pretty perplexed and often just freeze. I don't know what to say or do."

Amanda responds, "It took me a few years to trust Erik and to realize that he wasn't going anywhere. As long as I am honest with him, he'll reciprocate and be real with me. If I start making things up or blaming him—and not owning my issues—I'll have an intense reaction to something he says or does out of the blue. When this happens, I ask Erik to remind me that this is past stuff and has nothing to do with us in the here and now."

In *Hold Me Tight*, clinical psychologist and distinguished researcher Sue Johnson explains that you can tell when one of your "raw spots" has been hit because there is a sudden shift in the emotional tone of the conversation. She explains, "You and your love were joking just a moment ago, but now one of you is upset or enraged, or, conversely, aloof or chilly. You are thrown off balance. It is as if the game changed and no one told you. The hurt partner is sending out new signals and the other tries to make sense of the change."

For instance, Amanda's fears of rejection due to her father leaving her family when she was young have made it hard for her to trust Erik. Her ex-husband, Brian, was also unfaithful before he left her. Even when Erik's actions were consistent with his words, she still found it difficult to trust him due to her fear of abandonment. She knows that he's nothing like her ex or her father, but being intimate with Erik sometimes triggers intense feelings of unworthiness and loneliness due to her past baggage.

FEAR OF ABANDONMENT

The scariest thing about falling in love is living with the knowledge that it might end. You are faced with a choice. You can come at relationships from a place of love and trust, or you can choose to be suspicious, doubtful, and wary. The most important thing to consider is whether your partner is worthy of trust. Have their actions matched their words? Does your partner treat you with respect? Is your partner reliable? Is your partner faithful and truthful? If the answer to these questions is yes, you must choose to trust. In chapter 5, you will learn more about how to work through trust issues and fear of abandonment that often surface for remarried partners who have felt betrayed.

As Amanda puts it, "Erik is trustworthy and loyal, but when things get difficult, I always feel like bailing out. I know I need to get over this, and Erik reminds me that he is there for me. It's just hard to remember that our marriage is different when I'm triggered from my past."

When you avoid dealing with memories from your parents' marriage and your own divorce, it can cause you to project inaccurate feelings and intentions onto your partner. For example, if your mother suffered from depression when you were growing up, and your father was gone a lot, you may have become a "parentified child" who took on too much responsibility. As an adult, you could be overbearing or controlling with your partner if you are not conscious of this pattern and take steps to overcome it. Becoming more aware of emotional triggers is an important step toward building trust and intimacy with your partner.

EMOTIONAL TRIGGERS

If you're not aware of your emotional triggers, let alone how to handle them, your second marriage will be more turbulent. Many times, I have seen unacknowledged triggers create suffering and chaos. Becoming more conscious of intense reactions and not denying them or becoming defensive is the first step to coping effectively. Identifying your emotional triggers is vital to a healthy second marriage. Bringing to consciousness those triggers that provoke extreme responses from you will lessen your risk of sabotaging your relationship by withdrawing or issuing ultimatums, such as threatening to end the relationship.

It truly is worth putting in the effort to explore your emotional triggers. The more aware you are, the less you'll be ruled by past relationships. Exploring your triggers is an ongoing process. The first step is actually to *commit* to the process by discussing the concept of triggers or "hot buttons." For instance, you might reflect on how you notice a sudden shift in the emotional tone of a conversation. Describing triggers will help you and your partner raise self-awareness.

Some Simple Ways to Identify Your "Hot Buttons"

How is your body reacting? Notice any tense muscles, increased heart rate, hot or cold flushes, tingles, or any physical changes that generally indicate contraction (or physically reacting from what your partner says or does). Ask yourself, "What is the first reaction in my body? Do my fists clench? Does my breathing speed up? Does my face turn hot or red? Do I feel like fleeing the situation? Do I feel frozen or unable to move?" Mentally note these reactions and even write them down. Remember that physical reactions can be subtle all the way to extreme, so don't rule anything out.

What thoughts seem intense or repeat themselves? Look for *extreme* thoughts with *opposing* viewpoints (i.e., someone or something is good/bad, right/wrong, nice/evil, etc.). You don't have to do anything else but be aware of these thoughts without reacting to them. Let them play out in your mind. What story is your mind creating about the other person or situation? I recommend simply listing these thoughts in your journal or in a notebook to enhance your self-awareness.

Who or what triggers an intense emotion? Once you have become aware of your physical reactions, notice when your spouse's words or actions trigger extreme physical and emotional responses within you. Sometimes you'll discover a single object, word, smell, or another sense impression that triggers you. Other times you'll notice that you're triggered by a certain belief, viewpoint, or overall situation. For example, your trigger could range from anything such as loud sounds to a partner who is overly controlling and opinionated. However, you may have a whole series of triggers (most people do), so be vigilant and open to perceiving a whole range of things that set you off. Remember, it's important that you record these triggers in some kind of journal (either printed or digital). Writing them down will help cement them in your mind so that you remain self-aware in the future.

What happened before you were triggered? Sometimes there are certain "preconditions" to being triggered—for example, having a stressful day at work, waking up "on the wrong side of the bed," going to a certain uncomfortable place (such as the bank or a doctor's office), or listening to the children argue. Virtually anything could set the stage for being triggered later on. When you identify your emotional triggers, you may be able to prevent yourself from being triggered in the future simply by slowing down and reflecting upon them once you're aware of the trigger prerequisites.

What needs of yours were not being met? When we're triggered emotionally, it can usually be traced to one or more of our deepest needs or desires not being met. Take some time to think about which of your needs or desires were being threatened:

- Acceptance
- Autonomy
- Attention
- Safety
- Love
- Respect
- Predictability
- Being liked
- Being needed
- Being right
- Being valued
- Being treated fairly
- Being in control

Becoming aware of your body, thoughts, unmet needs and desires, and certain people or situations that set you off will help you get a better handle on your emotions—to not overreact or lose control. For instance, you might feel overwhelmed by attending a family event and either freeze, feel like arguing with someone, or even have a strong desire to leave. By being aware of your triggers, such as feeling threatened by being with close family members, you'll be better able to cope.

Five Ways to Cope with Triggers

Now that you have become more aware of "triggers" by tuning in to your body, thoughts, and unmet needs, work on becoming more aware of certain situations or words, or your partner's actions, that seem to trigger these reactions. The following is a list of some ways to help you cope more effectively with extreme emotions such as anger and fear so that you will be able to be calmer and more reflective.

1. **Remove your attention from the person or situation and focus on your breath.** One thing is certain, your breath is always there with you—it is part of you and accessible, and therefore a reliable way to relax. Focus on your in-breath and out-breath for a few minutes. Breathe in through your nose and exhale through your mouth as you count to ten. Thinking about a pleasant place can help you relax. Try imagining yourself in your favorite place. If your attention goes back to the triggering person or situation, pull your attention back to your breathing.

2. **Take a break.** Remove yourself from the situation. Walk away for five minutes and cool down. If you're speaking with someone, excuse yourself temporarily and say that you need to go to the bathroom or somewhere else. Return when you are feeling calmer and more centered.

3. **Find the humor in the situation.** Practicing this suggestion is not always possible, but you might be surprised how much laughter and pleasure lightens your mood and perspective. When I say find the humor in the situation, I don't mean necessarily laughing out loud. Instead, look at the situation from a different perspective and find the humor in it.

4. **Ask yourself why you are being triggered.** Your emotional triggers may have a way of blindsiding you. To offset this, ask yourself, "Why am I feeling so fearful or angry?" Understanding why you're being triggered will help you regain a sense of calmness, self-awareness, and control.

5. **Do not gloss over your feelings, but do not act on them.** Trying to resist your feelings isn't the solution. However, you can delay your emotional reactions. For instance, if you're feeling enraged by someone, instead of exploding at them, consciously set those feelings aside to experience and unleash later in a healthy way. You might choose to express this anger by screaming in your room or doing an intense workout. However, be

very careful not to repress your emotions. There's a fine line between consciously delaying your emotions and unconsciously suppressing them—this is why it's so important to practice the self-awareness suggestions in this chapter.

Healthy intimate relationships provide couples with a safe place for speaking out and voicing both positive and negative emotions without fear of negative consequences. Often, having gone through a divorce (your own but also your parents') can leave you with a fear of failure in relationships. This fear may make it difficult for you to be vulnerable with an intimate partner. If you spend more time second-guessing your partner's comments or reactions than examining your own behavior, this next section is tailor made for you!

IF IT'S INTENSE, IT'S YOUR OWN

When you feel intensely hurt or angry with your partner, it is common to want to blame them. It may seem obvious to you at that moment that your spouse is the person who needs to change. In reality, it's often your own baggage that's influencing your emotions. According to marriage counselor Mona Barbera, the truth about that kind of pain doesn't come from your partner's words or actions. As she explains in her cutting-edge book *Bring Yourself to Love*, "As I like to tell my clients, if it's intense, it's your own." Barbera suggests that when you deal with your own internal pain, your partner won't easily trigger an intense reaction when they do something that hurts or disappoints you. She writes, "It is hard to think clearly when you get tangled up with your partner."

However, when you're blaming your partner or distancing yourself from them, it doesn't make the pain go away. You still have to deal with your partner, who is probably angry with you for being blamed, attacked, or abandoned. In some cases, you will get the opposite reaction from what you really need—to feel loved. This is really a core issue for many people who sabotage relationships.

Todd and Megan, both in their midforties, personify this pattern. They have been remarried for seven years and are raising three children in a blended family. "I've been unhappy for some time," complains

Megan. "I've asked Todd to be more considerate of my needs, but things don't appear to be changing. It feels like I'm at the bottom of his list." To this, Todd responds, "Megan just doesn't make me happy anymore and things just aren't getting better." The common thread in these statements is this couple's focus on "fixing" the other person rather than on taking specific actions to change their part in an undesirable relationship dynamic.

Unfortunately, Todd and Megan are trapped in a vicious cycle of blame and defensiveness due to their emotional baggage and unwillingness to accept what they each contribute to their negative pattern of interactions. Since Megan felt ignored by her ex-spouse, she is quick to blame Todd when she feels left out or hurt by his actions. On the other hand, after dealing with an unhappy first marriage and a bitter divorce that lasted several years, Todd is easily frustrated with Megan because he just wants things to run smoothly.

Trying to change someone can be deadly for an intimate relationship. Instead, in a healthy partnership, your focus needs to shift away from how to "fix" the other person and toward a broader perspective of how to repair your relationship. The first person you need to examine is yourself. (In chapter 8, you'll learn more about how trying to change your partner can be damaging to your remarriage.)

Like all challenges in life, greater awareness and willingness to work on an issue can spark change. Successful remarried couples use productive disagreements, which are more like discussions than arguments, to improve their sense of security and communication. According to stepfamily expert Patricia L. Papernow, it can take a remarried family up to four years to reach a state of equilibrium, but with time and patience, you can create the kind of remarriage you need to thrive. Over time, many of the kinks in your relationship will smooth out as you weather the storms of remarriage together!

Four Action Steps for a Loving Dialogue

Be prepared for your discussions to be intense sometimes, especially when controversial issues and emotional baggage come into play. Each of you will have your own way of reacting to comments and concerns.

Since there will be disagreements, it is essential that you each show respect and kindness. Practice the following steps for thirty minutes each day with your partner. Then plan a special activity to do together each week. You may want to modify or add steps to your dialogue.

1. **Offer unconditional loving-kindness to your partner.** This includes support and compassion if they are upset (rather than justifying your position). When you are engaged in an argument, find a quiet time and place to talk. Set ground rules for respectful conduct, such as "No name-calling or yelling is allowed."

2. **Seek to use soft emotions when expressing feelings such as fear or hurt, rather than anger and disappointment.** Also, genuinely aim to understand your partner's point of view, without debate, criticism, or judgment, when they express tender emotions. It's normal for emotions such as fear to come up when your emotional sensitivities are being triggered. Remember that love and caring take time to develop in a remarried family, and fear can turn into anger if it's repressed.

3. **Don't take things personally when you disagree.** Imagine that your partner's concerns have nothing to do with your character or worth. If you find yourself getting triggered, picture that there aren't any threats, assaults, or insults in your partner's statements. They're just speaking about what upsets them, but it doesn't change your value or worth. If your partner says something hurtful, such as "You're too sensitive," resist the temptation to respond with a counterattack, such as "You're too critical." Instead, let them know you feel hurt, take some personal space, and agree to talk when your emotions have simmered down.

4. **Brainstorm ways to creatively deal with your partner's concerns.** Be sure to ask your partner to express their concerns fully before you speak or offer a solution. This will help both of you communicate more effectively, repair any misunderstandings or hurt feelings, and problem-solve solutions.

Focusing on being especially compassionate when there's a rough spot can go a long way toward creating a safe emotional space for both of you. This safety net can help promote intimacy and understanding without winners or losers (no one wins). The relationship wins when you both generate a solution within the context of a loving relationship. You don't have to let your past dictate the decisions you make today!

4

Don't Keep Secrets about Money

earning how to have productive, low-conflict discussions about money is essential to handling remarried finances in a healthy way. Money is a touchy subject for all couples, but the financial considerations of a second marriage are more complicated than a first marriage, often involving child support, alimony, and the multifaceted expenses of blended families. Common concerns include who pays for school and college expenses for children—yours, mine, and ours. Some remarried couples might want to consider a prenuptial agreement if they have survived financial infidelity, have unequal assets, or simply feel it's wise to protect their assets prior to walking down the aisle.

Couples who remarry often bring financial baggage with them, including obligations, responsibilities, and stressors—especially if they have children from their first marriage. This pressure can be compounded by the financial strain of having one or more mutual children. Some remarried couples bring debt from a previous marriage into the union that needs to be addressed during the early phase of blending two families. Because the average age of remarried couples is older than first-time married ones, saving for retirement can also be a particular concern for many couples in second marriages.

In *Money Advice for Your Successful Remarriage*, financial expert Patricia Schiff Estess explains that people always have a need for money, but remarried couples with children are worse off economically relative to other married people. She theorizes that they may experience ongoing money worries because they simply have more financial obligations than other married couples due to child support and alimony payments, as well as leftover debt from a previous marriage. The ongoing expected and unexpected expenses of children as they grow up are often the responsibility of biological parents and stepparents. In spite of the fact that stepparents are not legally responsible for their spouse's children, life is not exactly simple, and the vast majority of stepparents take on some financial responsibility for their stepchildren. This is primarily due to caring about their well-being and because their lives intermingle over time.

Despite the fact that financial issues and money problems are the number one subject couples argue about and a leading cause of divorce, there are very few studies of stepfamilies' financial preparations. One study by researchers Lawrence H. Ganong and Marilyn Coleman discovered that only one-quarter of remarried couples had discussed their finances prior to marrying. It's no wonder, since money matters trigger intense emotions for many people and are a major cause of stress in marriage and a primary reason why couples divorce.

In my case, I was a single parent raising two school-age children when I met my second husband, Craig, and fell in love. Truth be told, I had accumulated debt from living beyond my means as a single parent, and I was embarrassed to tell him about this fact. Wanting to impress Craig with my financial independence, I felt ashamed about my debts and feared losing him. But after several years together, it was becoming more obvious to him that I didn't enter our marriage with a clean financial slate, and I realized that by keeping secrets about my debt and financial obligations, I was breeding mistrust between us. Since money was such a hot-button issue in my first marriage, I was used to concealing debts and purchases for myself and our children. However, I was starting to feel uncomfortable with my financial infidelity because I love Craig and want our marriage to stand the test of time.

If couples have not established a bedrock of trust and vulnerability together, they might be more prone to committing financial infidelity. If you consistently feel uneasy because you can't trust your partner, even minor mistakes or errors in judgment can make you feel vulnerable, in spite of your partner offering a good explanation for their actions. In other words, by keeping secrets or lying to your partner, you put your relationship in jeopardy because your partner may have lost a sense of trust and security that couples need to thrive and grow resilient together.

IS KEEPING SECRETS ABOUT MONEY THE SAME AS LYING?

Trust is fragile in a remarriage. Secrets and lies endanger trust because they block intimacy and are a form of betrayal. Keeping secrets and lying by omission are the same as lying. However, people often rationalize keeping secrets because they think telling the truth will make things worse, or they are trying to protect themselves. Usually they lack confidence in their ability to fully disclose and explain money troubles or issues related to past or present financial mistakes. In reality, a pattern of keeping secrets in a remarriage is a red flag that the relationship is unhealthy and the couple has unresolved trust issues from prior relationships.

For example, Tamara and Calvin, whom you met earlier, were raising three children in a stepfamily and dealing with ongoing feelings of mistrust. For the first few years of their relationship, Calvin kept secrets from Tamara about a debt he owed to his former business partner. They had tied the knot after a rushed six-month engagement and had not adequately talked about their past. Suddenly, just as they were celebrating their second anniversary, Calvin got an email from his former business partner, demanding thousands of dollars to pay off a loan that they had taken out together. Tamara happened to be cleaning the house and saw the email on Calvin's computer screen. She was horrified.

To make matters worse, Calvin became very defensive when Tamara attempted to discuss the email and the debt with him. Sadly, they were unable to be vulnerable with each other and have an honest conversation, and Calvin's financial infidelity and subsequent defensiveness sparked animosity and mistrust between them that lasted for many years.

Tamara explains, "I love Calvin, and he's basically a good person, but he never told me the details about his debt to Alex. If I understand something, I'm much better able to process and deal with it. But it's like Calvin had this deep, dark secret and didn't trust me enough to share it with me. I was finally able to drag the details out of him and found out that he owed Alex over $50,000. This was a hard pill to swallow, but the worst part was his dishonesty."

When your partner withholds important financial information from you, regardless of their reasons, it's normal to lose faith in them. Any time someone keeps secrets, especially about something as important as money, they run the risk of losing their partner's trust forever. It is usually a formidable challenge to regain it. The mistrust will linger in the back of your mind—mistrust about your partner's love for you, fear of abandonment, and so forth. So much about trust is walking the talk. All too often, when a person isn't feeling safe enough in a relationship to be honest and open with their partner, it's because they don't believe that their partner truly loves them and they fear losing them, or they are overly protective of their own interests.

WHAT IS FINANCIAL INFIDELITY AND WHAT TO DO ABOUT IT?

What we're talking about here is financial infidelity, consciously or deliberately lying to your partner about money, credit, and/or debt. We're not talking about occasionally forgetting to record a check or debit card transaction but rather a situation where one partner hides a money-related secret from the other. According to the National Endowment for Financial Education, two in five American adults (41%) have committed financial infidelity.

Sometimes financial infidelity goes unnoticed for years, while in other cases a partner may suspect it's happening but use rationalization or denial because they have trouble believing that their loved one would be deceitful. This is especially true during the "romantic stage," an early period of remarriage when couples tend to wear rose-colored glasses and want to see the best in each other. This can cause people to overlook mistakes or flaws in their partner's character. We will discuss distinct stages related to financial issues and remarriage later in this chapter.

Susan, a remarried woman I interviewed, puts it like this: "I was mostly disgusted with myself and embarrassed when Jeremy found out about my secret account. How could I rationalize doing to my second husband what my ex had done to me? I know this is an excuse, but I just felt so insecure about money and felt like I had to hide some in case Jeremy decided to take off suddenly like Sam did. I'm not sure I'll ever recover from the fact that Sam took off with my savings and all the cash I had."

After attending couples counseling sessions, Susan and Jeremy, both in their midforties and childless, were able to get to the root of Susan's problems with secrecy about money. They discussed how Jeremy fed into it by being very controlling and withdrawn whenever Susan tried to engage him in a conversation about finances.

Jeremy reflects, "I came to realize that I wasn't an innocent bystander and Susan was reacting out of issues from her first marriage. Our counselor helped us see that we both contributed to the problem. After several months of therapy, we began having regular and honest discussions about money and we're getting stronger as a couple."

WHY DOES FINANCIAL INFIDELITY HAPPEN?

Often financial infidelity can be a symptom of deeper issues in a marriage. As with Susan and Jeremy, it can have roots in feelings of insecurity and a need for protection or control. Like many couples, Susan and Jeremy rarely spoke about their problems, so it was easy for Susan to feel entitled to stash away funds in a secret account.

Poor communication skills combined with baggage from the past can be disastrous for a remarriage because it destroys trust and intimacy. Likewise, when couples are dishonest and one or both of you try to gain control or achieve security by withholding important financial information, the fabric of your remarriage can be seriously damaged.

Eight Red Flags of Financial Infidelity

1. **You find credit card statements for an account you were not aware of.** You notice paperwork for an account you know nothing about. The spending was disguised or kept secret from you, and there is often a significant balance.

2. **Your name has been removed from a joint checking, savings, or credit card account.** You probably don't find out about this right away, and your spouse probably has a reasonable explanation for covering up the real reasons they are making this move without telling you, such as excessive spending, debts, or investments.

3. **Your partner becomes overly concerned about collecting the mail.** They might even leave work early to make sure that they collect the mail before you do.

4. **Your partner has new possessions that they attempt to hide from you.** When you ask about them, your partner seems too busy to talk or they change the topic.

5. **Cash or money in your savings or checking account goes missing.** Your mate doesn't really have a good explanation for this, and they brush it off as a bank mistake or they minimize the loss.

6. **Your partner becomes overly emotional or defensive when you want to discuss money.** They may yell, accuse you of being insensitive, and/or start crying when you bring up finances.

7. **Your partner lies about expenses and when you confront them, they get defensive.** They use denial as a defense mechanism and refuse to admit that they have a problem.

8. **Your partner seems very worried about money and overly interested in budgeting.** While this can be a good thing in the long run, it may be a sign that they are being deceptive, siphoning money into a secret account, or have a hidden spending problem.

The first step in dealing with financial infidelity is admitting that there's a problem and fostering a willingness to get professional help. Both people in a relationship need to be honest about their present and past financial mistakes so that they can truly repair the damage done. That means bringing out every statement, credit card receipt, bill, checking or savings account statement, loan, or other evidence of spending.

Next, both partners need to make a commitment to work through issues together. The person who was betrayed needs time to adjust to the details of the breach of trust, and this does not happen overnight. Likewise, the person who is the perpetrator of the financial infidelity needs to be completely transparent and willing to make a promise to stop the destructive behavior. They must change their daily habits of spending and/or hiding money, lending money to others, or even gambling. If someone has a gambling addiction, they will need to seek specialized treatment for this problem before couples counseling can be effective. In any case, feelings of anger, betrayal, and grief need to be dealt with if a couple is going to regain trust. Keep in mind that it takes time to do this, and couples counseling can be highly beneficial in this process.

Four Steps to Owning Up to Financial Infidelity in Your Remarriage

1. **Understand that your partner may need time to process your disclosure.** When you first tell them about your secrecy, they may be in shock and feel deeply hurt and betrayed.

2. **Share details about your past and current debts. Keep in mind that you will be discussing emotions as well as numbers.** For instance, Jeremy said to Susan, "I felt so hurt when I found out about your secret bank account." Share details about your past and current debts, as well as your spending habits. Full disclosure is highly recommended so that your partner can begin to rebuild trust.

3. **Offer your partner reassurance that you have made a commitment to change.** You may need to do this by showing them bank and/or credit card statements and having weekly meetings.

4. **Commit to doing whatever is necessary to rebuild trust with your partner.** This includes working to rid yourself of debt and spending habits that are contributing to any financial problems in your remarriage. Consider counseling sessions as a couple to gain support and a neutral party's feedback for at least eight to twelve sessions or until you see improvement.

Remarried couples often underestimate the challenges of blending two distinct worlds and buy into the myth that love will conquer all. They avoid talking about finances because it stirs up conflict. Critical junctures in a marriage such as buying a new home, starting a new job, or adding one or more mutual children to the family can spark anxiety about money.

BUILDING FINANCIAL TRUST IN FOUR STAGES

Understanding the following stages can help you build trust in your partner after getting remarried, especially after financial infidelity has occurred. Remember that there are degrees of financial betrayal and trust issues, and one size does not fit all.

1. **Romantic stage.** You typically wear rose-colored glasses while dating and first married. You are so happy to have found love the second time around that you might be reluctant to disclose debts and financial obligations. Be aware of this and seek to be more open and honest with your partner because keeping secrets can breed mistrust.

2. **Keep-the-peace stage.** Once you have lived together for a while and struggles emerge, it's normal not to want to rock the boat.

During this phase, it's crucial to sit down with your partner, away from your children, to discuss your income, financial responsibilities, debts, and budget. Remarried couples should also discuss their financial histories and realize this conversation can have emotional overtones.

3. **Reality-sets-in stage.** Once you have been dating or living together for a while, it's a good idea to confront money issues. These include any prior debt you and your spouse brought to the union, the expenses of your biological and stepchildren, spending styles, budgeting issues, and a myriad of other related topics. It's best to tackle these issues early on in your relationship to promote full disclosure and honesty. Now is not the time to be coy or beat around the bush. Keeping secrets or concealing debt or financial responsibility usually backfires and won't engender trust and good communication with your partner over time.

4. **Acceptance stage.** If you and your spouse stay together for over a decade, and money issues follow you, you will likely reach a stage when you are tired of arguing about money. It's time to accept and surrender. You and your spouse are now motivated to find ways to pay off debts, finance college, and plan for retirement. Unfortunately, couples who have been keeping debt secrets or overspending or have experienced a decline in income due to job loss or poor investments may feel a sense of panic at this stage. Wise couples seek financial help when this happens, and they approach their money troubles with a "united we stand" mind-set rather than allowing financial strain to divide them and lead to breakup.

With time and patience, you will be able to identify your fears and concerns. Remember, there is no "right" or "wrong" way to deal with issues such as unequal assets, child support, alimony, and private school and college expenses. Also remember that feelings are not "good" or "bad"; they are just real emotions that need to be identified, processed, and shared effectively without blame.

Money issues are often buried so deeply in our emotions that it's difficult to know what we believe or where our money attitudes come from. In *Debt-Proof Your Marriage: How to Manage Your Money Together*, financial expert and author Mary Hunt puts it this way: "Of all the issues in your marriage, money has the greatest potential to ruin your relationship. That's the bad news. The good news is that knowledge is power, and learning why money is so difficult will help you make a huge leap toward financial harmony."

What I learned from listening to the stories of couples who struggled with financial pressure and financial infidelity is that arguments about money are usually not really about money but stem from our history with it. And for better or worse, our relationship with it really starts during childhood and is a blend of family background and our unique take on the role it plays in our happiness. Layer in our experiences in our first marriage and it's no wonder things get messy.

ARGUMENTS ABOUT MONEY ARE RARELY ABOUT MONEY

Maybe it was your father being laid off from work, your mother complaining about making ends meet, or your divorced parents fighting about child support. Or growing up with an alcoholic parent who was unable to contribute much to the financial success of your family. No matter your stresses, you may have promised yourself that your life was going to be different and you'd be able to stay out of debt and live a peaceful life in the home of your dreams. In my case, I remember telling myself I would never get a divorce, talk about money in front of my children, or marry someone who was self-employed like my father, who as a freelance artist struggled to support five children.

For the most part, your family and relationship history will impact your emotions and behavior related to finances. For instance, Tara, 48, whom you met previously, was raised in a single-parent home where money was scarce, and her mother complained about not receiving regular child support from her father. When Tara divorced in her late thirties, she promised herself and her ex-spouse that she wanted to keep things amicable and work out financial issues fairly. Having adjusted reasonably well to being a single mom for a few years, Tara was blindsided when she met Conner, 49, who proposed after dating only six months. He proclaimed that he was eager to have his first child (her third) and believed that they needed to rush to tie the knot so they could get started.

In order to move ahead quickly with their plans of expanding their family, Tara and Conner got married without taking much time to successfully navigate the reality-sets-in or acceptance stages. When Conner announced to Tara that he was going to graduate school to further his career and advance from high school teacher to principal, all she thought about at first was more money being spent on his degree. Tara also worried about his increased work demands. Conner's ambition scared her because her ex-spouse was a workaholic who spent little time with her or their two children. Because Tara and Conner had difficulty being vulnerable with each other and having honest discussions about money, they began arguing a lot and lost some of the positive feelings and closeness that they had during their courtship and first year of remarriage. They never seemed to find time to discuss the hurdles that they would be facing as a remarried family raising three children.

In addition, Tara and Conner both entered their remarriage with significant financial baggage. For instance, Tara's ex-husband betrayed her financially by wiping out their checking and savings accounts before he left, and Conner's ex-wife was very controlling about money. Once they realized how different their backgrounds and perspectives were, they were able to calmly discuss their goals and create a budget that worked for them based on their mutual interests and dreams.

FINANCIAL BAGGAGE FROM YOUR FIRST MARRIAGE

Since financial stress is a major cause of divorce, it makes sense that there will be plenty of baggage left over from a first marriage that might spill into a second marriage. Most people who have been through a divorce understand how resentment can build up when couples bring into their relationship not only sharply divergent attitudes about money but also baggage that can cause them to have unrealistic expectations or concerns about the financial contributions the other person might make to the household. Since money has such powerful emotional connotations, there aren't any simple solutions to the challenges that couples face.

One of the first couples I interviewed, Judith and Rodney, in their late fifties, struggled with money matters because Judith had difficulty staying within a budget and made too many credit card purchases. Married for over ten years, they were raising four children: two teenagers from Rodney's first marriage, ages 17 and 19; and two mutual children, ages 7 and 9.

Rodney laments about Judith's financial infidelity: "It's very expensive to raise kids, and yet Judith continues to have a shopping addiction and charges hundreds of dollars on clothes for herself and the kids that she and they don't need. I'm much more conservative about money and don't believe in using credit cards. We need to sit down and plan a budget, and Judith needs to stop overspending."

For couples like Judith and Rodney, it's important to build trust and openly discuss financial concerns. Ideally it's best to have open disclosure about finances prior to marriage. However, when this doesn't happen, the next best thing is to do so as soon as possible. There is no time like the present.

Judith puts it like this: "I had a lot of guilt because I kept my shopping addiction from Rod for so long. My guilt only went away when we started talking about my debts, spending habits, and our budget. It's still really hard for me to talk to him about money. I know he'll never trust me, and he'll probably leave me if I continue to overspend."

I cannot overstate how crucial it is for you to be open about money if you want your remarriage to succeed. If you work together to build a strong financial future, it's possible for you to be transparent and trust that your partner won't leave you or criticize you for past mistakes. However, when you have significant financial baggage, unequal assets, marry older in life, or feel the need to protect yourself if you were a victim of financial infidelity before, you may want to consider a prenuptial agreement.

WHEN DO YOU CONSIDER
A PRENUPTIAL AGREEMENT?

Most people considering marriage—whether the first, second, or third—shy away from making a prenuptial agreement. The very thought of such an agreement raises trust issues and can lead to explosive conversations. However, when people remarry later in life, many concerns arise that could be addressed in a prenuptial agreement. They include supporting each other through retirement and old age; leaving assets to children, stepchildren, and "mutual children," if the marriage is ongoing at the time of death; and ensuring a peaceful divorce if the remarriage fails. Further, a prenuptial agreement can be a vehicle to help you decide how to support yourselves during the remarriage and make mutual decisions about finances that feel fair to both of you.

Some experts believe that prenuptial agreements lead to breakups because they promote defensiveness, but others feel they encourage honest discussion about finances. For instance, Tamara might have considered a prenuptial agreement had she known that Calvin owed $50,000 to his former business partner. In my case, Craig and I had fairly similar incomes and assets when we were engaged, so we decided not to draw up a prenuptial agreement before we got married. However, we met with an attorney and established a trust for my two children from my first marriage that included provisions for all three of our children in the event that I die before Craig. I felt that establishing an estate plan would provide for Craig, ensure that my assets be distributed fairly among our three children, and promote a sense of fairness for my two children from my prior marriage.

On the other hand, there are plenty of scenarios where a couple entering a remarriage might want to consider a prenuptial agreement. It can protect a more affluent partner when a couple has unequal assets, retirement funds, homes, and sometimes children from a prior marriage. It can also give people greater peace of mind if they were victims of financial infidelity in their first marriage or have concerns about having funds for retirement. Since the divorce rate for second and third marriages is between 60 and 73 percent, compared to 50 percent for first-time married couples, it's reasonable enough to want to protect your assets and ensure for a nonadversarial divorce if the marriage fails. Whether or not you choose to have a prenup, I highly recommend openly discussing the details of your past and current finances. In my experience, transparency often prevents divorce, and it's certainly better to know if you will have trouble discussing finances prior to marriage rather than after the complications of remarriage set in.

Ultimately it boils down to this: finances are essential to every aspect of your life, and discussing them openly provides you and your partner the best opportunity for building the foundation of a strong remarriage.

The Budget Overview

Here is the essential financial information that remarried couples need to discuss even if they do not have a prenuptial agreement:

- Assets: stocks, savings, belongings, etc.

- Debts: credit cards, loans, alimony, child support, etc.

- Obligations: children, parents, and pledges to charities and institutions

- Insurance: life insurance (amounts of coverage and who your beneficiaries are)

- Retirement savings

- Belongings of value such as expensive jewelry or cars and items in a safe deposit box

It's a great idea to type up a list of the items above and sign it together. You can adjust the items or add to them as they change. Some couples may prefer to meet with a lawyer and draw up a formal agreement, but others will want to do so informally, sign it, and keep a copy in a safe deposit box.

DEALING WITH DEBT IN A SECOND MARRIAGE AND MAKING A BUDGET PLAN

According to a recent "Couples and Money Study" from Fidelity, more than half of all couples surveyed said they carried debt into their relationships and 20 percent admitted that it had a negative impact. Among respondents who were concerned about debt, almost half said that money is their biggest relationship challenge and 67 percent said they argue about money regularly.

In order to deal effectively with bringing debt into a remarriage, you must make a commitment to having regular, open dialogues about money, follow the steps to deal with financial infidelity if it exists, and develop a budget plan geared toward a debt-free remarriage. Fortunately Mary Hunt's *Debt-Proof Your Marriage* is a good resource for building a budget plan. This list summarizes her suggestions with my own advice added:

1. **Write a record of spending.** This is a detailed list of your average monthly income and a detailed recording of where your income goes. This list becomes your baseline and it will include debts from previous marriages (credits cards, loans, etc.).

2. **Review your record at the end of one week.** Discuss the spending that took place without criticism or anger. Try to be as businesslike as possible, and avoid overreaction or drama if you want your partner to continue sharing.

3. **Develop a monthly record based on four weekly records.** You can label it something like "Bonnie and Jeff's Monthly Spending Record." Be sure to total up all categories of expenditures.

4. **Look at money leaks and laundering.** Leaks (money that is pouring out of your bank account) and laundering (spending that's kept secret or skimmed to avoid confrontation) will make it hard to build trust and allow you to reach financial success in your remarriage.

In order to keep a record of income and expenditures for over a three-month period, place everything into a category (see item 1 above), explains Patricia Schiff Estess in *Money Advice for Your Successful Remarriage*. At minimum, you'll want the following categories and should feel free to add more and revise:

- Basic housing costs: rent/mortgage, insurance, utilities, water, fuel, etc.

- Phone: cell phones, landline, etc.

- Housing upkeep: repairs, furniture, equipment, appliances, household help, etc.

- Groceries

- Meals in restaurants and takeout

- Entertainment: recreation, movies, plays, concerts, community events, etc.

- Clothing: purchases, dry cleaning

- Transportation: car payments, gas, car repairs and maintenance, subway, bus fair, tolls, etc.

- Vacations: airfare, gas, hotels, car rentals, meals, entertainment

- Education: private school and college tuition, online learning fees, certification programs, textbooks, preparatory instruction and training

- Medical: co-pays and monthly contributions to health insurance; out-of-pocket expenses, including medicine

- Family: childcare, child support, allowances

- Savings and investments: pension and retirement plan contributions; investments, including real estate

- Charity and gifts: church contributions, alumni donations, nonprofit organizations, etc.

- Debt: interest and principal payments you're making monthly

- Taxes: federal, state, local

- Personal: pocket money that's hard to keep track of and used for beverages, snacks, etc.

Don't forget to add up everything on this ledger and try keeping as little cash in your pocket as possible so you can better track your expenses. Once you have a clear view of your assets and expenses, you'll be in a better position to come up with a detailed budget plan. Examples of different ways to do this can be found online or in Mary Hunt's *Debt-Proof Your Marriage*. Before you make up your detailed budget plan, take time to decide which money management system is the best one for your remarried family.

MONEY MANAGEMENT: YOURS, MINE, AND OURS

Coming up with a system of managing your money that you both agree with can be a challenge. This may bring up the issues of unequal assets, debts, and differences in your philosophies about spending, saving, and so on. Stepfamily researcher Barbara Fishman interviewed sixteen middle-class stepfamilies and found that most tend to adopt either a *common-pot* or *two-pot* economic system. In the common-pot system, economic resources are pooled and distributed according to need regardless of biological relatedness, whereas in the two-pot system, economic resources are divided and distributed mostly according to biological lines. Fishman's findings suggest that concern for the good of the family underlies the common-pot economic system, whereas the two-pot system encourages economic independence and personal autonomy. However, distinguished family researcher Kay Pasley studied ninety-one remarried couples and found few differences between the happiness and satisfaction of remarried couples when comparing their financial management styles. Truth be told, no one system of money management is perfect; it is really a matter of what couples are comfortable with. The list below outlines three basic styles:

> **Common-pot system.** All of a couple's money is combined into a collective checking and savings account. This includes debts, child support, and each partner's income. Couples literally pool their financial resources together.

> **Two-pot system.** Couples keep their incomes, payments, bills, and debts in two separate individual checking and savings accounts and handle all child-rearing and household expenses on a fifty-fifty basis.

> **Three-pot system.** Each partner handles personal expenses of themselves and the children they brought to the marriage, while both contribute to a third account that's used for the upkeep of the entire family (mortgage or rent, food, household repairs, insurance, vacations, etc.).

Overall, studies show that higher-functioning remarried families pool finances and have higher levels of commitment, trust, and family cohesion using the common-pot system compared to families who keep their money separate. Further, couples who simply endorse the belief system that their money should be pooled have more positive interactions and higher marital quality than those who don't. Remarried couples who discuss beliefs about financial management, come to an agreement, and share resources enjoy higher levels of marital well-being when compared with those who avoid dealing with these issues.

In terms of stepfamilies, another common issue—particularly for families of some means—is who will pay for private school and college tuition. Many couples feel comfortable with the three-pot system in order to make things somewhat fair for partners who don't have children or who might resent paying for the educational expenses of their stepchildren. On the other hand, I have interviewed and counseled many couples who don't have strict boundaries regarding educational expenses and feel agreeable and happy to pitch in.

In our family, the common-pot system has worked well for over two decades because it prompts us to have full disclosure about finances and to rely on each other for financial and emotional support. When my husband first suggested that we adopt this method, I resisted it due to my former pattern of being secretive about my debts and spending habits. But in the long run, using this method has brought us closer together through regular communication about money and sharing resources. In my life, the things that I resist often are just those things that allow me to learn the most valuable lessons; adopting the common-pot system of money management is one of those things.

Other couples may find that the two-pot or three-pot system works well for their relationship. The key to success is being able to discuss your options openly and to come to an agreement or compromise that suits your personal and family objectives. The beauty of open disclosure of finances is that you're allowing each other to be vulnerable about one of the touchiest topics for all couples. It's quite a hurdle to jump over, and you can celebrate together with your favorite meal, picnic, beverage, or walk in the park!

A HOME OF OUR OWN: MOVING IN AND MOVING ON

For most remarried couples, deciding where to live before or after marriage elicits mixed feelings and can spark the flames of conflict. After all, the expressions "home is where the heart is" and "there is no place like home" strike emotional chords for a reason. After a divorce, some people sell the property owned with their former partner, divide assets, and move into different residences. For others, one partner buys out the other one and stays in the home. Either way, divorcing families usually experience some emotional upheaval. When a remarried couple is making the decision about where to live when they merge their households, it can be a time of emotional turmoil, and partners can become territorial and tense. The degree of stress engendered by moving in together can depend on many factors, such as whether there are school-age children (who might benefit from staying in the same district), how far the commutes are to each partner's workplace, and the financial advantages or disadvantages of living in an existing residence versus buying a new home together.

For instance, Andrea and Karl had been dating for four years and were engaged when they discussed moving in together. They couldn't agree where they would live because Karl worked fifty miles from the town where she lived with her two children. When she divorced three years prior, Andrea had purchased a home close to her ex-husband's, in the same school district where her two children, Debra and Tommy, ages 10 and 13, had been attending school.

Fortunately, Andrea and her ex-husband had sold their marital home and believed that they had a fair agreement and comfortable situation where their children could spend close to equal time with both of them. While Andrea would have been happy to move closer to Karl's work, her children and ex-husband balked at the idea of moving to a new town and starting fourth and seventh grades in new schools. Ultimately Andrea and Karl moved into her home temporarily and made plans to look for a home that would allow them to start fresh in a community that might make it easier for her children to have stability and spend time with their father. Karl's negotiating chip was that he could pick the style of the home and have a home office so that he could work from home to minimize his commute. Although this was not an ideal situation for Andrea and Karl, they were becoming more comfortable with their decision the last time we talked and believed it was a good compromise.

Andrea puts it like this: "I know it was a lot to ask Karl to commute much farther to work, but his kids are grown, and I had to tell him that not keeping Debra and Tommy in the same schools was a deal breaker for me. He wants to be a loving stepdad and so was willing to make compromises as long as we bought a home together and he had some say in which one we purchased."

Andrea and Karl's story is fairly typical of the remarried couples that I interviewed. About 70 percent of them reported tension and financial stress related to selecting a residence. Most of them wanted to write the first chapter of their new marriage in a home neither one of them had lived in before. The following list are things to consider when getting over this hurdle and moving on to a peaceful coexistence. But moving into a new home is no panacea, and children often have to adjust to living in two homes and to living with a stepparent and maybe stepsiblings after their parents' divorce.

Five Things a Remarried Couple Needs to Consider When Moving In Together

1. **Where will you buy or rent?** In the same community where the children living with you are going to school? Close to noncustodial children so you can see them often? Near supportive friends or relatives? Near or far from a former spouse? In a community where you have lived and/or feel comfortable?

2. **Who is responsible for the down payment on the mortgage?** This can be a particularly thorny issue when partners have unequal assets.

3. **What is the best way for the house to be titled on the mortgage or deed?** This is an important consideration for wills and estate planning.

4. **Do you plan to have one or more mutual children?** If so, you'll need more space for a growing family.

5. **How much space do you need for children?** This gets tricky when considering children who spend mostly weekend time with you or only visit occasionally. You want all of your children to feel comfortable in their new residence but, in some cases, you'll probably need to consider your resources and explain to your children that "sharing is caring."

No matter how hard we might try to keep our home a neutral place and even change décor after a former spouse moves out, most remarried people feel that ghosts from the past can linger and they want to start fresh in a new home regardless of whether there are children involved. When redecorating, keep in mind that both of you need to have enough of yourselves in the house to feel comfortable. It's a good idea to discard as many pieces of furniture and nonessential items as possible to help you both start fresh in your new life together. If one or both of you have children, make sure they have a say in decorating their rooms, and invite them to be active in painting and cleanup of their new space!

FINANCES AND THE MUTUAL CHILD

Children born into stepfamilies, or mutual children, have a unique endowment, according to psychologist Anne C. Bernstein. In *Yours, Mine, and Ours*, Bernstein explains that even if their parents stay married, "ours" children usually inherit one or more siblings born into a former marriage, and at least one of their parents and the children from a previous marriage have endured loss. Further, one of the many losses following a divorce that isn't often discussed openly in the remarried family is financial, yet it can create resentment among family members competing for resources.

Once Michael, their "ours" child, arrived, Tara and Conner struggled financially with the strain of raising three children, trying to pay off debt and live within a budget. While Tara wanted to provide equally for all three of her children, she worried that her two teenagers would hold grudges against their younger half sibling if they were forced to go to state colleges, or they had to take out large student loans. Preparing financially for their "ours" child and being more transparent about finances before they married would have reduced their conflict and helped them plan more thoughtfully for themselves and their children's future.

STEPS TO TAKE BEFORE (OR AFTER)
A MUTUAL CHILD ARRIVES

According to Patricia Schiff Estess, deciding to have an "ours" child is one of the most difficult choices remarried couples can make, and it's not the right one for all families. Because most remarried couples are older and already have one or more children when they wed, some parents are happy to forgo the possible advantages of adding a mutual child. However, if a couple decides that they are ready to take the plunge and have another child, the following steps are suggested by experts such as Schiff Estess to protect family members.

Beef up your emergency fund. It makes sense that when you add one or more new members to the household, expenses will increase and urgent situations and emergencies will occur. As a rule of thumb, Schiff Estess recommends having three to six months' worth of living expenses readily available for an emergency.

Update and increase your insurance. You'll want to add the baby to your health coverage and any life insurance plans you have. You should also consider whether you have adequate disability insurance in the event of an accident or serious illness.

Consider claiming an extra withholding allowance. This means you will pay less in taxes. Consult an accountant or financial adviser about this matter first, but many families feel relief when they have more expendable income on hand.

Start an education plan. Consider doing this for all of your children and think about tax-exempt savings bond funds. Gift money from relatives can be useful to add to this fund. If you buy US EE savings bonds, they will accumulate interest tax-free when you own them. And if you cash them in during a year when you pay college tuition, you may be able to avoid paying taxes on the accumulated interest.

Revise your estate plan. First, drawing up a will that considers the long-term financial well-being of all family members can be reassuring to young adult children who may have concerns. You'll need to examine your wills and decide on a guardian for the mutual child or children in the event that both of you die. It needs to be clear who will take care of the youngest member(s) of the family. This decision shouldn't be left up to the children after a death when they may not be thinking rationally. In terms of dividing assets fairly among children, it needs to be discussed first between the couple and then with a lawyer who specializes in estate planning. Often a trust is set up for children that spells out the details. Once the new will and/or trusts are established, parents and stepparents need to sit down with their children (when they are about age 15 and older) and explain things, encouraging them to ask questions. Remember that money is not everything; be sure to include heirlooms such as jewelry, furniture, and family mementos.

Having a child together can bring great joy but blur financial boundaries. For instance, the common-pot system would make it easier for a family to accommodate a new child, but the two-pot or three-pot system, where funds are managed separately, would be more challenging. If you have difficulty choosing the best method of dividing assets and budgeting money, it's a good idea to sit down with a financial planner, mediator, or counselor. Remember that conflicts about finances are common for all couples; your remarriage will become a lot more complicated with the addition of one or more mutual children. On the plus side, an "ours" child can help family members feel more secure if remarried parents maintain their commitment to stay together and work through conflicts amicably.

CREATING A FINANCIAL VISION FOR YOUR FAMILY

The first step in understanding and communicating your different perspectives about money as a couple is being able to identify how your background and unique take on money matters influence your feelings about money. Then look at how your emotions affect your discussions and ways of dealing with financial decisions. It's essential that you be open and honest about money and your past history with it. In fact, you might consider using a mediator or counselor if discussing financial concerns greatly increases the stress in your relationship.

When couples have a shared vision about finances, the inevitable ups and downs of marriage are less bothersome. Creating a larger context of meaning in life can help you avoid focusing only on the little stuff that happens and keep your eyes on the big picture. If done thoughtfully and respectfully, discussing your financial goals and writing them down will elicit a feeling of trust between you and your partner. Taking time to process your dreams can bring you closer. According to John Gottman, couples who talk about their hopes and dreams with each other openly are more likely to prioritize time and resources, including finances, and are more likely to create a sense of purpose as a couple and find happiness.

Four Action Steps for Creating Financial Success in Your Remarriage

1. **Set ground rules for your money discussions.** Create ways to have productive and loving talks about money matters with your partner. Remember, conversations about money are sensitive and can trigger intense feelings and fears, so have these discussions during times when you'll be alone and not distracted by TV, chores, or other events and situations.

2. **Use active listening skills.** Truly listen to what your partner is saying and try to understand the feelings behind the words. Validate their feelings by offering responses such as "That must have been hard for you when your ex betrayed you and took off with most of your savings. I'd love to hear more about how this experience affected you."

3. **Fully disclose your financial history.** This includes your feelings about money, assets, and debts. Be sure to ask questions such as "How long have you wanted to travel more? You seem very interested in it."

4. **Solve the differences and challenges between you rather than debating who is right.** For instance, choosing options for handling money—a common-pot, two-pot, or three-pot system (or a combination of them)—can empower you as a remarried couple and help you stay on track.

While none of these steps will be a breeze, take comfort in the fact that by being vulnerable and sharing information with your partner, you are building love and trust. Close your eyes and imagine sitting down for a cup of coffee or glass of wine and being able to talk about your debts, budget, and financial issues without withholding information or getting defensive or angry at your partner. Now open your eyes and make a plan to talk about money—you are more than halfway to accomplishing your goal of authenticity and financial freedom.

5

Don't Let Mistrust Stop You from Being Vulnerable and Intimate

I believe that remarriage is a sacred union that should be nurtured with love and attention. However, after the honeymoon period was over in my second marriage, I was keenly aware that feelings of mistrust surfaced and wreaked havoc on our day-to-day existence. It was the little things that caused us distress, such as when I'd question Craig about being fifteen minutes late when meeting me for dinner or he'd criticize my parenting in front of our children because he thought I was too lenient. It took us several years to build a trusting relationship that could weather the storms of remarried life.

In my experience, mistrust can be one of the most destructive issues in a remarried relationship if it's not dealt with successfully. Building trust in a second marriage is really about the moments of connection that allow you to feel safe and truly believe that your partner has your best interests at heart. However, most of the remarried couples that I interviewed for this book spoke about feeling suspicious at times over minor issues that were usually indications of underlying mistrust in their partner's intentions. Mistrust can play itself out in many ways. It doesn't always mean that you're scanning your partner's cell phone for text messages or searching their pockets for evidence of an affair.

Usually mistrust is just a lingering thought in the back of your mind that your partner doesn't truly love you. If you believe that your partner truly loves you and wants the best for you, you will trust them.

For instance, Michelle, 47, lacked trust in Paul, 56, during their first few years of remarriage because she endured infidelity by her former spouse. Michelle and Paul were raising four children in a stepfamily when they met me in my office to discuss their challenges with trust. Michelle was often suspicious of Paul's actions when he was late coming home and when they went to public places where he would mingle and chat with strangers. Fortunately Michelle was able to let Paul know that his behavior made her uncomfortable, and he was more than happy to give her reassurance. Paul explained that as a speech pathologist he'd always been outgoing and comfortable talking to many people. Simple measures, such as Paul calling when he ran more than ten minutes late from work, helped Michelle feel safe and build trust in him. Paul wasn't interested in changing his extroverted nature but he was glad that Michelle could explain the source of her mistrust and they could discuss it openly.

Michelle reflects, "At first I felt embarrassed to admit that I didn't trust Paul, because he's such a fine person and is admired by so many people. Plus, he's a great stepdad to my four boys. But I realized that we wouldn't be able to move ahead and be truly intimate if I didn't feel more confident that he wasn't going to betray me like my ex did."

BUILDING TRUST LEADS TO INTIMACY IN REMARRIAGE

This chapter features remarried couples, such as Paul and Michelle, who experience different degrees of emotional disconnection as a result of trust issues. My hope is that through their struggles and triumphs, you will be able to learn to extend trust to your partner and deal with underlying obstacles that prevent you from achieving lasting love.

Being able to trust your spouse is the bedrock of an amazing second marriage, and those couples I interviewed who were able to achieve secure attachment and stay emotionally connected were able to risk being vulnerable. As a result, they enjoyed the sensuality and passion that goes along with intimacy. All relationships have tension at times, but it is important for partners to use that tension to become more emotionally connected and physically affectionate, and to achieve a mutually satisfying marriage.

Happy remarried couples are able to identify whether their trust issues stem from their present relationship or are emotional baggage from past betrayals. If you understand your own history, and strive to understand your partner's past, you can stop repeating toxic patterns. It is possible to deal effectively with ghosts from the past by extending trust to each other through words and actions that are consistent with a loving second marriage.

In other words, because a second marriage comes with baggage from a first marriage, it's essential for a couple to openly discuss emotional triggers, past experiences, and trust issues early on in their relationship so they don't become disengaged. Sustaining an open dialogue about your thoughts, feelings, and desires will strengthen your emotional connection.

Emotional intimacy, trust, and vulnerability are essential ingredients that will help you feel securely attached to your spouse and satisfied with your remarriage. A new relationship is often exhilarating, intense, and exciting, but what sustains remarried couples is fostering intimacy by being vulnerable and building trust day by day. Once the daily stressors of living in a remarried family set in, it can be a challenge for couples to extend goodwill to each other and remain committed to staying married. The primary way couples can do this is by deepening their attachment though daily dialogue that is transparent without fear of abandonment or loss of love.

TRUST IS AN ESSENTIAL ELEMENT OF INTIMACY

Lisa and Ryan, both in their late forties, have been married six years and are raising Ryan's two daughters from his first marriage. Lisa heard about my study from a friend and she sought me out, wanting to find ways to improve her remarriage. Lisa describes her second marriage as happy and successful but feels it is a daily struggle to be a full-time stepmother to Ryan's teenage daughters, Marisa and Victoria. She does not have her own children, but she was eager to take on the role of stepmom. Like many of the remarried people I interviewed, Lisa finds herself comparing her two marriages, especially when she is feeling uneasy or mistrustful of Ryan's intentions.

Lisa describes her second marriage as one that allows her to grow, whereas her first one was unhealthy and stifled her individuality. She reminds herself that she's lucky to have a partner who is totally committed to working on their marriage and invested in developing a true friendship characterized by trust and intimacy rather than fear of separation. She knows she's fortunate to have married Ryan, who is a good man. Lisa is learning to differentiate her mistrustful feelings derived from her ex's ending their marriage suddenly due to financial infidelity, from small breeches of trust such as Ryan returning home thirty minutes late from work or forgetting to text her on a busy day.

Lisa reflects, "I realize marriage is not always perfect. I learned the importance of sharing my feelings honestly in my first marriage. I'm usually the quiet one. I shut down. Ryan will patiently invite the conversation, and I am still learning to disclose my feelings without fear of losing him. He proves every day that he doesn't judge me."

Ryan relaxes on the couch beside Lisa and says gently, "My first wife was super demanding, and I could never catch a break. When I fell for Lisa, it was because of her easy-going personality. I want her to feel comfortable talking to me about anything. I reassure her all the time that I won't desert her like her ex did. I'm here for her every day, no matter what."

Ryan's heartfelt disclosure and interest in Lisa opening up to him illustrates how trust is an essential element of intimate relationships that can only exist when people feel safe enough to be vulnerable with their partner.

A SENSE OF SECURE CONNECTION IS KEY

Fear of intimacy and lack of connection are often signs that one or both people don't feel emotionally safe within the relationship. Further, lacking confidence in your partner's trustworthiness can cause you to feel disconnected and distressed, which can lead to insecure attachment in your marriage.

Lisa never felt comfortable being vulnerable with her first husband because she didn't believe he truly loved her. By withholding her thoughts, feelings, and needs from him, she played it safe but put her relationship at great risk. As a result, when Lisa met Ryan, it took her a couple of years to feel comfortable opening up to him.

Lisa reflects, "I didn't want to be that rebound person since Ryan was newly divorced, so I didn't allow myself to be vulnerable and tell him how I really felt until I felt secure in his love for me."

It is through being vulnerable that we achieve a level of emotional safety with our partner. It's the primary way to strengthen a marital bond and keep love alive. Thus you'll be able to reestablish a secure emotional attachment and preserve intimacy in your marriage.

Sue Johnson, author of the landmark book *Hold Me Tight*, uses the concept of *primal panic*, a term coined by neuroscientist Jaak Panksepp, to explain why some distressed people, who are driven by intense fear of loss, might resort to demanding behaviors when they seek reassurance. Others might withdraw in order to achieve a sense of soothing and to feel protected. This is especially true for remarried individuals who have endured infidelity and betrayal.

For instance, when feelings of disconnection arise, instead of being vulnerable and sharing your true feelings, you might become demanding rather than thoughtful and patient in your actions. A demand-withdraw pattern then develops. According to Sue Johnson, the longer this pattern persists, the more negative it becomes. One way to change it up is to focus on your part in the dynamic and stay in the present moment. This will allow you to bond with your mate through emotional closeness, conversation, touch, and sexual intimacy because you aren't concentrating on your fears of not getting your needs met.

Lisa puts it like this: "Ryan accepts me for who I am. He knows that if I feel upset it's best to hold me rather than back off. He knows that if he holds me close and tells me to breathe, it will help me. It's the touch that helps people stay close. If you don't give your spouse the touch and the love and say, 'I'm here whenever you need me,' how will they know?"

Lisa continues, "I tell him 'You do everything right.' But if he started to yell at me when I'm in panic mode, I don't know what I'd do. I tell him, 'Just hold me, just be there for me.' It's the little things that matter. Like when he comes home and has had a tough day and says his back is killing him, I give him a massage. It wipes all my mistrust away, and we are close and connected."

In the six years that Lisa and Ryan have been married, they have become masters at being vulnerable with each other and have a satisfying sexual and emotional relationship. Instead of focusing on each other's flaws and looking to blame each other, they spend their energy fostering a deeper connection. Lisa and Ryan have learned to give each other the benefit of the doubt and have put an end to the demand-withdraw pattern so many couples develop. Instead, they are shedding the baggage from their first marriages and healing the past through being vulnerable and emotionally connected.

VULNERABILITY: THE KEY TO EMOTIONAL INTIMACY

While self-sufficiency and autonomy can help you weather the storms of life, they can also prevent you from achieving the love and intimacy you deserve. For an intimate relationship to be balanced, partners must be able to depend upon each other and feel that they're needed and appreciated for the support they give. If you've been let down in the past, the prospect of needing someone can be frightening. Opening up to your partner can make you feel vulnerable and exposed, but it's the most important ingredient of a trusting, intimate relationship.

In *Daring Greatly*, Brené Brown defines vulnerability as uncertainty, risk, and emotional exposure. Indeed, the act of falling in love is the ultimate risk. Love is uncertain. It is inherently risky because your partner could leave without a moment's notice, betray you, or stop loving you. Putting yourself out there also entails a greater risk of suffering due to the criticism from others or feeling hurt when things don't work out. Brown explains that vulnerability is the core of all emotions and feelings. She writes, "To feel is to be vulnerable. To believe vulnerability is weakness is to believe that feeling is a weakness." She believes that we fear being vulnerable because we associate it with dark emotions such as fear, shame, and sadness—emotions that we are reluctant to discuss, even when they have a profound impact on all aspects of our lives.

The ultimate risk is allowing yourself to be vulnerable enough to love your partner in an authentic way, which requires letting go of any fear of being hurt or abandoned. It is possible to be vulnerable and close to others without losing parts of yourself. By doing this, you will be able to form a secure attachment with your partner and feel emotionally safe with them.

By being vulnerable and taking risks, Lisa has been able to overcome her fear of abandonment and stop withdrawing from Ryan in order to protect herself. She has also been able to lessen her feelings of unworthiness and shame resulting from years of living with her former husband's rejection and betrayal. Now when Lisa feels fearful, she is more likely to ask Ryan for a hug or verbal reassurance of his love for her. Ryan is happy to respond in a positive way and feels appreciated by his wife. It comes down to Lisa trusting herself and having the confidence to be able to handle rejection or potential conflict. Lisa's courage to face her fears head on has allowed this couple to connect on a deep emotional level and to raise Ryan's two daughters from his former marriage successfully. In order to do this, it's important to gain insight into the source of your fear about being open with your partner.

WHAT DRIVES YOUR FEAR OF BEING VULNERABLE WITH YOUR PARTNER?

Take a moment to consider that you might be sabotaging your remarriage out of fear of being vulnerable. If you're afraid of showing weakness or exposing yourself to your partner, for instance, you might be unaware that fear is preventing you from being totally engaged in your marriage. You may be freezing out the opportunity to love your partner deeply because you're afraid to be authentic and share your innermost thoughts, feelings, and needs with them.

- Are you fearful of exposing parts of your personality that your partner may find unacceptable?

- Does keeping a distance make you feel safe and in control of your emotions?

- Are feelings of shame stopping you from exposing your true feelings or talking about tough topics?

- Do you fear that your partner will abandon or betray you?

Couples who are successful in creating lasting love understand that their habitual responses, such as distancing themselves or being demanding, can create and maintain positive or negative patterns of relating. Examining your own protective behaviors that have become habits is a good way to build intimacy with a partner. Instead of asking your partner to change, work on altering your own negative habits. Sharing vulnerable feelings is about saying how you feel, rather than expressing your thoughts or criticisms about your partner's actions.

If you wonder what to do if you are paralyzed by fear or unable to risk being vulnerable with your partner, there are some simple steps you can take. First, you need to acknowledge it. Fear does not go away on its own; it tends to morph into something else. Trying to deal with everyday hurts by bottling up your emotions and deny-ing they exist doesn't work because it can drain you of energy. And research shows that attempting to minimize or ignore negative thoughts or feelings might actually intensify them, causing some people to explode with emotion.

In *Hold Me Tight*, Sue Johnson explains that we all have "raw spots" that make us reluctant to show our vulnerabilities to others at times. For example, Suzanne and Keith, a remarried couple in their late thir-ties and childless, both have emotional sensitivities that cause them to fear expressing their true feelings. Suzanne explains, "It's really hard to tell Keith how I feel. When I tell him I need him, a voice in my head says that I shouldn't need him so much. I feel scared." Therefore, instead of self-disclosing, Suzanne becomes increasingly clingy and demanding and goes into the primal panic mode.

Instead, if Suzanne and Keith could be more transparent and express their authentic feelings, they would begin to connect in a more honest and direct way. For instance, when Suzanne complains that Keith works long hours to avoid spending time with her, rather than get defensive, he might say something such as "I wish I could come home earlier, too, because I really miss you. Can we make a plan for the weekend?"

Likewise, rather than criticizing Keith and accusing him of being intentionally withdrawn and purposefully unavailable, Suzanne could be vulnerable and say something such as "I really miss being with you when you're working. I love you." It really comes down to both partners risking being open and stopping the destructive cycle of complaining, blaming, and feeling emotionally disconnected from each other. Truth be told, being vulnerable allows you to establish a secure emotional connection with your partner and to stop pointing fingers at each other when you are feeling out of touch emotionally.

Five Ways Vulnerability Leads to Emotional Intimacy

1. Vulnerability increases your sense of worthiness and authenticity.

2. Vulnerability helps you feel close and connected to your partner—yet achieve your own sense of identity.

3. Vulnerability helps you ask for what you want and avoid stonewalling (shutting down or distancing yourself from your partner).

4. Vulnerability allows you to build trust in others and become fully engaged in an intimate relationship.

5. Vulnerability allows you to open your heart—to give and receive love fully.

Trust and vulnerability are essential aspects of achieving intimacy in relationships. According to Brené Brown, disengagement is the most dangerous factor that erodes trust in a relationship. The only way to avoid this is to risk being vulnerable with your partner by asking for help, standing up for oneself, sharing unpopular opinions, and having faith in yourself and your partner. The ultimate risk is being willing to fall in love, which requires letting go of control and fear of being hurt or rejected.

Four Steps to Allowing Yourself to be Vulnerable with Your Partner

While all relationships present risks, they are risks worth taking. Even if you have been abandoned or cheated on, you can surrender your shield and allow your partner in. A healthy partnership is within reach if you let go of fear and believe you are worthy of love and all of the gifts it has to offer.

1. **Visualize yourself in an honest and open relationship.** This will help you work toward allowing yourself to be more vulnerable and open with your partner.

2. **Challenge your beliefs and self-defeating thoughts.** These undermine your ability to accept nurturing and support from your partner.

3. **Remind yourself daily that it is healthy to accept help from others.** Asking for help is a sign of strength rather than weakness. Don't let your fear of rejection or past hurt stop you from achieving the love and intimacy you deserve. Practice being vulnerable in small steps since it takes time to adopt new behaviors. Keeping a journal and/or talking to a therapist can help you make progress.

4. **Give yourself permission to be vulnerable.** Allowing yourself to take risks will help you develop a more trusting relationship with your partner, a relationship in which you can be comfortable sharing your dreams and being your authentic self.

VULNERABILITY AND TRUST GO HAND IN HAND

Being vulnerable was a tremendous challenge for Judith, 58, when she met Rodney, 59, over a decade ago. Both divorced and raising four children, they had plenty of baggage from their first marriages and both were fearful of rejection. As you learned in chapter 4, Judith had a lot of difficulty being transparent about finances with Rodney; she overspent on unneeded items and kept secrets about this from him. During the first few years of their remarriage, many of their disagreements stemmed from the difficulty Judith had in feeling safe enough to be vulnerable due to her strict Irish Catholic upbringing and her first husband's emotional abuse. Essentially Judith had spent her first marriage waiting for the other shoe to drop, and it took her a few years to build trust with Rodney.

Judith puts it like this: "It took a lot for me to be close and intimate with Rodney because I was raised in an environment where I was put down for speaking up. My first marriage was so dysfunctional that we had horrible communication and awful sex."

She explains, "When I'd get upset, Rodney would ask me what was wrong, and it would take me awhile to tell him what I wanted. He began to realize that things might bother me that don't bother other people. Then he started reassuring me that it was okay to feel hurt when his daughter would say bad things about me or when I was jealous of the time he spent with his son. We both began to understand that we're not going to deal with all of our issues, but we love each other enough to be there for each other."

Rodney responds, "We always try to make time to kiss each other before leaving the house. I love that Judith is such a beautiful person and takes good care of the kids and me. We walk the dogs together, which gives us time for adult conversation. We're in love and make love often."

As Judith's and Rodney's words illustrate, intimacy can be an important source of comfort and provide predictability in an uncertain world. Truth be told, when your partner makes a bid (such as reaching out for a kiss), your first response should be to turn toward them. As silly as it sounds, you can have romance in the kitchen or grocery store if you are receptive to your partner's request for connection. In addition, physical affection can lead to sensual communication and better sexual intimacy, something we'll be looking at closely in chapter 6.

THE IMPORTANCE OF TURNING
TOWARD EACH OTHER

I always tell remarried couples that if they want to strengthen emotional intimacy and deepen their love, they need to remember to *turn toward each other*. This means showing empathy, responding appropriately to bids for connection, and not being defensive. Asking your partner open-ended questions is also a great way to increase emotional closeness. If you only ask questions that require yes or no answers, you close the door to intimate dialogue. In other words, take your time and make love to your partner with words.

Judith and Rodney's story demonstrates the importance of being able to turn toward your partner when they make a bid for connection. According to John Gottman, a tendency to turn toward your partner is the foundation of trust, love, and a dynamic sex life. After studying thousands of couples over forty years, he discovered that we have three ways of responding to our partner's overtures and that turning toward our partner is an incredible way to deepen intimacy.

Bid Examples

"I had a tough day. Can you cook dinner
   tonight even though I said I would?"

"Did you notice when you came home that I washed the cars?"

Turning-Toward Response

This type of response enhances your emotional bond with your partner.

"I'm tired too but I can heat up leftovers and
   make a salad since you look beat."

"I didn't notice you washed my car. Thanks
   for telling me so I can check it out."

Turning-Against Responses

Some couples have habits of turning against each other's bids for attention or they get defensive or shut down, sometimes without even knowing it.

> "You promised to cook tonight. Can't you
> see that I'm watching the news?"

> "Why do you always want credit for
> doing things around here?"

Turning-Away Responses

Finally, this type of response creates disconnection and resentment between partners because there isn't any verbal exchange or validation of your partner's bid for attention.

> You pick up the newspaper as your
> partner approaches you.

> You turn on your computer when your partner
> makes a request or starts a conversation.

When Judith met Rodney, she was not sure she was ready to fall in love again since she had only been divorced two years. What won her over were the ways he responded to her overtures and made her feel appreciated. This was especially important to her because her first husband had always been quick to give her the silent treatment when she gave him a bid for connection.

Judith says, "Rodney treated me well from the beginning. I recall that I could tell by his facial expressions that he was happy to see me, and he always went out of his way to be kind and compliment me. We were strongly attracted to each other."

Judith and Rodney's marriage has not been free of challenges. In fact, they experienced several years of turmoil with Rodney's younger daughter, Samantha, who harbored a grudge toward her dad for many years. Rodney believes that Samantha was a victim of parent alienation stemming from her mother's bad-mouthing him. Additionally, Samantha had openly disapproved of Judith and even spread rumors about her on social media. What saved their marriage was trust.

Because every marriage has tension, knowing that you trust each other enough to go through challenges together is the glue that holds you together and makes your second marriage stronger.

Cultivating this sort of relationship is one of the greatest challenges for remarried couples. No one is perfect, but the best partner is the one who is willing to go on the journey with you. "The moment he would tell me he had to go on a trip for work, I'd be worried he wouldn't return," says Judith of Rodney. Although Rodney was not perfect, he was always open and trustworthy. In addition, any transgressions he made were not so large that he and Judith could not work through them.

Although every relationship is different, it's important for you, as a remarried person, to realize how you can be your own saboteur. If you mistrust your spouse without good reason, you run the risk of damaging your relationship. In Judith's relationship with Rodney, she realized that because he's a reliable person and would not cheat on her or go out of his way to hurt her, she must trust him. He has proven himself to be loving, kind, and trustworthy. By second-guessing Rodney, or feeling anxious about his whereabouts, Judith wasn't holding up her end of the bargain in the marriage.

Trust is built and maintained by small and large actions over time. If trust begins to waver, fear may overwhelm you, and doubt and suspicion may grow. You are faced with a choice: come at your relationship from a place of love and trust, or choose to be suspicious, doubtful, and wary. The most important thing to consider is whether your partner is worthy of trust. Have their actions matched their words? Does your partner treat you with respect? Are they dependable? Are they faithful? If the answer to these questions is yes, you must choose to trust. Of course, it's possible that you'll end up getting hurt. However, if your partner has shown you trustworthy behavior, you should reward them by showing trust in return.

TRUST WILL BRING YOU CLOSER

It's impossible to establish emotional and sexual intimacy without trust. As the stories in this chapter illustrate, learning to trust is one of the biggest challenges faced by individuals entering a second marriage. Getting remarried can actually intensify trust issues. Because of the breakup of your first marriage, you might approach relationships warily and come to expect the worst. It may seem at times as if you are wired to recreate the past. However, with courage and persistence, you can learn to trust again and restore your faith in love.

One of the hardest things about trusting someone is learning to have confidence in your own judgment. Trust is about much more than finding signs that your partner has been unfaithful. It's about believing they have your best interests at heart. Every person is born with the propensity to trust others, but through life experiences you may have become less trusting as a form of self-protection. Falling in love and getting remarried can be invigorating, but it can also be scary at the same time. An inability to trust a new partner may take on several forms, ranging from feeling they are dishonest or secretive to doubting they are going to keep their promises or be dependable.

Take a moment to consider this: your partner is not solely responsible for creating mistrustful feelings. In most cases, you must take equal responsibility for creating an atmosphere of safety and security in your relationship. In order to begin the process of overcoming mistrust, ask yourself:

- Does my fear of loss and abandonment
cloud my perspective and cause me to
overreact to my partner's actions?

- Is my mistrust coming from something that is actually
happening in the present, or is it related to my past?

- Do I feel comfortable asking for what I need
and allowing myself to be vulnerable?

- Do I bring my best self to my interactions with my partner?

- Do I possess self-love and allow myself to be loved and respected?

Many relationships are sabotaged by self-fulfilling prophecies. If you believe your partner will hurt you, you can unconsciously encourage hurts to emerge in your relationship. But day by day, if you learn to operate from a viewpoint that your partner loves you and wants the best for you, you can enjoy trust in your remarriage.

INTENTIONALLY CULTIVATING EMOTIONAL INTIMACY CAN KEEP A SECOND MARRIAGE STRONG

Experiencing emotional intimacy with a partner is one of the most satisfying experiences in life. But for many remarried couples, it's almost as if they're on a tightrope, balancing feelings of security with tension. This can cause them to experience anxiety when they are off balance but create a sense of calm when they are in harmony with each other. In *Hold Me Tight*, Johnson explains, "To stay on the rope we must shift with each other's moves, respond with each other's emotions. As we connect, we balance each other. We're in emotional equilibrium."

This may be especially true of remarried couples who don't share a long history of responding to bids for connection and learning to trust each other. For instance, Rodney and Judith are beginning to understand the importance of sharing emotions and affection with each other.

Rodney reflects, "When I've had a tough day at work and can look forward to spending time with Judith unwinding at the end of the day, it helps lower my stress level. I used to feel that we were missing the mark, but lately we're more in tune with each other's day. I tell Judith to let me know if she wants me to grab takeout on the way home, so we can have more time to relax."

Emotional intimacy can only occur when two people are devoted to taking total responsibility for their own feelings and needs. Remarried couples must be aware of their personal experience in the moment and committed to working together as a team. It's not possible for a couple to do this without having a deep emotional connection. Ideally, both partners need to talk about their feelings in terms of positive need, instead of what they don't need. Positive need is a recipe for success for the listener and the speaker because it conveys information and requests without criticism and blame.

Since many remarried couples marry on the rebound, they often have not had the time and opportunity to work through trust issues from their first marriage. In some cases, they might live in the past and mistrust their new partner based on issues from their prior marriage. These issues might stem from sexual or financial infidelity, emotional or sexual abuse, abandonment, or a combination of any of these betrayals that might linger in the mind and emotions of the remarried person.

For instance, Kelly tends to blow things out of proportion when she feels mistrustful of Mark, her second husband. In her midthirties, she is a teacher whose first marriage ended due to infidelity. She has two daughters from her first marriage, ages 9 and 13, and Mark's 10-year-old son spends weekends with them. Kelly married Mark on the rebound after a brief courtship, and she often reacts with fear and suspicion when he returns home late from work and there is the slightest imperfection in his explanation as to why.

When Mark is even a little delayed coming home, Kelly often responds with anger and she doesn't listen to his side of the story. She goes straight to accusation: "You're always late and you don't care about me." In the past, Mark would react negatively, but he is learning that Kelly just needs reassurance, so he calls if he has to work late or is stuck in traffic.

Kelly puts it like this: "When triggers come up with Mark because he takes longer to get home from work, I always question him; I give him the third degree. But I'm learning not to overreact. He's aware that I have trust issues and he's learning to answer my questions without getting mad or defensive."

When Kelly acts with suspicion at minor inconsistencies in her husband's explanation about why he's late, she knows she is blowing things out of proportion. She has learned to recognize that she might be reenacting painful memories of her first marriage and arguments she observed between her parents in her childhood home. It's important for Kelly not to respond to Mark from a place of fear and mistrust and for him to reassure her rather than show anger or get defensive.

Through consistency, Mark is working on showing Kelly by his words and actions that he's there for her. He is deeply committed to her and doesn't have a history of betrayal in prior relationships. Likewise, Kelly must learn to examine her thought processes. Is her self-doubt and mistrust grounded in reality or is it a fragment of her past? She must be willing to challenge her negative thinking—to free herself from the blueprints of her previous life.

How does Kelly do this? She must be willing to let go of self-defeating patterns—she must be willing to trust and be vulnerable with Mark. Often intimate relationships, such as a second marriage, reawaken childhood fears and cause people to grapple with love, trust, and commitment. Once Kelly and Mark can work through these issues together, they can build a healthy marriage and enjoy the security that is there for the taking.

More than 40 percent of the remarried couples in my study grappled with trust issues. Trust is much more than a feeling. It is an acquired ability and takes time to cultivate when you've endured divorce. When you sustain the loss of a relationship due to broken trust, it can make you smarter and more keenly able to extend trust to those who are deserving of it. You can learn to trust your instincts and judgment when you honestly deal with your fears. If you're able to come to a place of self-awareness and understand the decisions that led to trust being severed, you can start to approach others with faith and optimism.

Four Action Steps to Build Trust in Your Remarriage

1. **Challenge mistrustful thoughts.** Ask yourself, "Is my lack of trust due to my partner's actions or my own issues, or both?" Be aware of unresolved issues from your past relationships that may be triggering mistrust in the present.

2. **Trust your intuition and instincts.** Have confidence in your own perceptions and pay attention to red flags. Be vulnerable and ask for reassurance if you feel mistrustful.

3. **Don't assume your partner has bad intentions.** If your partner lets you down, it may just be a failure in competence—sometimes people simply make mistakes.

4. **Listen to your partner's side of the story.** Believe that there are honest people in the world. Unless you have a strong reason to mistrust your partner, have faith in them.

For a happy remarriage to work, you must be able to trust each other. If learning to trust again is something you have been struggling with, it will impact all aspects of your marriage. But as the stories in this chapter have illustrated, you're not alone in this world. Many people successfully work through trust issues and go on to have long-lasting and successful second marriages. Remember that you have the power to break free from the hold mistrust has on your life!

I've started to notice that I stay up late to avoid having sex with Adam or I leave my shirt on when we are intimate. Things aren't right between us, and I blame myself for putting on extra weight. **MELISSA, AGE 48**

6

Get Sexy and Fall in Love All Over Again

Like all long-term relationships, remarriages go through dry patches. Remarried couples often tell me that they lack passion and go long periods of time without enjoying sexual intimacy. New studies show that the average person in a relationship has sex once a week. Sex, however, doesn't necessarily mean satisfying sex, and partners often experience differences in sexual desire.

Laura, 42, a middle-school teacher, came to my office complaining that her husband, Kevin, 41, an electrician, was more interested in having sex than she was, and she'd been withdrawing from him for some time. In fact, they usually went to sleep at different times and rarely cuddled or showed physical affection. Married for eight years, Laura and Kevin are raising five children in a blended family and both remarried on the rebound. Due to their quick courtship, they had few opportunities to get to know each other's preferences and needs for sexual and emotional intimacy before they tied the knot.

As Laura and Kevin describe their second marriage, they speak about the glory days when they were dating and passion ran high. However, over the last couple of years, their sexual intimacy has declined, and they can't remember the last time they made love and had time alone, away from their children. Most of their conversations are about work, chores, their kids' activities, and mundane aspects of their stale marriage.

Laura puts it like this: "Kevin and I love each other and want to get back on track but we're always with the kids. We don't really know how to be intimate and close because we had dysfunctional first marriages and we're rarely alone. But we haven't given up and want to stay together."

Couples who have the most successful second marriages understand the importance of cultivating emotional, physical, and sexual intimacy. As you learned in chapter 5, emotional intimacy occurs when you're vulnerable enough to share your thoughts, feelings, wishes, and dreams with your partner in a loving way without fear of rejection. You must feel worthy of being loved in a close relationship and be able to be vulnerable and let down your armor in order to become emotionally available to your partner. This might be a challenge if you've been betrayed by your former spouse. Many divorced and remarried people have learned to avoid intimacy by putting up walls to protect themselves from emotional pain.

Sexual and emotional intimacy are closely connected. Sexual intimacy is more than just having sex, and includes all manner of touching, such as hugging, holding hands, and tender touch. These are all great ways to affirm your love for your partner. Physical affection sets the stage for sexual touch that's focused on pleasure. Without emotional and physical intimacy, your remarriage and sex life might feel insufficient and monotonous. A good sexual relationship is built on emotional intimacy and physical closeness. In other words, if you're hoping to improve the amount of passion in your remarriage, you need to first work on being emotionally and physically close with your partner.

In fact, sex that's satisfying to both partners will help you sustain a deep, meaningful bond. Carving out time to connect sexually is especially challenging for remarried couples who have busy schedules. It's hard to set limits on young children who crave attention and have legitimate needs, and to care for teens who may need emotional support and transportation to social, extracurricular, or school events.

Kevin laments, "We used to try to go to bed at the same time and have sex at least a few nights a week, but lately Laura tells me she is too busy because she has to grade papers or pay bills. It's really starting to put a wedge between us because my first marriage was unhappy, and one thing that drew me to Laura was her strong sex drive. She used to buy sexy nightgowns, and we'd light a candle and have a glass of wine to get in the mood. I can't tell you the last time we did that. I don't want to settle for a lonely marriage again."

Truth be told, 60 percent of the remarried couples that I interviewed said that they felt extremely lucky to find a passionate partner in the first several years of their courtship and marriage, but the passion dwindled sharply due to the challenges of remarried life and blending families. Some people stated that they desired to break free of a boring sexual routine—to do something wild and exciting—but they're not sure how to go about it. Others felt that they didn't need to have sex weekly but were worried that their partners would stray over time if they didn't satisfy them.

Ask yourself, "Is the quality of my sex life affected by baggage from my former marriage?" If so, eliminate your prior notions and former patterns of sexual intimacy and start fresh with your new partner by exploring their desires and passions. Be vulnerable and share your preferences and hidden desires. In doing so, it's possible to stay sexy and intimate throughout the course of your daily lives as a remarried couple.

Judith puts it like this: "It took me a while to realize that Rodney was nothing like my ex and he really does love me in a totally inclusive way. What I mean is that he values my views on things, thinks I'm smart, likes to do things with me, and also finds me very sexy. Rodney likes it when I'm playful with him and touch and kiss him passionately."

This sense of deep respect for each other and a passion that goes beyond the act of sexual intercourse is a sentiment expressed by many of the remarried people in my study. It's being comfortable with vulnerability and trusting that the other person has your back and accepts you with all of your flaws, your less-than-perfect physique, sexual hangups, and performance anxiety during times of insecurity or tiredness. Judith and Rodney, whom you met earlier, were remarried in their early forties and each had a lot of baggage to deal with in addition to raising four children in a blended family with high-conflict ex-spouses.

Rodney says it well: "I love Judith for who she is, and she's nothing like my ex or anyone else I've met. I can be free to be myself without worrying about being judged. I used to worry about my sexual prowess and staying power, but what matters to Judith is our closeness. We communicate well in all aspects of our life and I never thought that was possible."

CULTIVATING SEXUAL INTIMACY IN YOUR SECOND MARRIAGE

A good sexual relationship starts outside the bedroom. Remarried couples who have the most successful relationships understand that cultivating intimacy means achieving a balance of tension and connection. Moments of connection such as touching, talking, or making love are all part of the glue that holds intimate relationships together. If remarried couples want great sex, they need to put their energies into forming a physical and emotional relationship that satisfies both partners.

Is it possible to fall back in love? In *I Love You, But I'm Not in Love with You*, author Andrew G. Marshall answers that question. He argues that it is possible for couples to rekindle love by building a better understanding of themselves and each other, and ultimately building a stronger, more passionate connection. He explains that *limerence*, a term coined by psychologist Dorothy Tennov in her landmark book *Love and Limerence*, is the early phase of falling in love characterized by elation and passion. Marshall writes, "Someone under the spell of limerence is bound tightly to his or her beloved, however badly he or she behaves."

What happens to one's feeling of love after limerence is gone? Marshall calls the next phase *loving attachment*, the type of love characterized by a deep connection, sexual intimacy, and the ability to tackle the challenges of life together. Marshall suggests that the two main culprits that destroy loving attachment are neglecting physical intimacy and not accepting each other's differences.

DOES FALLING OUT OF LOVE MEAN
THE END OF YOUR MARRIAGE?

When we met in my office for an interview, Hannah, 43, and Matt, 45, told me that they've been married for eight years and are raising two teenagers from Hannah's first marriage. Matt's 10-year-old daughter visits them two weekends a month. Their urban lifestyle is hectic and focused on their children's schedules and work. Most of their conversations revolve around routine aspects of their blended family.

Hannah puts it like this: "I love Matt, but I'm just not in love with him anymore."

When Hannah drops this bombshell, Matt responds, "I thought we were doing okay, I really did. Even though we don't have sex much anymore—it just seemed like a phase we're going through. I was shocked when Hannah started talking about separating and even took her kids and slept at her mom's house for a few days."

Hannah explains that her feelings have been building up for years and that she feels guilty because she's starting to fantasize about being single. Matt tells her, "I'm devastated and feel so betrayed. You have no loyalty to me—there's no way I saw this coming." He feels blindsided and needs to find ways to express his love for Hannah so they can reignite the passion they experienced before the stresses of blended family life set in.

As Hannah and Matt describe their typical pattern of relating, it comes down to Hannah seeking out Matt for emotional and sexual intimacy and Matt distancing or pulling away. Matt describes his disengagement from Hannah as a struggle. He says, "It just feels hard to meet her expectations for always being so close. By the time I hit the bed most nights I'm exhausted. I just don't have the energy I used to because I own a plumbing business and I'm on call for emergencies."

By all accounts, Hannah and Matt were close emotionally and sexually during the early years of their remarriage, but over the last few years their sex life has dwindled because they do not make their marriage a priority. They rarely spend time together without their children, and they've become more like roommates than husband and wife. Their pattern of pursuing and distancing can be changed, but only if they are willing to work on identifying it and coming up with a plan to alter it.

Hannah reflects, "I'm aware that when I come on too strong with Matt, he gets flooded and shuts down. My immediate reaction is to feel afraid and to try to get him to open up. I had the same problem with my ex-husband, and I know it's making things worse for us. I want to get close to Matt without smothering him."

According to distinguished psychologist and author Harriet Lerner in *Marriage Rules*, "It's always easier to point the finger at our partner than to acknowledge our part in the problem. In order to truly connect with a distant or distancing partner, we need to identify the problem and take steps to change it." Since the pursuer-distancer dynamic is so common among remarried couples, we will examine it closely.

THE PURSUER-DISTANCER DYNAMIC

According to experts, the most common reason couples fall out of love and stop being sexually intimate is because of a pursuer-distancer dynamic that develops over time. Sue Johnson identifies this pattern as the "protest polka," and says it is one of three "demon dialogues." She explains that when one partner becomes critical and aggressive, the other often becomes defensive and distant. John Gottman's research on thousands of couples reveals that partners who get stuck in this pattern in the first few years of marriage have more than an 80 percent chance of divorcing in the first four or five years.

Why is this relationship pattern so common? Gottman found that men tend to withdraw and women tend to pursue when they are in intimate relationships. Further, he explains that these tendencies are wired into our physiology and reflect a basic gender difference. In his classic "Love Lab" observations, he notes that this dynamic is extremely common and is a major contributor to marital break-down. He also warns us that if it's not changed, the pursuer-distancer dynamic will persist into a second marriage or subsequent intimate relationships.

Partners in intimate relationships tend to blame the other person when their needs are not being met. A pursuer-distancer dance follows, which intensifies the dynamic. Couples report having the same fights repeatedly. After a while, they're no longer addressing the issue at hand and a vicious cycle of resentment, frustration, and anger develops and never gets resolved.

While all couples need autonomy and closeness, many partners struggle with the pursuer-distancer dance and feel chronically dissatisfied with their degree of intimacy. When the pattern of pursuing and distancing becomes ingrained, the behavior of one partner provokes and maintains the behavior of the other. It's normal to feel a sense of disappointment when your desire for emotional and sexual intimacy doesn't match your partner's, and a pursuer-distancer dynamic can develop in the bedroom. While this dynamic is one of the most common causes of divorce, don't panic! Lacking sexual intimacy is a common struggle for hard-working couples balancing jobs, parenting, and intimacy.

In *Wanting Sex Again: How to Rediscover Your Desire and Heal a Sexless Marriage*, sex therapist Laurie J. Watson writes, "Most sexual concerns stem from an interpersonal struggle in the marriage." She describes the tug-of-war between being too close and too distant from a partner as a repetitive pattern of one person being the pursuer and another being the distancer.

In many cases, the distancer retreats and seeks out alone time when under stress, and this intensifies their partner's need for closeness, thus their desire to pursue. The problem is that if this pattern becomes deeply entrenched, neither person gets their needs met. Sometimes a distancer realizes too late that their partner is severely distressed and they have already started making plans to end their relationship.

HOW TO DEAL WITH A DISTANCER OR PURSUER

Let's examine how the pursuer-distancer dynamic usually works by looking at a typical scenario with Suzanne and Keith, whom you met earlier. Suzanne's demands for more sexual intimacy are her way of motivating Keith to open up, so she can gain reassurance from him. In this case, the ways that Suzanne and Keith respond to each other backfire, creating a negative pattern of interpersonal relating.

"Let's talk about why we're not spending time together anymore," Suzanne complains, as her husband reads the newspaper and turns away from her bids for connection. She says, "How can we get along if we don't work on our problems?"

Keith responds, "I'm not sure what problems you're talking about. We're getting along okay. All couples go through hard times."

Suzanne feels increasingly frustrated with her attempts to draw out Keith. Meanwhile, Keith resorts to his typical distancer strategy, perhaps stonewalling her attempts to communicate by giving her the silent treatment. As she continues to express more disappointment in Keith, he further withdraws. If this pattern isn't reversed, it's easy to see how they can both begin to feel criticized and develop contempt for each other—two of the major warning signs that their marriage is doomed to fail, according to John Gottman.

It's no wonder that many of the interactions between couples become deadlocked in the pursuer-distancer dynamic. Partners can end up in a stalemate and are left feeling bitter and disillusioned about their marriage. Repair work begins with expressing your intent in a positive way and taking responsibility for your part in this negative cycle. This can be done by saying things such as "I'd really appreciate it if you'd cook dinner tonight since I'm behind on projects at work and need to work late."

Without recognizing it, many pursuers come on stronger than they intend to, not realizing that being in the "pursuit mode" may cause their distant partner to withdraw even more. Likewise, by pulling back, a distancer may cause their pursuer partner to pursue more vehemently. Watson suggests that couples entrenched in this pattern try switching roles to find out firsthand what it's like to walk in their partner's shoes. This can be a way to enhance empathy, awareness, and possibly even jump-start a new behavioral pattern of initiating and responding to sexual advances from your partner. In general, most couples can balance their needs for closeness and separateness in terms of sexual intimacy if they develop more vulnerability, compassion, and sensitivity to their partner's needs, both inside and outside of the bedroom. A good first step is to establish more emotionally intelligent dialogue that allows both people to feel heard and validated.

Dialogue to Grow Closer Together

Here is a possible dialogue for remarried couples who want to learn about each other and grow together emotionally and sexually.

> Partner A: I feel left out when you don't open up to me. I'd like to know what you're thinking when I share my feelings with you.

> Partner B: It sounds like you'd like me to share more of my thoughts with you when you're talking about your feelings. I can work on that.

> Partner A: I feel hurt when you read the paper when we're eating dinner because I'd like to learn more about your day and get close to you.

> Partner B: You'd like me to be more engaged with you during dinner. I wasn't aware that your feelings were hurt. I do get tired in the evening after working all day, but I'll try to interact more because it's important to you.

> Partner A: When we have loving sex, I feel closer to you. I'd like to talk about ways we can please each other sexually and both get our needs met.

> Partner B: I feel closer to you too, even though it's hard for me to open up and talk about sex. Let's try to find ways we can both get our needs met sexually and be more intimate.

Practiced daily, this type of dialogue will create a stronger emotional and sexual connection between you and your mate. Couples who spend at least thirty minutes daily in conversation with each other and express love, affection, and admiration will foster a closer bond and thrive both in and out of the sheets.

BUILDING A GREAT SEX LIFE IS
ABOUT EMOTIONAL CONNECTION

What is different about couples who have a dynamite sex life? This is what *The Normal Bar* authors Chrisanna Northrup, Pepper Schwartz, and James Witte wanted to find out in their online study of seventy thousand people in twenty-four countries. Their findings have amazing implications for remarried couples.

Couples with a great sex life all do the following:

- They say "I love you" every day.

- They kiss each other passionately for no reason.

- They give each other surprise gifts.

- They know what turns their partner on and off erotically.

- They are physically affectionate, even in public.

- They keep playing and having fun together.

- They cuddle.

- They make sex a priority, not just the last item of a long to-do list.

- They stay good friends.

- They can talk comfortably about their sex life.

- They have weekly dates.

- They take romantic vacations.

- They are mindful about turning toward each other.

In sum, the results of this comprehensive study validate my belief that couples should strive to stay close, affectionate, and interested in each other if they desire a satisfying sex life. Learning ways to connect with your partner on all levels is challenging but worth undertaking. The oldest couple in my study, Dan and Priscilla, personify the findings of this study. Both in their late sixties, they are going strong after thirty years and raising six children in a blended family. They know what it means to have a sensual and happy remarriage.

Dan says, "Priscilla still looks sexy to me, even after forty years and lots of ups and downs. When she makes me a special snack and encourages me to pick up my tennis racket to volley with her, there's no better high. We don't need a cocktail to get in the mood for sex because we are excited to be in each other's company and enjoy spending time together."

The reality is that successfully cultivating daily moments of intimate connection can result in a deeply fulfilling second marriage.

But what about couples who have not been able to stay connected emotionally and sexually? It's easy to understand how couples can drift apart, letting their baggage and busy schedules get in the way to the degree that they stop being vulnerable and intimate with each other.

DEALING WITH DIFFERENCES IN SEXUAL DESIRE

A lack of sexual passion is one of the most common problems that brings couples to therapists. During the early phase of marriage, many couples barely come up for air, lost in the excitement of falling in love. Unfortunately, this blissful state does not last forever. Many remarried couples complain that they've found themselves in the middle of a serious dry spell in their sex life or they're mismatched in terms of their sexual desires. It's not uncommon for one partner to be more highly sexed than the other, and this can create a sense of emotional and sexual disconnection.

Once a couple stops having sex, there's sufficient evidence to believe that it's a fast and slippery slope into sexual famine. Broaching this topic with your partner can be especially difficult if you do not feel connected emotionally or have lost trust due to financial or sexual infidelity in the past or present. However, if you feel disconnected from your partner sexually, they very likely share your feelings and may even feel some relief if you bring up the elephant in the bedroom.

When I met with Adam and Melissa, a childless remarried couple in their late thirties, there was a clear imbalance in their degree of sexual desire. Melissa found herself avoiding Adam and making up excuses so she didn't have to be intimate. During our sessions, she realized that she hadn't really resolved the mistrust and fear of abandonment that she experienced both as a child after her parents divorced and during her first marriage. Since her first husband left her suddenly and never looked back, she worried that Adam would do the same if they became too close.

Adam puts it like this: "It was hard at first when Melissa brought up that she doesn't feel like having sex much anymore. But in a way it helped me get some things off my chest, and I realized she really does love me and wants to get back to feeling sexual with me. She's just fearful of me leaving."

Melissa responds, "It was good to take time in our sessions to talk openly about the obvious problem that we have with giving each other sexual pleasure and being close. I tend to blame myself because I've put on a few pounds and feel insecure. But one book I read said that the more sex we have, the more we'll want to have."

Four Tips to Help You Deal with Differences in Sexual Desire

1. **Stop making excuses and start having sex more often.** Couples tend to blame fatigue, work, kids, and so forth, but they just need to start having sex more often. In fact, sex can be an aphrodisiac. The more sex you have, the more sex you want. Many people report that having sex jump-starts their engine, allowing their body to begin producing more sexual hormones that can remind them how much they enjoy making love, and want to do it more often.

2. **If you feel your sex life is wanting, it's likely your partner does too.** If you can be vulnerable and have an open discussion, you'll probably find that you aren't alone in feeling that your sex life is going through a serious dry spell. There is relief knowing that you're not alone, and talking about it might be the beginning of real change.

3. **Variety is the spice of life, so be receptive to talking openly about sexual fantasies and desires.** It could be that you've always fantasized about having wild, passionate sex on the kitchen counter or in the bathtub. Or maybe you want to try different positions. Plan an erotic night when intercourse is optional, but you reconnect with your partner, make out, get naked, and talk about your fantasies and desires.

4. **Understand that it might take time to get in the groove sexually.** It might feel awkward when you have sex after a hiatus but keep it up and things will improve over time. If you try some of the above suggestions and don't see progress after a few months, it's a good idea to get help from a therapist. Be sure to look for a sex therapist or a counselor with training in helping couples with issues related to sexual desire and frequency. Believe me, you're not alone and help is available!

THE ART OF SENSUAL COMMUNICATION

Making love to your partner with words and talking about sex as a form of foreplay can enhance sexual intimacy. Sex talk can definitely spice things up when the demands of jobs, kids, and the household are piling up. All it takes is the right attitude and a willingness to try to be more sensual. After all, a great sex life is about the quality of your marriage, not just the alignment of your bodies.

When was the last time you talked to your spouse about your sexual needs? Most of us go through life feeling shame about our sexual desires and we suffer from distorted beliefs, such as "My partner should know what I need." However, you will be more likely to get your sexual needs met if you state them directly as a bid for connection and patiently wait for a response.

Being more sensual in your communication with your partner includes talking about how attracted to them you are, how sexy you think they are, and what you look forward to during your lovemaking. Saying something such as "I love it when we make love in the shower and have plenty of foreplay" can enhance your experience later on.

Flirting with your partner can also bring joy and help you feel more sexually in tune with each other. Remarried couples who never stop flirting enjoy less tension and higher sexual chemistry. Judith and Rodney learned the value of flirting early on in their relationship. They thrive on new ways to ignite their mutual passion and sexual chemistry—especially in the morning when the house is quiet and Rodney's daughters have left for school. Lately it is common for them to take a shower together or enjoy making love before rushing off to work.

Many of our preconceived notions about what might please our partner sexually aren't based on fact. These notions might even prevent us from reaching out to our partner to ask about their preferences, such as where, when, and how they would like to make love. Likewise, we might not feel comfortable discussing our own likes and dislikes. However, one of the key elements of a great sex life is being able to talk about your preferences and show your partner what you desire. No one is a mind reader. Being clear about your sexual desires is a gamble worth taking.

In fact, most sex therapists recommend that making time to focus on pleasure, rather than orgasming, can bring couples unpressured, playful sexual intimacy. This works best when couples agree to go slower, communicate, try different positions within each sexual encounter, and take turns pleasing each other rather than being goal-oriented in their sexual touch. Scheduling at least one date night a week when you don't focus on work or your family can help you rekindle passion because you're making sexual and emotional intimacy a priority.

Seven Tips to Help You Rev Up Your Sexual Intimacy

1. **Tell your partner daily that you love them.** Be bold and declare your love openly. Great sex is yours for the taking if you learn to express your love freely and generously to your partner. This includes displaying your love and affection for them in public.

2. **Focus on physical affection.** Hold hands with your partner, cuddle more often, initiate sex more, demonstrate your love through touch, and kiss passionately daily. Holding hands, hugging, and touching can release oxytocin (the bonding hormone), which causes a calming sensation. Studies by psychologist Julianne Holt-Lunstad, of Brigham Young University, show that oxytocin is released during sexual orgasm and affectionate touch as well. Physical affection also reduces stress hormones—lowering daily levels of the stress hormone cortisol and increasing a person's sense of relationship satisfaction. When you have the time, enjoy sharing a massage before sleep!

3. **Allow tension to build.** Our brains experience more pleasure when the anticipation of the reward goes on for some time before we get the actual reward. So take your time, share fantasies, change locations, and make sex more romantic. Avoid talking about problems or criticizing each other. Sexual arousal plummets when we focus on the negative aspects of our partner's behavior. Instead, stimulate erotic energy by teasing or flirting with your partner.

4. **Make sex a priority.** Set the mood for intimacy earlier, before TV or work dulls your passion. A light meal, your favorite music, and a delicious glass of wine can set the stage for great sex. Make sure to get enough sleep because better sleep practices can help alleviate sexual problems. Satisfying sex can also help those suffering from sleep problems. Practice reducing your stress levels by exercising, going for counseling, and sharing your feelings and thoughts with your partner.

5. **Break the pursuer-distancer dynamic by walking in each other's shoes.** Mix things up to end any power struggles. For example, distancers need to practice initiating sex more often, and the pursuer can try being shy and quietly seductive—perhaps encouraging the distancer to move toward them.

6. **Try a variety of activities and sexual practices that bring you both pleasure.** Have fun courting your partner and practice being more romantic by writing loving text messages or notes and planning special dates. Demonstrate erotic interest by giving your partner a passionate kiss or breathing in their ear. Talk about sexual fantasies, express your sexual preferences, listen and respond to what your partner wants, and make love in different positions and locations.

7. **Practice being more emotionally vulnerable during sex.** Share your innermost wishes, fantasies, and desires with your partner. If you fear emotional intimacy, consider engaging in individual or couples therapy. For instance, the best way to deal with differences in sex drives is by communicating openly and respectfully about your needs while being receptive to what your partner's desires might be. Rather than criticizing your partner, show them what turns you on!

Fortunately, there are some simple things you can do to restore the spark you once had as a couple. In fact, even if you are not a touchy-feely person, increasing physical affection and emotional connection can help you sustain a deep, meaningful bond. Paul and Michelle, whom you met earlier, are a busy couple raising four children in a stepfamily and yet they've discovered that the secret to keeping their sex life vibrant is to take time at least a couple nights a week to be both emotionally and sexually intimate and make time away from their children a priority.

Michelle explains, "I noticed that our passion started to diminish during our second year of living together as a family. Between activities for the kids, work, and family commitments, we weren't finding time for us. Then Paul booked us a room at a Marriott sixty miles away on the Cape and asked me to find family to babysit and pack my bag for the weekend. Since it really helped to ignite our sex life, we now go away for the weekend once or twice a year and it's really paying off."

Being more sensual in your communication with your partner includes talking about how attracted to them you are, how attractive you think they are, and what you look forward to during your time alone together. Saying something such as "I love it when we cuddle on the sofa and have plenty of touch" can enhance your emotional intimacy. The following steps will help you enhance sensual communication if practiced over time. If you don't see progress after a couple of months, it's a good idea to seek out marriage counseling.

Four Action Steps to Enhance Sensual Communication

1. **During the next two days, focus on using nonverbal ways to connect with your partner in order to increase your level of intimacy.** Try to smile more, touch your partner more frequently, sit close together on the couch, or offer reassurance with a gentle stroke of your hand if they seem to need it.

2. **Decrease pressure to have sex by minimizing discussions and containing your own worries about sex.** Psychologist David Schnarch, author of *Passionate Marriage*, coined the term *holding on to yourself* to describe the importance of partners becoming more comfortable with their own level of sexual tension and not always going with their instinctive desires to either pester (pursue) or start running (distance).

3. **Increase physical affection by doubling the amount you touch your partner daily.** Having an additional point of physical contact during a kiss with your partner creates a deeper sense of intimacy. Connect with more than one part of your body, such as putting your hand on your partner's cheek when you kiss. Hold hands, give them a massage, and show your love through

touch twice as much as you have been. Parting in the morning and reuniting at the end of the workday are good times to practice this ritual.

4. **Randomly leave "I love you" sticky notes or send loving text messages at least once a day for a week.** Think of fun and special places to leave these notes. Examples are the shower, lingerie drawer, or a briefcase or purse. Text messages can include romantic content. For instance, "I can't wait to hold you tonight—I love you!"

Responding positively to your partner's overtures for emotional and sexual connection will help you bring out the best in each other and keep your second marriage fulfilling and sexually satisfying. Sex in a good marriage serves its purpose to enhance vitality and satisfaction. Give your partner the gift of love and passion today. The good vibes that you feel after sex can help you feel close for days!

Keith doesn't listen to me anymore. In the
beginning, I felt I could tell him anything,
but we're just not communicating very
well lately. **SUZANNE, AGE 38**

7
Don't Make a Big Deal about Nothing . . .
But Do Deal with Important Issues

One of the most vexing aspects of remarriage is that most misunderstandings that lead to arguments arise out of insignificant issues—they seem to come out of nowhere. One of the reasons might be that we are continuously testing our partner to see if we are loved unconditionally or risk being left. As you learned in chapter 3, people who remarry often have emotional baggage from their first marriage that can set the stage for mistrust and a pessimistic mind-set about their second marriage. And when couples have differing expectations and needs, discussions about trivial matters (such as what to eat for dinner) can spiral downhill quickly into major quarrels.

Take, for example, this conversation between Maria and Jason, a childless couple in their late fifties who have been remarried over a decade. Their dialogue illustrates the inconsequential nature of most arguments between remarried couples. They both admit that their sensitivities from their first marriage set the stage for feelings of vulnerability, defensiveness, and fear of rejection.

Jason: What kind of salad should I make
for our company tonight?

Maria: A green salad, what else?

Jason: What do you mean, "What else"?

Maria: Well, we usually have green salad, but I guess we could make something else.

Jason: Does that mean you don't like my green salad?

Maria: No. I like it but go ahead and make something else.

Jason: Not if you want green salad to go with our grill.

Maria: I don't. Make a fruit salad instead tonight.

You can see how Jason and Maria's miscommunication and misreading each other's intentions set the stage for a disagreement. When Maria added the tag "What else?" to her response, the underlying meaning was "You're a jerk for asking; you should have known." Understandably, Jason would interpret Maria's comment as critical and demanding (she wanted Jason to read her mind) and lacking in directness and clarity.

In *That's Not What I Meant!* linguist and author Deborah Tannen explains, "Things seem to get worse in close relationships that continue over time because we don't realize that communication is inherently ambiguous and that conversational styles differ, so we expect to be understood if there is love. When misunderstandings inevitably arise, we attribute difficulties to failure: our own, or the other's, or a failure of love."

According to Tannen, the more contact people have with each other, the more opportunities they have to do things that can be misunderstood. In fact, talking more usually makes the problem worse because different ways of speaking are at the root of the difficulty. In this chapter, you'll learn ways to take risks, adjust unrealistic expectations, communicate more effectively, and deal with disappointments and misunderstandings in the context of a loving remarriage.

THE SOURCE OF MOST REMARRIED
COUPLES' MISUNDERSTANDING

We've all said things that our partner interpreted much differently than we hoped they would. As illustrated in Maria and Jason's dialogue, we often communicate by way of meta-messages or secondary communication, including indirect cues. In other words, how a piece of information is meant to come across isn't always how a listener interprets it. Therefore seemingly benign comments can lead to awful feelings and a sense of putting your foot in your mouth.

Lisa puts it like this: "Ryan accepts me for who I am most of the time, but the other day he came home, scanned the living room, and said loudly, 'There's enough moisture and garbage in this family room to fertilize my garden.' To which I responded, 'If I'm such a terrible housekeeper, why don't you hire a maid.'"

Although Ryan didn't outright accuse Lisa of not cleaning up, his meta-message was clear. Ryan didn't ask about the source of the mess in the family room. If he had, he would have found out that his teenage daughter Marisa had had a group of friends over for a study group and left a mess because they were in a hurry for soccer practice.

Ryan reflects, "Sometimes it seems impossible to say what I want to say about Lisa's behavior without her getting on the defense. Just the other day, I was trying to show her how to load our new dishwasher correctly and she said, 'You always blame me when the plates go in backward when it's usually your girls or their friends that do it. You never cut me a break.'"

This situation is common for busy remarried couples such as Lisa and Ryan, who are juggling work and running a household with kids. Because Lisa is a relatively new stepmom who hasn't yet earned her stepdaughters' trust, they perceive her as an outsider. Further, Lisa and Ryan appear to both be hyperfocused on trying to prove a point and more concerned with being "right" than achieving harmony in their relationship. They also both have their own filters based on past communication patterns and their own unique relationship histories.

FILTERS THAT PREVENT GOOD COMMUNICATION

One of the common barriers to positive communication is that what our partner hears is often very different from what we are trying to communicate. In *Fighting for Your Marriage*, psychologist Howard J. Markman and his colleagues explain that we all have filters (or non-physical devices in our brains) that change the meaning of information we hear. These include distractions, emotional states, beliefs and expectations, differences in communication style, and self-protection. As with other filters (e.g., coffee filters), what goes into our communication filter is frequently different from what comes out. For example, if Jason walks in the door and asks, "What's for dinner?" Maria may interpret that as a complaint, whereas he might simply be saying he is famished from a long day at his office.

At times, we have all experienced the utter frustration of feeling that our significant other misunderstood us. After all, we thought we were being clear, concise, and explicit about our thoughts and feelings. Being able to identify and discuss some of the key filters of communication is crucial to feeling better understood by your partner.

Like most remarried couples, Suzanne and Keith, whom you met earlier, display a communication style that illustrates a common problem for remarried couples. In their late thirties, they tend to argue over silly things that reflect the baggage they brought to their remarriage. For instance, Suzanne may come home exhausted after her busy day working at a local college and see Keith on the computer. Because he works at home in the technology field, this is no surprise, but instead of turning toward Suzanne when she makes a bid for connection, Keith turns against her response and changes the subject, rather than establishing a connection. Not only does Suzanne feel misunderstood, she is irritated after a long day at work. Here is how one conversation went:

> Suzanne (*thinking she wants to go out and have fun after a difficult day*): I'm exhausted, and you haven't started dinner. Let's grab a bite at the new Cajun café in town—they're having music and a great special tonight.

Keith (*with frustration climbing*): Why do we always have to go out just because you're too tired to cook. I work hard all day too. You're always tired. Just because I'm on the computer, it doesn't mean I'm having fun.

Suzanne (*confused because she just wants to enjoy a night out with Keith and her friends*): Why can't we enjoy a dinner out one night a week when we both make good money? I'm not always tired but I want to hear the band at the café—a lot of my friends will be there.

Keith (*feeling angry*): I never said you didn't make good money. I know you make more money than I do and that bothers me. I know you'd rather be with your friends than me, but you don't have to get nasty.

Suzanne: You never do anything wrong, do you?

We all have plenty of filters that create misunderstandings. They affect the way we see, hear, and perceive the words our partner uses. They stem from our emotions, life experience, family and relationship history, and cultural background. According to Markman, distraction is perhaps the most common cause of feeling misunderstood by our spouse.

Common Distractions

Do you believe you have your partner's attention when you speak to them? Are internal factors such as thinking about something else, worrying about bills, or feeling tired stopping you from focusing on what your mate wants to tell you? External factors such as children, TV, cell phones, or background noise might also be a big obstacle to effective communication.

With anger in her voice, Suzanne reflects, "It seems like Keith often has the TV on when I'm trying to talk to him. We rarely get to talk and it's like I have to schedule an appointment to talk to my husband."

Keith responds, "Our schedules are just really different. Suzanne wants to talk right away when she walks in the door and I like to watch the news and unwind after a long day. I'm not opposed to talking, it's just bad timing."

Like Suzanne, I often complain that my husband, Craig, watches too much TV, especially when one of his favorite hometown—Philadelphia—sports teams is playing. Since he's a loyal Eagles fan, he was glued to the TV when the Eagles and New England Patriots were playing live for the 2018 Superbowl. Because I needed to ask him an important question, I was feeling frustrated with his intense focus on the game and ability to tune me out. Fortunately we had been married for over two decades by then, so I politely asked him to mute the TV so we could chat. In times past, I would have turned off the TV or continued to talk to him while he was watching the game, causing tension between us.

Emotional States

Let's face it—our moods greatly affect our communication. If we're in a bad mood, we're more likely to perceive what our partner says negatively. This point is illustrated by Lisa's bad day and her negative interaction with Ryan when she returns home from picking up Marisa from a soccer game.

Lisa (*in a frustrated tone*): You have no idea how much traffic there was in town.

Ryan (*in an icy tone*): Are you saying you didn't want to pick up Marisa?

Lisa (*feeling defensive*): I'm just aggravated because we haven't eaten dinner and I haven't had a chance to go grocery shopping this week.

Ryan (*rolling his eyes*): Would you prefer I do the shopping even though you agreed to do it since I work more hours than you do?

Lisa (*feeling angry*): I never said I wouldn't do the shopping.
It's just been a busy week with my dad in the hospital
and I didn't expect so much traffic after the game.

In *The Dance of Connection*, Harriet Lerner explains that when the emotional climate of a relationship is spontaneous and relaxed, we can let go of a lot. And when we're in a good mood, we might cut our partner some slack. But the opposite is just as true.

Let's take this dialogue with Lisa and Ryan over again. Lisa comes home from picking up Marisa from a soccer game. It's obvious that she feels frustrated as she throws her car keys on the counter and sighs. Instead of getting defensive, Ryan sees her frustration and acknowledges that she's had tough day.

Lisa (*in frustrated tone*): The traffic was bumper to
bumper, and it was such a waste of time!

Ryan (*in a calm, loving tone*): I'm so sorry you had to deal
with horrible traffic. What a waste of your time when you've
had such a busy week and are worried about your dad.

Lisa (*giving Ryan eye contact*): Exactly! The last thing I
needed was to be stuck in traffic after a difficult week.

Ryan (*in a soft, loving tone*): My week has been busy too, so
why don't we get take-out Chinese or pizza. What do you
prefer tonight? I'm happy to run out and get it for us.

Without being explicit, Ryan and Lisa acknowledged that Lisa's bad mood was a filter. Ryan responded with empathy and understanding. While being in a bad mood does not excuse awful behavior, it's a reason why couples often get into arguments about trivial matters and tend to dig their heels in, which can lead to escalating disagreements and a tense home environment. Many emotional filters can color your interpretation of what your partner says—and your response to them.

In this second example, Ryan was able to turn toward Lisa by offering her active listening, support, and a solution (Chinese takeout). In *The Science of Couples and Family Therapy*, John Gottman explains that couples have many "micro-attachment injuries"—small moments when our partners aren't there for us. He believes that many of these moments are innocent rather than mean-spirited. Gottman writes, "However, a mindful awareness of how and when our partner expresses a small need can, over time, make a huge difference."

Beliefs and Expectations

Many crucial filters have to do with how you think and what you expect from your partner. As you will see in this disagreement between Tara and Conner, an unrealistic expectation can have a negative impact on a couple's communication. Conner has recently started graduate school, and he and Tara are raising three children in a stepfamily.

> Tara (*in an icy tone*): I thought you said that you'd be home from class by 7:00 p.m. I knew when you started back to college that you would leave us behind. I have too much responsibility for the house and our kids.

> Conner (*in an angry tone*): You don't have much faith in me. I had to stay after class to get notes from another student since I missed our last class.

> Tara (*looking disappointed*): Well, we could have eaten dinner together because the kids are all home tonight. But you didn't think it was important to call and let me know you were running late.

Here, Tara's belief that Conner's return to college is an attempt to abandon his family has led her to have negative beliefs and expectations. Instead of giving him the benefit of the doubt, she makes accusations and assumes the worst of him. In *Fighting for Your Marriage*, Howard J. Markman explains, "In general, you will be disappointed or happy in life depending on how well your perceptions of what is happening match what you expected—what you think should be happening. It's not surprising, therefore, that expectations play a crucial role in how happy your marriage will be."

For instance, if we believe someone is trustworthy, we might "pull" behavior consistent with our expectations and focus on the times when they follow through rather than let us down. In Tara's case, her expectations of Conner being inconsistent and untrustworthy have caused her to have a negative lens when she's evaluating his words and actions, and she's focusing on small matters rather than looking at the big picture.

Differences in Communication Style

Maria and Jason, both in their late fifties, have been seeing a marriage counselor for a year to help them develop positive ways of communicating. During our interview, Maria, an articulate and outgoing middle-school teacher, praised Jason for attending couples counseling sessions when they went through rough patches.

Here is how Maria puts it: "Jason and I argue a lot about trivial matters such as household chores, but I don't really feel that these are the issues we're disagreeing about. Most of our negative and critical comments come from past relationships. Jason tends to shut down when we argue, and this just makes me angrier because that's what my father and my ex did to me. It's hard not to take it personally when he's late coming home. I know he's not late on purpose—he runs his own electronics store."

Jason reflects, "I know I need to communicate better with Maria. I love her, and I don't tell her enough. I should text or call when I'm running late. Then I like to come home and watch TV because my job running a small business is stressful. When Maria turns off the TV and demands I talk to her, I feel resentful. This leads to her criticizing me because she feels ignored."

Maria and Jason's central problem is a common one for remarried couples. It's not that they never communicate with each other; the issue is that much of their dialogue is negative and critical, and they almost speak a different language. There are many "hidden issues" that come to the surface when they argue because they often sweep feelings under the rug. Destructive patterns of relating are common among couples who got married older and have baggage. They also reflect the stresses and storms that come with a second marriage.

Conflict does not have to be problematic or caustic to a relationship. What matters most in the success of a marriage is how you deal with the problems that arise. According to John Gottman, negative behaviors that can be caustic to a relationship include criticizing (especially personal attacks about the character of your partner), showing contempt or disrespect by trying to make your partner feel worthless (eye-rolling, name-calling, mimicking, etc.), being defensive, and avoiding or stonewalling. Unfortunately, these patterns can become a habit, and issues that are ignored for too long are rarely resolved because they can leave partners feeling hurt and resentful.

Maria explains, "This morning I was going through the bills and Jason was heading out to the gym. I asked him to sit for a few minutes so we could discuss finances. He could tell by my tone that it was important, but he kept telling me that he needed to go. He doesn't listen to my concerns about his overspending and my suggestions about how we could cut back. It seems like Jason never wants to talk about important issues and my resentment is growing every day."

During tough conversations, it's helpful to choose battles wisely—that is, to distinguish between what is and what isn't worth making an issue about. Bickering can lead to the demise of a relationship. It's like chronic warfare that erodes the quality of a relationship and makes it tough to discuss difficult topics. When dealing with differences with your partner, the key is to listen attentively, understand each other's perspective, rein in defensiveness, and stop criticizing and blaming each other.

Self-Protection

In second marriages, one of the biggest hurdles couples face is how to approach difficult conversations without getting defensive or trying to prove a point. This leads to an unfortunate pattern of attack and defensiveness where both partners believe they must prove they're right and defend their positions. After all, it takes two people to contribute to a miscommunication or dispute. According to psychologist Daniel B. Wile, if this pattern continues over time, it can diminish love and respect between partners. The following are ways to curb defensiveness before it becomes a bigger issue.

Four Ways to Curb Defensiveness

1. **Keep a calm composure.** While it is natural to raise your voice and get agitated when you feel attacked, lower your voice and adopt a friendlier tone. If you feel yourself taking things personally, press the pause button and suggest a ten- to fifteen-minute break before continuing a conflictual conversation. You might say, "I'm trying to listen, but I can feel myself getting defensive. Can we start this conversation again in fifteen minutes?"

2. **Listen to your partner's side of the story and validate them.** Instead of focusing on your own agenda and the points you want to make, ask your partner what's bothering them and really listen before responding. When you respond, validate their perspective and use a soft start-up, such as "I value your input and I'd love to hear more from you." Be sure to use good eye contact and reassuring touch to comfort your mate.

3. **Focus on the issues at hand.** When you focus on changing your partner, you miss the opportunity to work together to come up with a solution. You are no longer on the same team. Instead, focus on the issues at hand to meet both of your needs. Stay in the moment and resist the urge to bring up old issues or touch on your partner's raw spots.

4. **Take responsibility.** If you focus more on your part of the problem, you'll be less likely to point your finger at your partner or take things personally. Reflect on how your words and actions might make your partner feel and be accountable for

your impact. By taking responsibility for his part in the dispute, even just a small piece, Jason is validating Maria's feelings and they can begin to restore healthy communication.

Communicating love and admiration to your partner is a hallmark of courtship, yet as remarried couples settle in to dealing with the stresses of day-to-day life, these comments start to fade in frequency. You may not express gratitude for your partner aloud because it may not come naturally. Instead, you might make a big deal over trivial issues and miss the big picture. Becoming conscious of these dynamics is the key to changing them.

Six Strategies for Increasing Communication and Creating Loving Intimacy

1. **Be sure you first understand, and then seek to be understood.** Respond to what your partner is really saying in the moment. Be attuned to their experience, more than your own.

2. **Freely communicate your admiration and fondness for your partner.** You might say, "You are such a special person and I am lucky to have you as my partner."

3. **Catch your partner doing something "right" and compliment them for it.**

4. **Practice offering mutual gratitude on a regular basis.** For instance, you might say, "I'm so grateful that you work so hard, and I can see you had a hard day. I'd like to get you some iced tea and hear about how your day went."

5. **Turn toward your partner.** Look for opportunities—when they make a bid for attention, affection, or any other type of positive communication. Overtures often display themselves in basic but powerful ways, such as a smile or pat on the shoulder.

6. **Remind yourself of your partner's positive qualities and express your positive feelings out loud several times each day.** In *The Science of Trust: Emotional Attunement for Couples*, John Gottman suggests increasing the number of positive comments you make to your partner in order to establish a good relationship. Listen to their point of view and adopt his rule of maintaining a five-to-one ratio of interactions—for every negative interaction, you need five positive ones.

HOW TO USE "I" STATEMENTS

When one partner communicates effectively, it encourages their partner to do the same. Communication affects how safe and secure we feel in our relationship as well as our level of intimacy. It's a challenge to be honest with a person who you cannot trust. You might worry they will respond in a negative or hurtful way. For instance, Maria will get more feedback from Jason when she shares her feelings honestly, and takes responsibility for them, rather than criticizing him.

Now that they are aware of this ineffective pattern, they're working on ways to listen and respond more positively to each other to improve the quality of their communication. One fairly simple yet highly effective way to short-circuit this negative cycle of relating to your partner is the use of "I" statements. An "I" statement is an assertive statement about your thoughts or feelings that doesn't place blame or judgment on your partner. It makes it more likely your partner will hear what you say and not get defensive, in contrast to a "you" statement, which is negative and usually places blame on the other person and causes them to become defensive.

Accepting responsibility is the most important aspect of communication, and using "I" statements is a good way to do this. There are three aspects of using "I" statements effectively:

1. **State your emotion.** "I feel . . ." It is a self-disclosure, referring to "I," and expresses a feeling. It must be expressed by stating how you feel, not "You make me feel" etc.

2. **Describe your behavior or conditions related to your feelings.**
   "When you . . ." Refer to the other person's observable
   behavior or the conditions that are relevant for you to feel
   the way you do. State the facts without opinions, threats,
   criticism, ultimatums, judging, mind-reading, or other
   words or behaviors that might create defensiveness.

3. **Explain why those conditions or your partner's behavior
   cause you to feel this way.** "Because . . ." Explain why
   you experience this emotion when your partner does the
   behavior. Also include how you interpret their behavior and
   any tangible or concrete effect their behavior has on you.
   Be especially careful about not being blameful when you
   describe the "because."

For instance, when our children were growing up, I'd often feel criticized by my husband, Craig, when he'd make comments about me being too lenient with them. An example of how I could have used an "I" statement might be "I feel hurt when you make comments about me being too easy on our kids. When I'm offering to do their chores, it seems that you interpret that as me being a pushover, when I'm simply trying to be loving and supportive toward them. When we have this misunderstanding, I don't feel understood or appreciated by you."

ACTIVE LISTENING AND VALIDATION

Being an active listener requires that you put your own agenda aside and focus on what your partner has to say. It means that you're willing to suspend your own concerns, needs, and thoughts temporarily so that you can be fully present with your partner and tune in to the meaning of their words, tone of voice, and nonverbal communication. In active listening, the listener gives feedback as a way to better understand and clarify what the speaker is saying. In essence, the listener is validating what their partner is saying and helping the speaker feel a sense of being understood and being close and connected.

Likewise, with active listening, the listener is checking to make sure they've accurately heard and interpreted their partner. This behavior reduces the chance for misunderstandings and disagreements. It's akin to placing an order for flowers on the phone and asking the florist to repeat your order back to you for clarity and accuracy. It's especially important to listen actively to your partner if they seem upset about a problem in your relationship or family and you've been arguing a lot.

Couples need to realize that active listening is not the same thing as giving advice. While we might perceive ourselves as being helpful by giving instructions or explaining how to do something, our mate might interpret this behavior as our need to be "right." You might know you are right, but ask yourself, "Is it more important to be right or to be happy? Is it worth destroying a relationship by trying to prove I'm right?" There's nothing wrong with giving advice when our partner asks for it, but most suggestions are unsolicited and come across as keeping score rather than being helpful.

Further, invalidation tends to make difficult problems worse in remarried families. In earlier chapters, you met Judith and Rodney, a remarried couple in their late fifties who are raising Rodney's two teenage daughters from his first marriage and their two mutual children. When Judith felt hurt by her stepdaughter's negative comments, she wouldn't always share it with Rodney because he would jump to giving her advice, and she knew she'd feel judged or criticized by him.

Most people rush to try to solve their partner's problems by offering suggestions and skip over validation. What Judith craves is being listened to and validated. She continues to feel challenged by being a stepmother to Samantha, who has spread negative rumors about her. However, if Rodney validates her feelings by acknowledging that he "gets it" and still loves her, Judith will be more likely to share her thoughts and feelings with him and feel understood. The important part is validation. After all, fixing a problem comes later, and most people are capable of solving their own problems. What they want is to be seen and heard.

Judith reflects, "It's hard being a stepmom to Samantha because she's close to her mother and I think she bad-mouths me. But sometimes

I just want Rod to listen and try to understand my pain. I don't feel this way about his other daughter. She's younger and bonded with me from the beginning. Honestly, I don't have much hope things with Samantha will change, but I just want Rod to see how hard it is to be the recipient of her negativity."

Keep in mind that this isn't a normal way of communicating, and it may feel awkward at times. However, if a remarried couple agrees to try it out, active listening and validation are powerful ways to enhance communication about sensitive topics. For instance, Judith and Rodney are both feeling stressed about Judith's relationship with Samantha, but when Judith feels that Rodney understands her experience, they can both focus on the big picture—their goal of having a strong, loving partnership!

THE TWENTY-MINUTE DAILY CONVERSATION

I mentioned earlier that a twenty-minute stress-reducing conversation each day can help couples feel more connected. (Thank you, John Gottman, for the basic idea.) We're talking about a face-to-face conversation where partners take time to ask questions, get to know each other, and build shared meaning. Preferably, this conversation needs to be about whatever is going on outside of your relationship. This isn't the time to discuss struggles between you. The twenty-minute conversation can encourage couples to build trust and intimacy if they both honor this time together.

Four Action Steps to Have a Stress-Reducing Conversation

1. Decide together to make the twenty-minute conversation happen. It can happen in the morning or after work, as long as it happens regularly.

2. During this conversation (and at other times), acknowledge and show appreciation for your partner. Validate their feelings and tell your mate specific things they do that

you love. For example, "I love it when you make me breakfast—your coffee is delicious!"

3. Make a commitment to implement this twenty-minute conversation as a daily ritual. It may feel awkward at first but will get more natural over time.

4. Consider including questions that give you and your partner the opportunity to explore new areas of each other's lives. Possible questions to include:

   • In what ways do we operate well as a team and what ways could we improve?

   • How is our relationship different from others that have not worked out?

   • When did you first realize you were interested in pursuing a relationship with me?

   • What was your favorite vacation?

   • What is one of your secret ambitions or dreams?

Sometimes remarried couples are so absorbed in their problems that they forget to see their partner as a person. You can strengthen your relationship by learning more about your partner and discussing their thoughts and feelings. If you try to answer the above questions about your partner first, and then compare answers (or interview each other), you are on the path to building authentic love and improving the quality of your second marriage.

8
Manage the Flames of Conflict

after a quick phone conversation confirming a location at a nearby café, Erin and Ron, whom you met previously, agreed to meet me for a follow-up interview. As you might recall, theirs is an unusual love story. They were childhood sweethearts, drifted apart in college, and reconnected over social media after their subsequent marriages and divorces to others and their unlikely reunion.

Erin reflects, "We've been married a couple of years now, and when I saw you at the mall and you asked how we were doing, it was hard to keep it short. I'm so glad we could get together and explain what we're going through with Tommy and Cole, because we don't want to let it pull us apart."

During our interview, Ron was forthcoming about their recent problems related to raising Erin's two teenage sons, whom he referred to as good guys who are just plain lazy. The "chore war" usually starts at 6:00 a.m., as Ron is returning home after working third shift as a night auditor at a large resort hotel, and Tommy and Cole are struggling to get ready for the morning bus ride to their high school classes.

Ron says, "I just didn't raise my two kids this way. They didn't leave their crap around, and they made their own breakfast and did dishes. I think Erin spoils her boys because she feels bad that she initiated the divorce. I'm not trying to be their dad, but I can't take much more of their disrespect and chaotic lives. It's starting to put a wedge between me and Erin, and our house is a mess."

With intensity in his voice, Ron explains that he raised two children who turned out to be successful adults and he feels justified in his complaints about his two stepsons' behavior. On the other hand, Erin was laid off six months ago and says she doesn't mind cleaning up and making breakfast for her sons.

Erin reflects, "After being a single mom for a few years, it's nice to be home for a change and be able to nurture my boys—they've been through so much stress with the divorce. Ron is just too uptight about the house. He was never like that when we were dating in college, and he's just going to have to learn to relax his expectations of my boys if we're going to get along. I refuse to spend my days yelling at Tommy and Cole to pick up."

To this Ron responds, "Why can't Erin see that we need to teach Tommy and Cole a lesson about being accountable. They'll grow up to be irresponsible adults who rely on others to get by. Maybe if she worked like I do she'd see that productivity depends a lot on being organized, and our home is a disaster waiting to happen."

In this exchange, it's clear that both Erin and Ron feel they must defend their positions. Each has a strong need to prove they're right, and each has developed an unfortunate attack-defensive pattern of relating. It can happen in the most mundane conversations in a remarried family. You and your spouse are discussing chores, finances, or who will prepare dinner, and suddenly your partner says that you (or your child) are not doing your share or living up to your end of the bargain. That's when knee-jerk reactions are easy, and full-blown arguments typically follow.

Conflict doesn't mean the end of your remarriage, and it can actually make it stronger. There are always going to be disagreements; you cannot avoid them entirely. What you can do, however, is become skilled at recovering from disputes by talking about your perspectives afterward. In this chapter you will learn how to have an effective recovery conversation. A general principle of recovering from conflict is to avoid focusing on being "right," and to deal with conflict using a collaborative rather than adversarial approach by avoiding trying to prove a point.

STOP TRYING TO PROVE A POINT
AND MAKE REPAIR ATTEMPTS

What Erin and Ron need is a way to stop blaming each other and to eliminate their pattern of trying to prove a point. The first step toward changing this dysfunctional pattern of relating is awareness. They can benefit from developing a team approach to conflict resolution—realizing that working together is more important than being right. When each partner asserts their position and differences are addressed, a resolution is possible and a partnership is formed. What matters is preserving love and attachment and getting back on track after a dispute.

In *The Seven Principles for Making Marriage Work*, John Gottman describes repair attempts as the secret weapon that emotionally intelligent couples employ that allows their marriage to flourish rather than flounder. A repair attempt is any statement or action—verbal, physical, or otherwise—intended to diffuse negativity and keep a conflict from escalating. In over forty years of research in his classic "Love Lab" studies, Gottman discovered that the number one solution to marital problems is to get good at repair skills. He explains that repair attempts allow a couple to get back on track after a fight and are an important way to avoid resentment.

For example, after Tommy and Cole got on the bus one day after a particularly heated dispute over a pile of dishes left in the sink, Erin approached Ron offering physical affection (putting her arm on his shoulder and kissing him on his cheek) and made breakfast for them. While they ate, Ron and Erin had a calm recovery conversation, which allowed them to process their earlier disagreement, each owning their part in it and expressing their views on how to deal with household chores. Rather than rupturing the bond in their relationship, Erin's repair attempt helped bring them closer. Since Ron appreciates being touched as a sign of love, he was comforted by Erin's loving touch and kiss on the cheek.

In the beginning of their relationship, Erin and Ron were so elated to have discovered each other that they focused more on their similarities than differences. After a while, emotional baggage from past relationships was causing them to overreact to triggers (such as a messy house) and they started to become more critical and defensive with each other. They lost sight of the loving feelings that brought them together in the first place.

Erin puts it like this: "We tend to get irrational and dig our heels in when we fight—like we did in high school and college. Ron would say, 'You're always right, Erin; you know you're always right.'" Erin pauses and continues: "This would infuriate me even more. So now I say, 'I don't want to always be right. I want you to understand where I'm coming from. And if that means we can't talk about this right now, I'm going to go in the other room and read until we cool off. When I come back, we can talk.'"

Ron explains, "Usually one of us will say 'I love you and I want to get though whatever we don't understand. Can we be friends?' That's what gets us through our fights—we are best friends. I used to think arguing was a bad thing, but I'm learning to fight fair."

Every relationship has its inevitable difficulties, and conflict goes with the territory. Sometimes remarried couples avoid conflict because it signified the end of their first marriage or led to bitter disputes that never got resolved. But avoiding conflict backfires in intimate relationships. Bottling up negative thoughts and feelings doesn't give your partner a chance to change their behavior.

One of the secrets of a good second marriage is learning to choose battles wisely, distinguishing between petty issues and truly important ones. For example, Ron learned that arguing over dishes left in the sink was hardly worth the battle. Rather than keeping score, he and Erin sat down with Tommy and Cole and discussed a schedule for chores and family responsibilities and stated their expectations in a positive way. Everyone contributed to the discussion, and Cole developed a chart—he enjoys graphic art. Ron and Erin were surprised that her boys bought into the plan as long as they could take Friday off and have pizza delivery with their friends—without their mom and stepdad hovering or demanding cleanup right away!

DEAL WITH HIDDEN ISSUES

As we saw in chapter 7, when trivial issues are blown out of proportion, you should suspect *hidden issues*. For instance, the argument between

Erin and Ron earlier in this chapter isn't really about Tommy and Cole's messiness; it's about power and control in the family. Further, when people don't feel recognized for what they have to contribute and safe enough to express negative feelings, they might blow up a trivial issue, such as leaving dishes in the sink.

In *Fighting for Your Marriage*, psychologist Howard J. Markman and his colleagues explain that hidden issues are a sign that couples are keeping score, don't feel recognized, and aren't working as teammates. He explains that hidden issues reflect the unexpressed expectations, needs, and feelings that, if not attended to, can cause great damage to your marriage. Markman believes that most couples deal with issues only in the context of events. In other words, the only time couples pay attention to an issue is when they are fighting about it. In a healthy relationship, partners draw out untapped possibilities in each other rather than focusing on each other's flaws.

PATTERNS THAT CAN ERODE THE QUALITY OF YOUR RELATIONSHIP

Happily married couples battle against negative patterns of relating rather than against each other, according to Markman. In *Fighting for Your Marriage*, he advises couples to watch for the four patterns that can erode the quality of a relationship: escalation, invalidation, negative interpretations, and withdrawal and avoidance.

> **Escalation.** This occurs when you focus on trying to prove a point or upping the ante. For instance, if you walk away or ask for a little space when you feel that your buttons are being pushed, this can defuse an argument. When escalation is short-circuited, according to Markman, it's usually because one partner backs off or says something to de-escalate the argument, breaking the negative cycle.

> **Invalidation.** You put down the thoughts, feelings, or character of the other partner. This behavior can be subtle or direct. The best way to avoid invalidating your partner is to show respect

for them and acknowledge their different perspective. For instance, when Craig doesn't finish a home repair, I could say, "I realize you have your own time table for getting the basement finished and you would rather go for quality than speed."

Negative interpretations. You consistently interpret your partner's motives negatively. For example, if Ron is angry at Erin for being too lenient with her two sons, he might say, "You are such a pushover, they take advantage of you." He may fail to realize that she just asked her sons to mow the grass.

Withdrawal or avoidance. You withdraw from or avoid important discussions. This can involve one or both partners shutting down during an argument or being unwilling to engage in a conversation about a particular topic or issue. The pursuer-distancer dynamic discussed in chapter 6 is common among couples where one partner withdraws or avoids.

For remarried couples, it is especially important to avoid negative patterns of relating because misunderstandings can easily be heightened due to emotional baggage from a former marriage. This can cause some people to seek revenge or engage in other destructive behaviors that are highly detrimental to a remarriage. Truth be told, you won't be able to resolve all conflicts, but that doesn't mean your marriage has to suffer. It's more a matter of which issues you can live with and manage successfully. For instance, when we disagree about where we want to go for vacation, I'll ask Craig, "On a scale of 1 to 10, how much do you want to do this?" By picking and choosing our battles, we argue less!

CAN A SECOND MARRIAGE THRIVE WITH UNRESOLVED CONFLICTS?

Many couples buy into the myth that if a marriage is healthy all issues get resolved. However, it's not the presence of conflict that stresses the relationship; it's the manner in which partners respond to each other.

Positive, respectful communication about differences—developing tools to repair disputes such as stating requests in an affirmative way—helps keep a marriage thriving. Differences of opinion between mates can make a marriage stronger as long as they aren't deal breakers and both people agree to accept their differences.

For instance, some problems in a relationship never get resolved because both people dig their heels in and are unable to listen to each other. As a result, neither partner is able to get their point across. This is one of the reasons why Gottman's research finds that 69 percent of problems in a marriage don't get resolved, but they can be managed successfully if couples have repair skills.

We can use conflict as an opportunity for growth. When each partner approaches the other as an equal, working through some conflicts can actually nourish rather than drain a relationship. Other times, couples might agree to let things go and repair hurt feelings. They might accept that a compromise can't be reached because their viewpoints are so vastly different.

Most of the time, remarried couples can work on trying to repair conflicts. For example, Wendy and Michael, both in their late thirties, childless, and in their second marriage, endured bitter divorces and have trust issues that lead to arguments over safety and security. This is especially the case when they are out socially, when Wendy admits to feeling more insecure. However, she is learning to reflect and take responsibility for her part in their disagreements rather than reacting with accusations and mistrusting Michael's intentions.

As they learn how to be vulnerable and discuss concerns that arise with each other in a timely and respectful way, they are strengthening their repair skills. They are beginning to embrace the notion that conflict is an inevitable part of an intimate relationship and that not all problems have to be resolved. This helps them bounce back from disagreements faster and build a successful, long-lasting relationship.

Wendy reflects, "Ninety percent of the time I trust Michael and believe he wants the best for me, and the other 10 percent is not a big deal anymore. Michael is not trying to hurt me on purpose when he comes home late or forgets to text me. He has proven his love day in and day out. Our arguments always simmer down when one of us does something kind or refuses to up the ante. I'm the one that tends to hold a grudge, but I'm learning to let go of resentment toward Michael."

In other words, instead of focusing on Michael's flaws and looking to blame him, Wendy is spending her energy fostering a deeper connection. She has stopped assuming the worst of Michael and demanding that he change.

Six Reasons to Stop Trying to Change Your Partner (Work on Yourself Instead)

1. **Your partner is not going to change.** You can't change a cat into a dog. Love just isn't enough to change a person's basic nature and upbringing. If you fall in love with someone who is reserved and you are more outgoing and need outward signs of affection to feel secure, you will feel chronically dissatisfied. Most likely these differences will eat away at loving feelings over time and erode positive feelings in your relationship.

2. **Rather than trying to "fix" your partner, focus on improving your own life.** Many people stay in dysfunctional relationships with the unconscious desire to change their partner. According to relationship expert Ross Rosenberg, people often stay in highly dysfunctional relationships to their own detriment because they don't know how to emotionally disconnect when they get caught up in a codependent (pleaser/fixer) dance with a partner who can't reciprocate.

3. **Focusing on changing your partner can prevent you from focusing on the issues at hand.** Ask yourself, "What am I trying to accomplish?" Avoid name-calling and don't attack your partner personally. Remember, anger is usually a symptom of underlying hurt, fear, and frustration, so keep things in perspective. Avoid defensiveness and showing contempt for your partner (eye-rolling, ridicule, name-calling, sarcasm, etc.).

4. **Focusing on changing someone allows wounds to fester.** Challenge your beliefs and self-defeating thoughts about your partner's behavior when you perceive it to be negative. Listen to your partner's side of the story. Are there times when you feel mistrustful or hurt even when they present evidence to the contrary about your grievance?

5. **Trying to change your partner interferes with your ability to move on.** Try to remember you're on the same team. Accept that people do the best they can and try to be more understanding. But this doesn't mean that you accept your partner's hurtful actions. You simply come to a more realistic view and give those actions less power over you. After all, none of us is perfect.

6. **Trying to change your partner can lead to the end of your relationship.** In *Why Marriages Succeed or Fail*, John Gottman suggests that criticizing your partner is one of the main causes of divorce. It's different from offering a critique or voicing a complaint. The latter two are about specific issues, whereas the former is an attack on the person. For instance, this is a complaint: "I was worried when you were late. We agreed that you'd call when you were running late." This is criticism: "You never think about me; you're so selfish!"

Fortunately, even if you're in a relationship that is heading in a bad direction, there are strategies that can set you and your partner on the right path again. Taking responsibility for your part in negative patterns of relating to your partner is the hallmark of a successful remarriage. If you embrace the notion that conflict is an inevitable part of an intimate relationship, and that not all problems have to be resolved, you will bounce back from disagreements faster and build a successful, long-lasting relationship.

CHANGE STARTS WITH YOU

Do you spend more time questioning your partner's words or actions than examining your own? Blaming your partner can feel good in the moment, but it can lead to anger and resentment. Conflict is not always a destructive thing in relationships. In fact, all couples argue. The difference between the couples that stay together and the ones who divorce is the way they repair after conflict. The key to having a happy second marriage is to stay engaged or connected during conflict and not withdraw from your partner or throw in the towel too easily.

In fact, Paul Schrodt, a professor at Texas Christian University, and his colleagues studied fourteen thousand participants and discovered that the most common reason why couples develop serious difficulties is that one or both partners withdraw and go into silent-treatment mode due to feelings of hurt, anger, and resentment. Schrodt also found that women are usually the ones who demand or pursue, and men tend to withdraw or distance.

In *Marriage Rules*, Harriet Lerner suggests that a good disagreement can clear the air as long as you are respectful and you repair hurt feelings. She writes, "It's nice to know we can survive conflict and even learn from it. Many couples, however, get trapped in endless rounds of fighting and blaming that they don't know how to get out of. When fights go unchecked and unrepaired, they can eventually erode love and respect, which are the bedrock of any successful relationship."

Eight Tips for Dealing Effectively with Conflict in Intimate Relationships

1. **Do not blame, criticize, or show contempt for your partner.** Talking about specific issues will reap better results than attacking your partner. For instance, this is a complaint: "I'm upset because you didn't tell me about spending money on new clothes. We agreed to be open with each other, and money is tight right now." This is criticism: "You never tell me the truth. How can I trust you?" Avoid defensiveness and showing contempt for your partner (eye-rolling, ridicule, name-calling,

sarcasm, etc.). Starting conversations with a soft and curious tone—for example, "Could I ask you something?"—will lessen your partner's defensiveness.

2. **Avoid character assassinations.** Don't attack your partner's character, values, or core beliefs. Remember that anger is usually a symptom of underlying hurt, fear, and frustration, so stop and reflect on your own emotions. Validate their perspective first, then share your viewpoint. When you feel like attacking your partner, ask yourself, "What am I trying to accomplish?"

3. **Don't make threats or issue ultimatums.** Avoid saying things you will regret later. Don't issue ultimatums, such as "I'm leaving if things don't improve," except in rare instances when there is a major relationship violation. In most cases, it's more effective to make a request in a positive way, such as "I'm too upset to talk now, so can we discuss this after dinner?" Take the *D* word (*divorce*) out of your vocabulary. Make a commitment to stay together (unless there is abuse) and accept that there will be difficulties as you deal with healing from past betrayals and everyday hurts.

4. **Approach conflict with a problem-solving attitude.** Avoid trying to prove a point. Instead, examine your part in a disagreement. Listen to your partner's requests and ask for clarification on issues than are unclear. Engage in a conversation with your partner that is productive, rather than shutting down. The relationship wins when both partners get some—but not all—of their needs met.

5. **Use "I" statements rather than "you" statements, which tend to come across as blameful.** For example, "I felt hurt when you purchased the car without discussing it with me" rather than "You are so selfish; you never think of what I need." I discussed ways to use "I" statements productively in chapter 7.

6. **Take a short break if you feel overwhelmed or flooded.** This will give you both time to calm down and collect your thoughts so

you can have a more meaningful dialogue. When emotions are high, people tend to repeat well-worn behavior patterns, and they are less flexible. Set up a policy where no disapproval (or criticism) is allowed between you and your partner for at least twenty-four hours during times of turmoil and high stress in your remarried family.

7. **Give your partner the benefit of the doubt.** Instead of focusing on your partner's flaws and looking to blame them, try spending your energy fostering a deeper connection. Avoid building a case against your partner. Instead, express positive feelings and gestures of love often and become skilled at demonstrating acceptance and gratitude in your words and actions.

8. **Practice having a recovery conversation after an argument.** Daniel B. Wile believes that your focus needs to be on listening to your partner's perspective, collaborating, building intimacy, and restoring safety and goodwill. A recovery conversation can reveal information about your relationship, lead to a resolution of the fight, and restore intimacy. Adopt a mind-set that views relationships as teachers. This will allow you to overcome setbacks after a dispute or miscommunication. Instead of focusing on the past, spend energy fostering a deeper connection with your partner.

Once you've learned to manage and resolve conflicts effectively, it becomes much easier to repair disputes and get back on track. If you find yourself struggling, tell your partner what is on your mind. For instance, say something such as "I feel flooded right now. Can you hold me or tell me you love me? I feel like attacking you, but I don't want to do that." Most of the time, you'll restore intimacy by being honest and open with your partner during times of high conflict or distress. It takes time and patience!

When I caught up with Erin and Ron for a follow-up interview, they were becoming more skilled at the art of dealing effectively with conflicts. While their early love affair had them feeling exhilarated about meeting unexpectedly and falling in love, they both realized it takes dedication and hard work to make a complicated second marriage thrive.

Ron says, "Erin and I are learning to get along better, mostly because I'm trying to be more realistic about our different standards of neatness and to be tuned in to what Tommy and Cole have gone through. I realize that my love for Erin is stronger than my need to be right."

Erin explains, "Ron still gets upset when I clean up after my boys, but he's learning to relax a bit and spends more time in his man cave, which he keeps immaculate and where he can chill. I'm also more reflective about how feeling sorry for Tommy and Cole won't help them grow up to be responsible adults, and it's better for me to leave their messes for them to clean up."

THE ART OF COMPROMISE

Most of us dislike conflict. Very few people were raised with healthy role models for dealing with differences. However, while conflict may appear to be a destructive force in relationships, it can actually help you achieve lasting love. In fact, differences can be a source of interest and fresh energy rather than a cause to prove a point or defend your position.

It appears that Erin and Ron have learned the art of compromise and viewing each other as allies, rather than enemies, in a battle against misunderstanding. For most of us, listening and accepting our partner's influence without getting defensive is a difficult skill to master. This is especially true when what our partner says is a trigger and hits a raw spot.

Erin reflects, "I'm learning to accept Ron's influence when we disagree. It's like when we're having financial problems, I let him have the final say. I'm trying to look at differences as an opportunity to change the way I look at things, because I can easily dig my heels in. This new way of looking at disagreements has helped me stay calm. Sometimes I feel upset about something Ron says about Tommy and Cole's messiness, but I try to remember that this is a touchy topic for me."

Couples will disagree—it's a given. Nevertheless, arguing with your partner is an opportunity to learn more about how to resolve differences and love your partner more deeply. Love means risking feeling vulnerable and sharing your feelings, thoughts, and desires, even if it could lead to a disagreement. Conflicting needs for closeness and space exist in all intimate relationships. When issues come up with either of these needs, it's essential that you discuss them with your partner and find creative ways to compromise.

What is the meaning of the word *compromise*? It's a settlement by which each side makes concessions. While this doesn't sound romantic, if you decide you want to save your marriage, you have to learn to negotiate, which is the essence of compromise. Negotiation is about diplomacy. It's a tool that will help you and your partner get on the same side and become intimately connected. Over time, productive arguments can actually help couples stay together. Happy couples learn ways to have fruitful disagreements—more like discussions than arguments—and not hold on to recycled anger or feelings of resentment.

DEALING WITH DIFFERENCES OF OPINION

Cheryl, 60, and Jay, 66, found out the importance of compromise early on in their second marriage. When Cheryl's daughter from her first marriage, Alexandria, and her two preschoolers joined their household (after their first wedding anniversary), it created somewhat of a crisis for their marriage. Alexandria was looking for employment and unable to support herself. She promised she would move out in six months, after saving up enough money to rent her own place. While Cheryl saw this as a golden opportunity to spend time with her daughter and bond with her grandchildren, Jay saw it as an intrusion on his personal space and new marriage.

Jay explains his position: "I was used to living alone after my divorce over the last ten years. The noise and chaos in our home rose dramatically—especially after dinner when the kids are usually watching TV in the family room, where I was accustomed to watching the evening news. They also stay up much too late, so we don't get any quiet time, except when they go to their dad's house for an overnight."

Cheryl rests her cheek on her palm and responds thoughtfully, "I know this is hard for Jay, but it's only temporary, and Alexandria and my grandsons need help right now. Besides, it makes me feel good to help her out financially, so I agreed not to charge her rent. Now you're just being petty."

About a month later, after following my suggestion of contacting a marriage counselor to help them learn to compromise, Cheryl called me to report the good news. They had attended two sessions with a trained therapist and they had already adopted several solutions to minimize Jay's resentment and Cheryl's defensive reactions.

Cheryl reports, "We ended up coming up with a plan where my grandsons would watch TV before dinner while we cooked. Alexandria agreed that they'd have playtime and bath time after dinner—one hour earlier—so that all the adults in the house could enjoy peace and quiet and the boys would get a better night's sleep. Alexandria also agreed to shop for groceries and cook one night a week when her boys where spending time with their father."

Due to their willingness to compromise, Cheryl and Jay reclaimed their home, and their grocery bill was reduced by Alexandria cooking one night a week. Most importantly, they were able to get back on track and restore their personal and couple time. Cheryl reported that Jay was feeling less resentful, and she even found him playing on the floor with her grandsons rather than watching the news one night. By being able to come up with compromises that they both felt good about, they strengthened their bond as a couple and improved their friendship.

The repair tools that Cheryl and Jay used—listening, attempting to understand each other's perspective, and compromising—allowed them to get back on track and support Cheryl's daughter and grandchildren. Their story illustrates how compromise can help couples maintain intimacy. When one or both partners shuts down or becomes critical, issues often get swept under the rug and are never resolved, leaving the partner who feels hurt—or both people—even more resentful. However, adopting a resilient mind-set and repairing hurt feelings can turn disconnection into intimacy.

Instead of trying to "fix" each other, Cheryl and Jay now focus on cleaning up the murky water that clouds their vision of their relationship. After they have come to a compromise, they can both give each other the space to understand and explain what is really going on rather than what they "think" the problem is. Once they realized that in every disagreement there are always two valid perspectives, it was no longer necessary for them to argue in order to prove they were right. They discovered that it was okay to disagree as long as they attempted to listen and understand each other's point of view—attempting to show empathy rather than making accusations or insults.

Compromise is an important tool to strengthen and preserve a second marriage. Discussing concerns that arise with a partner in a timely and respectful way will help couples become better at repair skills. Even happy remarried couples have stresses in their marriage; they have disagreements, frustrations, and anger. However, they don't let anger build into resentment because their dedication to each other is solid. Their strong connection along with the knowledge and skills to deal with the complications of remarriage are vital to beating the odds and seeing their remarriage succeed.

Following these action steps will help you build empathy for your partner, manage and resolve conflicts, reach compromises, and achieve positive engagement. Try these for one week and then discuss your progress with your partner over lunch at your favorite restaurant or diner to avoid rushing!

Four Action Steps to Learning to Compromise

Before you practice the exercise below, you and your partner need to write down one issue that is important to work on. It's important to identify the areas that both partners can be flexible about and those that are a challenge to consider worthy of compromise. For instance, a core need for you might be sitting down to a family meal on Sunday, but you're okay with takeout in the den on Friday night.

1. **Establish common goals that you and your mate can agree on.**
   Be sure to discuss any feelings you share on the issues you're discussing.

2. **Practice empathy by trying to imagine yourself walking in your partner's shoes.** Show willingness to help your partner meet one of their personal goals or dreams by asking how you can help them.

3. **Listen actively without making evaluative comments or asking too many questions.** To avoid defensiveness, reply to—rather than react to—your partner. When your partner identifies an inflexible area of area of need, ask for more clarification about why it is important to them and include their feelings, beliefs, and values on this issue.

4. **Write down one compromise that honors both of your needs, wishes, and dreams.**

Celebrate the fact that you worked on the art of compromise successfully, and remember that it's a work in progress!

It took Victoria and Marisa a long time to feel comfortable with me. It seemed like they felt that by being close to me they were betraying their mom, who had started a new family with another man. But things have gotten better because I've been patient and waited for them to come around. **LISA, AGE 47**

9

Embrace Your Role as a Stepparent and Create Positive Stepfamily Memories

during our third month of dating, my husband stated emphatically, "Your kids seem nice and I'm ready to be a stepdad." He was only the second man I dated after my divorce, and I was stunned by his eagerness to commit to a woman with two kids, as he was a 42-year-old bachelor with no children of his own. His only deal breaker, which he announced on our second date, was that he wanted to have a child of his own (biological or adopted) and he wouldn't bend on this request. Craig comes from a large family and at that time was an uncle to six nieces and nephews whom he loved spending time with in addition to enjoying many of his friends' children.

Fortunately I was receptive to trying to have a third child in my early forties and became pregnant fairly quickly. However, our adjustment to living together and Craig's struggles as a stepdad were evident shortly after we married. He was in for a rude awakening when he discovered that he wasn't going to earn his stepchildren's respect just by virtue of marrying me. He clearly had to earn it, day by day, by being there. In fact, any authority he tried to impose—for example, "Could you please hang up your jacket?"—was sometimes met with challenging remarks such as "You can't tell me what to do," or they ignored him. Craig later reflected that for about three years it felt as if our newly formed family went through some real growing pains that included having our own child, Catherine, who in the beginning was seen as a threat to my two older children because she took up a lot of my time and attention.

Another huge challenge we faced as a stepfamily was differences in our parenting styles. This included my unwillingness to accept feedback from Craig about any possible mistakes I made because he didn't have any experience as a parent when we wed. In addition, I tend to be a little more lenient than he is in my parenting style. Some of our differences played out in heated arguments in front of our children. I often made excuses for their behaviors that Craig found annoying, and he complained that I make things too easy for them. My common refrain when he asked that they do household chores was "It's not fair to ask them to do that since they help out at their dad's house too." I had to learn to allow Craig to find his footing as a parent and stepparent and to stop being so defensive when he tried to engage with me about my parenting style.

DIFFERENCES IN PARENTING STYLES

The most difficult aspect of remarried life for many couples is parenting. Remarried couples often have different parenting styles, and this can create a lot of conflict. Most remarried couples who have children from previous marriages aren't prepared for the complexities of living in a stepfamily. Further, couples might enter a second or third marriage with distinct expectations and assumptions, such as the new family will heal the hurts of the previous divorce, that can influence how well they accept the realities of stepfamily life and their adjustment to it.

It takes time for everyone in a stepfamily to adjust to living together. It is important for a biological parent to be aware that their spouse might feel ambivalent or left out and to back them up, so they do not feel taken for granted. If you discuss your roles and methods of raising children, it can help you and your partner navigate situations that arise. As a stepparent, it's also crucial for you to feel supported by your spouse. When this does not happen, it can lead to tension between you and your spouse, and you are likely to feel resentful, hurt, and overlooked. For instance, when I interviewed Deidra, she'd been divorced from Bob for several years and told me that one of their biggest struggles had been raising his two daughters from his first marriage.

As Deidra spoke about the breakup of her second marriage, she freely expressed her regret and sadness about the differences between her and Bob's approaches to parenting and how this contributed to their bitter divorce after eight years of remarriage. Deidra, 49, had married Bob, 50, when his two daughters were 6 and 12, and because he had full custody, the children lived with them full-time. Since Deidra didn't have children from her first marriage, there was a big learning curve for her to get used to being a full-time parent in her forties. While Colleen, 6, was generally more cooperative and even affectionate with Deidra at times, responding positively to hugs or cuddling on the couch on occasion, her older sister, Jessica, 12, was much more reserved and even hostile toward Deidra when she tried to discipline her or assert her authority.

Deidra reflects, "This was my second marriage and I really wanted it to work, but from the get-go there were big problems. Since Bob's ex moved out of state and was happy to relinquish her role as a parent to pursue a job in the entertainment industry, her daughters usually only saw their mother for Christmas and summer vacation. Jessica was constantly comparing me to her mom, and I came out as the villain. Since Bob worked long hours as a firefighter and I had retired early from my nursing career due to a back injury, I was the one who was home after school, and I did the cooking, childcare, and laundry."

She continues, "My upbringing was in a military family where respect and following the rules were musts. Bob's family was more lenient. He believed his daughters could do no wrong, shouldn't do chores, and were entitled to a lot of treats and gifts because they had dealt with their parents' bad divorce. It seemed like he was always trying to overcompensate for his wife leaving suddenly, when they were young, because she got a call from her agent about an acting job in Los Angeles."

One of the biggest problems that Deidra said led to the demise of her marriage to Bob was the lack of respect that his daughter Jessica had for her, and his unwillingness to intervene when his daughter was being rude. This dynamic led to many arguments that rarely got resolved; Bob was uncomfortable dealing with conflict and he usually sided with his daughters because he felt sorry for them. Deidra wanted Bob to support her and instead found that he showered his daughters with gifts and took her for granted. The last words out of her mouth as she left my office were "It was a no-win situation."

In another situation, Conner, 49, whom you met earlier, often felt like an outsider in the lives of his two stepchildren, although his second wife, Tara, 48, tried to make him feel included in their tight family unit after they wed. When his and Tara's mutual child, Michael, was born two years after they married, he thought things would get better, but they were worse for a while as everyone was getting used to living together. Through it all, Tara never gave up hope that her two older children, Shana and Teresa, would come around and warm up to Conner. Tara and Conner knew they couldn't rush things, since Tara's teenage daughters still spent Saturdays with their biological dad and resented their parents' divorce and her remarriage to Conner.

Three years after they married, the dynamics in their stepfamily were finally starting to shift a bit, and Tara and Conner were looking for opportunities to help Conner bond with his stepdaughters. Then one night, when Tara announced she had an open house at the school where she taught, Conner seized this opportunity to attend his stepdaughter Shana's basketball game.

Conner reflects, "She even invited a few friends out for pizza afterward. It felt good to hang out with Shana and her friends after the game. Tara had to work, so I stepped in. For once I didn't feel like an intruder in my stepdaughter's life. I played basketball in high school, so I gave her tips because she is new at playing. I wish I knew during the first couple years of our marriage that it would take time for my stepdaughters to warm up to me."

THE STEPFAMILY: NO SUCH THING AS AN INSTANT FAMILY

Tara and Conner found out that there's no such thing as instant love between a new stepparent and a stepchild. One of the most crucial things to learn about a stepfamily is that most children give love and trust to their parent naturally but feel that their stepparent must earn their love and trust over time. Children often don't have time to ease into the new relationship with a stepparent(s), and so the relationship can feel forced or unnatural. The biological parent can help their children bond with their new spouse if they make it clear that their marriage is solid and that disrespect toward their spouse won't be tolerated. If both parents try to plan enjoyable activities for all family members, and work as a team, it will help everyone build a foundation of trust and create positive stepfamily memories.

However, it's important to acknowledge that the stepfamily will never be just like an intact family. The couple may be in love and fulfilled in the marriage, but when there are children from a previous marriage, there's no honeymoon period. And in most cases, parents and stepparents have unrealistic expectations about some aspects of stepfamily life. Couples need to be aware that stepparents will have some ambiguity in their roles and level of authority. Also, the myth that loving your partner means loving their children immediately can create disappointment and resentment and has to be discussed openly. These discussions are crucial for the well-being of the remarried couple, and the biological parent should never assign blame or try to provoke shame in their spouse who has these feelings. It's completely normal for stepparents and stepchildren to feel uncomfortable with each other.

For instance, Lisa, whom you met earlier, became an instant parent to two stepdaughters, Marisa and Victoria, 13 and 16, and didn't have any prior parenting experience. Since her husband, Ryan, had full custody of his two daughters and they only visited their mother two weekends a month, Lisa plunged into her role with enthusiasm and was shocked at the hurdles she had to jump over to win her stepdaughters' respect.

Lisa puts it like this: "Ryan and I have a strong marriage that has weathered the storms of raising Marisa and Victoria for over six years now. When they were younger, they were more likely to listen to me and show some affection. But now that they are teenagers, they balk when I ask them to do dishes or clean up their room. Marisa even said to me the other day that her mother is a lot nicer and told me not to yell at her when I really wasn't even raising my voice. This really hurt me because I drive them to activities, cook their meals, and even help them with their homework."

Both Deidra and Lisa thought they could win over their stepdaughters by playing the role of mother and homemaker. Truth be told, a stepparent can never replace a stepchild's parent, and it can take many years to bond with your stepchild. This is especially true if you only see your stepchild a few days a week or some weekends.

Lisa says, "It seemed like they thought that by being close to me, they were betraying their mom. It's not like I haven't made mistakes, like the time I got mad at Victoria for talking back to me and said 'At least I'm here for you every day.' That was so mean, and even though I apologized a few times, Ryan reminded me about that comment for a few months. I have to accept that I'm only human, but it has been a long journey trying to forgive myself and have realistic expectations."

DISCUSSING EXPECTATIONS

Sometimes the gap between expectation and reality is very wide, yet there's usually no easy time, place, or way to share your expectations with your partner. As mentioned previously, most of our expectations about marriage come from the family that raised us. Or you might want your union to be like your friend's parents' marriage or your next-door neighbor's family because they always seemed so happy and free of conflict. Further, remarried couples also bring expectations from their first or second marriages. If you endured a difficult marriage, you might expect your new partner and their children to be the family you always dreamed of. It's these unchecked expectations that so often trip us up.

Because they don't know any better, instead of evaluating unrealistic expectations, many remarried couples blame themselves or the relationship itself once disillusionment sets in. When this occurs, partners can play the blame game and position themselves against each other, not beside each other. If you and your partner have an open dialogue about your expectations, the common concerns and disillusionments can become normalized and not seen as due to the flaws of either spouse. For instance, when Danielle, 48, was dating Tom, 52, getting to know his teenage daughter on weekends was enjoyable. And because Danielle is a physical therapist who works with children, she envisioned a warm, close relationship with Carrie. It wasn't until they were married for over a year and Carrie had her fifteenth birthday party at their home that Danielle realized that she hadn't entered her remarriage with her eyes wide open.

Danielle reflects, "Looking back, I should have seen it coming when Carrie pitched a fit because her dad and I wouldn't let her invite boys to her party and have a sleepover. Tom works Saturdays as a manager of a small store and I just didn't feel I could handle a group of girls with their hormones surging. We were also afraid that mixing boys in would lead to trouble since Carrie has always been a bit rebellious—especially since we got married. When we told her that no boys were allowed, Carrie became furious and said, 'You aren't my mother.' Her words were like a knife in my heart."

Unfortunately, Danielle struggled with feelings of guilt because she could not warm up to Carrie, and they have had an up-and-down relationship for years. Like Danielle, many stepparents are well intentioned and yet let unrealistic expectations of themselves and their role as stepparent create a "tyranny of the should" or unrealistic expectations that can lead to guilt, emotional distress, and marital unhappiness. The term *tyranny of the should* was coined by psychologist Karen Horney in the early 1900s to explain a tendency in some people to have a split between their ideal self and their real self, and the difficulty they have reconciling the two. In her case, Danielle told herself she "should" have felt closer to Carrie and so she fell short of her own expectations of how a good stepmother should feel and behave. She also felt disappointed in Carrie.

When you believe that you *must* or *should* do something, the demands imply a set of expectations, and it's common to set unrealistic standards. I encourage you to review this list of stepfamily "shoulds" and try to add some of your own to the list. Then discuss these with your partner over your favorite beverage.

Stepparent "Shoulds"

- Stepfamily life should be smooth because my partner and I love each other.

- My stepchildren should love and respect me because I married their parent and treat them respectfully.

- I dealt with old losses and baggage prior to getting remarried so they shouldn't affect my relationship with my new partner. Our stepfamily will heal the hurts of the previous divorce.

- Other people in my stepfamily should (or must) pitch in and share responsibilities and chores.

- If my love for my partner is strong enough, outside forces such as ex-spouses and relatives will never come between us.

Once Danielle and Tom started to calmly discuss their expectations, they were better able to deal with the stress and storms of helping raise Tom's daughter, Carrie. After they explored their "shoulds," they realized that they're a good enough dad and stepmom to Carrie, in spite of their flaws. As a result, some of their tension and conflict decreased. They came to accept the reality that we all make mistakes and stumble along the way, and learning from their blunders could help them get along better in the long run. Fortunately, children, like the rest of us, are resilient and will bounce back when you stumble. As long as you are committed to doing your best, to keeping lines of communication open, and to being kind and loving, chances are great that you will all be fine.

In addition to examining unrealistic expectations and "shoulds," going through this list of common mistakes will help you come to terms with the realities of stepfamily life. You may not relate to all of them. Keep in mind that there are different types of stepfamilies—one shoe doesn't fit all.

Six Common Blunders of Stepparents

Blunder #1   You try too hard to be liked and to win over your stepchildren. It's perfectly normal to want to bend over backward to win the approval of your stepchild(ren). However, giving in to their every whim can create an unfortunate dynamic. Having realistic expectations that it can take stepkids a few years to warm up to you and that gifts or bribes won't speed up this challenging process can help stepparents come down to reality.

Blunder #2   You expect to be an instant family or to have instant love. Patricia L. Papernow, author of *Surviving and Thriving in Stepfamily Relationships*, explains that it can take stepfamilies two to four years to successfully blend and that there is no such thing as instant love.

Blunder #3   You and/or your spouse tolerate disrespect from your stepchildren. Many stepchildren resent having a new stepparent and see them as a rival for their biological parent's attention. This can create an unfortunate situation where they might be rude, even if they're generally polite and well behaved. When her stepdaughter was disrespectful, rather than responding with anger, Lisa learned to pause, take a deep breath, and say something such as "You seem frustrated with me, but I won't tolerate rudeness." She also coached her husband, Ryan, about the importance of intervening with his daughters, even if she made mistakes or they were in a bad mood.

Blunder #4   You try to be your stepchildren's parent and discipline them too soon. Trying to discipline your stepchildren before you have established trust is a recipe for disaster. Instead, try to be a caring adult friend. Once you have earned their respect you might be able to give them corrective feedback in a noncritical way. This is especially true of teenagers and children who are actively involved with both of their biological parents. Do your best to tread lightly and try to establish a bond based on shared activities that you both enjoy. For instance, if you and your stepdaughter both enjoy dancing, going to a dance concert together may help you to connect.

Blunder #5 You have unrealistic expectations of instant acceptance. Many stepparents feel immense pressure to claim their rightful place in their new family. For instance, Janna, 34, who has been stepmother to George, 12, for ten years, says, "It doesn't matter if they are 5 or 15, they are someone else's child. You have to be a friend to them, and you'll never be their mom or dad." Your marriage won't flourish if you expect your stepchildren to love and accept you right away.

Blunder #6 You take it personally when your stepchildren prefer their biological parent. The role of a stepparent is tricky and most likely will get easier over the years. The key to success is not to take it personally when your stepchildren prefer to spend time with their biological parent. If you remember that being an adult friend and mentor to them over the years will pay off, it will help you cope with hurt feelings. Janna reflects, "I tried not to take it personally when George wanted to see the new *Star Wars* movie with his mom, even though he knows I'm a big fan. It's not about me. I'm the adult and he's the child. Instead, we streamed it on Netflix and had a blast watching it in our cozy family room with a bowl of popcorn."

SHATTERING THE MYTH OF THE WICKED STEPMOTHER

According to E. Mavis Hetherington, psychologist and author of the landmark three-decade University of Virginia longitudinal study of 1,400 divorced and remarried families, being a stepmother can be extremely challenging without much of a payoff. She discovered that whereas most stepchildren will come to appreciate and accept a stepfather, the situation with a stepmother is more difficult and the stepchild's resentment is more intense. She found that most stepmoms are expected to be nurturers who are responsible for running daily family life, even when they might have preferred to take a back seat. Hetherington also found stepmothers were demonized in situations where the husband didn't support his wife's efforts to parent and discipline, and where the husband's ex-spouse treated her as a rival. She was surprised that so many of the children she interviewed described their stepmothers as evil, malevolent, wicked, or monsters, and even gave them nicknames such as "The Dragon."

From the beginning of her relationship with her husband, Rick, Jillian found her stepdaughter, Kylie, 16, to be a challenge because she was resentful of Jillian and tried her best to alienate her from her husband's family. Jillian, a high school guidance counselor, expressed empathy to Kylie when she angrily stated that she wished that her parents where still together. During several of their conversations, Jillian let Kylie know that she was sorry that she was hurt by her parents' divorce. But in spite of her attempts to show compassion and appease Kylie's intense anger, Jillian found that her rage was often out of control and directed toward her. Fortunately, Rick was supportive and tried his best to intervene when Kylie unleashed insults, accusations, and verbal assaults toward Jillian.

Jillian reflects, "I understood how difficult the divorce had been for her and I tried to be empathetic to her feelings. But when she started to blame it on me, I thought it was time to sit down with her and explain that I didn't know her father when he was married to her mother. Of course, this conversation did not go over very well. For the next several years, she popped in and out of our lives, and a lot of her behavior was attention seeking."

Unfortunately, a common theme for the stepmothers I spoke with was that they experienced many rough patches in their role as stepmom, regardless of their efforts to be a kind, helpful peacemaker. In fact, 75 percent of the stepmothers I interviewed stated that their own behavior and feelings were just one factor in determining how well they were accepted and respected by their stepchildren. Other factors included being the victim of bad-mouthing by biological mothers and feeling like an outsider. However, one protective factor that emerged from my research and many other studies on stepparenting is an association between a spouse showing support and understanding about the challenges a stepmother faces and her overall sense of happiness with being remarried.

Jillian's attempts to be understanding and incorporate her step-daughter into their lives was a constant struggle, especially because she had two biological sons who were resentful of Kylie's angry outbursts and the drama she presented when she showed up at their home unannounced and demanded money or special treatment. Jillian's usual go-to was to try to convince her exhausted husband and wary sons that Kylie was wounded by her parents' difficult divorce and the victim of parent alienation because her mother had tried relentlessly to turn her against Jillian and Rick. After two years of constant turmoil, Jillian and Rick hit a brick wall from which they have not yet recovered.

Jillian says, "Then, just when I thought things had improved between us, I mentioned this to my mother-in-law and she said that Kylie was saying horrible things behind my back to other members of my husband's family. This new information was very hurtful, and I chose not to address it with her. These types of issues continued to the point that we no longer have contact with her; she has disowned her father and wants nothing to do with either of us."

Although being a stepparent is not easy for anyone, being a step-mother is the most challenging role of all. This may be especially true of stepmothers who help raise their husband's daughter(s) because they might see their stepmother as a threat to their relationship with their own mother or to have stolen their father's time and attention from them. If you are a stepmom in a situation where your stepchildren resent or disrespect you, it's crucial that you not take it personally. Hard as it can seem, try to empathize with their situation and give them time to come around.

WHAT ABOUT STEPFATHERS?

Unsurprisingly, stepfamilies headed by the mother where the stepfather joins the family seem to fare better. In her comprehensive study of 173 adults whose parents had divorced, psychologist Constance Ahrons learned that whereas fewer than one in three children with remarried parents think of their stepmother as a parent, more than half regard their stepfather as a parent. Fifty percent of those whose moms remarried were happy about it, but less than 30 percent were pleased when their dads remarried. Further, a recent study of 2,085 stepfamilies by researchers Valarie King, Lisa M. Boyd, and Maggie L. Thorsen found that stepfathers play a pivotal role in fostering feelings of family belongingness for adolescents residing in stepfamilies.

What are some of the aspects of being a stepfather that make this experience less of a struggle? In an effort to find out more, I conducted in-depth interviews of five stepfathers in my sample about taking on this role.

Tommy, 49, was proud to use his real name and considers himself a bonus dad to his two stepdaughters, Samantha and Meghan. He has a 10-year-old son, Steven, from his first marriage; Steven spends about 50 percent of his time with Tommy and his new stepfamily. Tommy survived a difficult divorce and never imagined being remarried. But then he met his second wife at a conference and was struck by the similarity in their values, which focus on serving others. Remarried for four years to Caroline, Tommy learned the role of stepfather well from his own stepdad, who moved in with him and his mother when he was seventeen. Tommy found that the skills he learned from his "bonus dad" were crucial to his own success.

Tommy reflects, "He didn't lay down an 'it's my way or the highway' rule. This was a huge parenting lesson that I would eventually use. He was very respectful and kind. He never raised his voice to me (or my mom). Just more lessons I would need in my 'toolbox.' I didn't set the rules my first day of moving in with the ladies. I let it organically grow. My wife has two daughters, 19 and 14. The ladies and I created our own bonds, and I started picking the younger one up from school on Mondays so we could do something together, like stopping for an ice cream. I learned about their interests. When it came time to propose to my wife, her oldest was the first person I went to for permission."

Another stepfather, Leo, 64, was eager to talk about the struggles and delights of marrying his wife, Janette, 63, who had a 3-year-old son, David, from her first marriage when they met. Leo and Janette have been married thirty-two years and raised David with two younger "ours" siblings, Alicia and Nick. As Leo talked about his role in David's life, he stressed that he knew he had it easy because David only saw his real father about twice a year, so he didn't have to compete with him.

Leo puts it like this: "David has always called me Dad and is affectionate. He's close to me and my wife and both sides of his family. When his dad reappeared in his life as he got older, he still wanted to spend time with me. It meant a lot to me that David still enjoyed going to Bruins hockey games with me."

THE INSIDER AND OUTSIDER

Many of the stepparents I interviewed described themselves as being an outsider in their family. This is because the stepfamily structure often puts parents and stepparents on opposite ends of a continuum when it comes to separateness and closeness. For instance, every time a stepchild enters a room or a conversation, the biological parent might consider themselves as an insider and the stepparent as an outsider. This happens naturally because children typically gravitate to the parent they are most comfortable with, an insider, when seeking support or nurturance.

It's normal for a stepparent to feel that they're left out or overlooked at times. This literally leaves them feeling like an outsider in their own family. If you had secure attachments growing up and good self-esteem, these feelings are easier to cope with. However, if you experienced some insecurity in your early attachments or felt abandoned or neglected as a child, you may find the position of outsider especially painful as you grapple with feelings of anxiety, sadness, or loneliness that remind you of your past.

Feelings of insecurity, jealousy, or isolation about not being included in your spouse's relationship with their biological children can be devastating if they're not acknowledged and worked through. These unresolved feelings can cause you to feel dissatisfied with your role and less tolerant of your stepchildren's rude, ambivalent, or distant behavior. Even Leo, who has been happily married to Janette for over thirty years and raised three children with her, describes his feelings of being an outsider as intense and troubling at times.

Leo reflects, "I wanted so much for Janette's son to trust me and not always run to her when he had a problem. I even felt jealousy because David was so close to Janette's parents, who they lived with when he was a toddler. It brought back feelings of insecurity I had as a child who was always overshadowed by an athletic older brother."

In *Surviving and Thriving in Stepfamily Relationships*, renowned stepfamily researcher Patricia L. Papernow explains, "The insider/outsider challenge emerges very early in stepcouple relationships and threads its way through all of the other challenges. It often remains present, though in somewhat softer form, even in mature, well-established stepfamilies."

Four Ways to Overcome Problematic Insider and Outsider Positions in Your Stepfamily

1. **Share your feelings about being an insider and outsider and seek solace and support.** Whether you are a biological parent or a stepparent, these negative emotions won't dissipate on their own if they're not dealt with. Practicing the active listening techniques outlined in chapter 7 will be beneficial in helping you work through these issues.

2. **Normalize the challenge by not overreacting.** Since these positions go with the territory in a stepfamily, it's important for stepcouples to view them as typical and not pathological. It's normal for outsiders to feel left out and for insiders to feel torn between the people they love and anxious about meeting their divergent needs. Since a biological parent is more aware of their children's strengths and vulnerabilities than a stepparent would be, it's a good idea for them to share some of their insights with their spouse, so they feel more included in the lives of their stepchildren.

3. **Carve out lots of one-on-one time with family members.** As a stepfather, Conner adheres strongly to this principle and tries his best to schedule time with his two stepdaughters and biological son at least once a month. He and his wife, Tara, carve out one night each week to go out to eat, have a long walk, or whatever they choose to enrich their bond.

4. **Establish family routines that can enrich relationships.** Such routines may include story time with young children or pizza-and-movie night with school-age children and teenagers. Look for family activities that you can enjoy and mentor your children and stepchildren in, such as teaching them to ski, play tennis or chess, and so on!

For some stepparents, acknowledging the issues of being an outsider and having their feelings validated is enough. Likewise, some biological parents can get relief from declaring that they've had enough of trying to meet everyone's needs and ask family members to cut them some slack. But for those bearing scars inflicted years ago, there might be more frequent triggers, and you might benefit from couples counseling to work through these bruises so that you can better adjust to stepfamily life and live in the present.

UNDERSTAND YOUR PARTNER'S VIEW

As a stepparent, you can benefit from learning more about your partner and their children's experience prior to your marriage. It's much easier for you as an outsider to become closer to the insiders in the family if you express empathy and caring toward your partner. Children who observe their stepparent displaying compassion and love to their parent will be more accepting of them. Why is this so? Because children often develop a very intense, protective bond with their parent after divorce. Your partner is important to you, and you are vital to them. It makes sense to show your emotions to your spouse, children, and stepchildren in a healthy way, so you do not develop resentment or leave them in the dark.

Just as a stepparent needs to try to understand their partner's experiences through their divorce and unpack emotional baggage that they bring with them, a biological parent can reap great benefits by gaining a better understanding of their partner's experience of being a stepparent who might feel left out or as an outsider. You grant your partner a valuable gift by encouraging them to talk about their perspective and air their feelings in a positive way during mealtimes and family meetings. It's also crucial for you as a parent to do everything within your power to assist your partner and your children in developing a closer bond. Simple gestures such as encouraging your spouse to attend your children's school functions or sporting events can help everyone connect and create positive experiences.

FOR STEPPARENTS: THE DIFFERENCE
BETWEEN BEING A FRIEND AND A PARENT

Think back to the time when you were anticipating being a stepparent. You may have experienced some excitement about the opportunity but some concern about the role you would play. Was it confusing? There is no instruction manual that comes along with being a stepparent. It's important to decide early on what kind of stepparent you want to be because this can help your stepchild adjust to having you in their life. It will also help you grow and continue to bond with your stepchild as they develop through different stages. Just like all parents, a stepparent must be flexible in taking on a role of parent or friend and have good boundaries. It is possible to adopt both roles as long as you understand the difference between the two, have realistic expectations, and proceed slowly.

Stepparent as Parent

If you are a stepparent who wants to take on the role of a parent, you're up for a challenge. You should first consider the age of your stepchild and their relationship with their biological parents. For instance, if your stepchild is younger than age 9 and/or has minimal contact with your partner's ex-spouse, you'll have an easier time of it. Otherwise, be ready for some heated battles and prepare to have your authority challenged. Comments such as "You're not my dad (or mom)" are common ways that children raised in stepfamilies express their anger about their parents' split and having to live with a stepparent.

When taking on the role of a parent, including disciplining your stepchild, you will show them caring if you do so gradually and in a loving way. This is especially true if your stepchild is young and has little or no contact with their other parent. Just be sure not to discipline your stepchild too soon after moving into the home. It will take time for your stepchild to get used to accepting you as their parent's significant other and they may test you and your authority. Tread lightly with preteens and adolescents who naturally try to test limits and want to assert their autonomy. It's usually best to connect with a preteen or teenage stepchild through activities that you both enjoy and not expect too much conversation or acceptance for the first couple of years.

Stepparent as an Adult Friend

Ideally the role of a stepparent needs to be as a supportive, friendly mentor who teaches by showing a good example. If you can do this most of the time, you will probably win the affection of your stepchild over time. If on occasion you need to set a limit (such as a bedtime or curfew), this will work out better if you have established a good rapport and clearly established your role as an adult in the new family who has authority but who cares and listens. This doesn't mean that you will always have an easy time of it or that your stepchild won't challenge you. However, they will be less angry and rebellious if they feel that you are on their side.

Try to show understanding when you sense your stepchild has divided loyalties between you and their biological parent of the same gender. They might also be struggling with the challenges of living in two homes. It's also a good idea to express empathy to your stepchild if their noncustodial parent is unreliable or inconsistent in their visitation. Suggest that you do something together such as go for a bike ride, bowling, or a walk to the park as a way to bond, show interest, and distract them. For teenagers, just being there for them, expressing compassion, and maybe watching TV or playing a video game together will probably be the most effective way to connect.

UNDERSTANDING YOUR STEPCHILD

Victoria was about 10 years old when her father, Ryan, married Lisa. In her view, she had little control over the events unfolding in her life, including her mother remarrying and starting a new family quickly. Even though Lisa seemed nice enough and obviously really loved her dad, it still didn't seem fair to Victoria that her life had to change so radically. When she met me for an interview, she was eager to share her perspectives as a stepchild. In her mind, nothing would ever be the same after her parents' split and she believes that parents ought to be more understanding about the stepchild's plight.

Victoria reflects, "I wrote on my closet door, 'January 18 was the worst day of my life'—the day of my parents' divorce. For me, divorce meant changes in where I lived, changes at school and with friends, and having to spend time with new adults I didn't particularly want to spend time with. No one asked me if I wanted any of those things to happen, but they did, without my consent, and sometimes without warning."

During our in-depth interview, Victoria speaks with anguish about both of her parents getting remarried around the same time. She explains, "I had a teacher tell me that if I loved my parents, I would accept their significant others because I'd want them to be happy. Inside I was screaming, 'What about my happiness?'"

These are hard issues, and there are no easy fixes, but following these tips can help you weather the rough times and be a supportive stepparent.

Eight Tips to Bond with Your Stepchild and Create Positive Memories as a Stepfamily

1. **Proceed slowly.** Take your time getting to know your stepchild. If you rush the relationship, it may satisfy your own unmet needs to be liked, but your approach could backfire. It's important to realize that you're not replacing your stepchild's other parent; your role is more of a mentor. Never make your stepchild feel as if they have to choose between their biological parent and you. Over time, everyone in the recoupled family can create a positive culture together.

2. **Respect your spouse's relationship with your stepchild.** And don't feel threatened by their close connection. Your partner will want to spend special time with their child, so try not to feel neglected by them. Make plans with your friends or with your own kids and graciously step out of their way.

3. **Develop a relationship with your stepchild through daily activities, hobbies, and shared interests to create positive memories.** Strive to engage in activities as a family unit as much as possible so everyone has an opportunity to make a connection. Sharing interests in sports or the arts can help you develop a bond. Spending time together, even if it's eating a

meal or watching a movie, can help weave the fabric of stronger stepfamily relationships.

4. **Understand your stepchild's view and have realistic expectations.** First, it's a given that your stepchild had a relationship with your spouse that existed before you came on the scene. They're likely to see you as a rival to both of their parents. Even if your stepchild seems to like you well enough, they will sometimes prefer you weren't in the picture and may express this by ignoring you or being indifferent or rude. Your remarriage effectively ends any hope of their mother and father reunifying and can reignite feelings of loss for your stepchild.

5. **Be sure to discuss roles and feelings about parenting with your spouse.** Sometimes a biological parent may not understand a stepparent's feelings of rejection. They may need you to tell them what they can do to support you. On the other hand, a biological parent may feel criticized and get defensive when their spouse offers unsolicited advice about parenting. Blending your sometimes-opposing styles of parenting and focusing on what you have in common will benefit all family members.

6. **Be courteous and respectful of your child's and stepchild's "other parent."** Keep in mind that it is likely that they would not have chosen to have their children live with them part-time. Stepparents need to stay out of interactions between biological parents working out holiday or vacation schedules, and biological parents need to be collaborative when planning family events.

7. **Realize that love often comes later.** Even if you don't hit it off with your stepchild, you can still develop a working relationship built on respect. If your stepchild does not warm up to you right away, that does not mean you have failed. Adopting realistic expectations can help you get through some rough spots. Be patient and try not to react with anger if your stepchild gives you the cold shoulder or is a little impolite sometimes.

8. **Cooperate with your partner, and talk, talk, talk.** Most of the talking will take place away from your children or stepchildren, but be sure to have cordial conversations and informal discussions about family rules, roles, chores, and routines with the kids.

THE MUTUAL CHILD

For many remarried people, having an "ours," or mutual child gives them the opportunity to "do it right," that is, to have a child who is lucky enough to have both parents live together. According to family researcher Kay Pasley, about half of all stepfamilies go on to have a child between them. While the experience of having a child can destabilize any family, a mutual child often provides a bridge for stepparents and stepchildren to connect and love this child that is "ours" and related to everyone. Even some of the parents who worried that having a child with their new spouse might be perceived as being disloyal by their existing children felt that their "ours" child helped their other children believe that their stepfamily was permanent. They benefited from the addition of a younger half sibling, according to stepfamily researchers Lawrence Ganong and Marilyn Coleman.

In *Yours, Mine, and Ours*, Anne C. Bernstein explains, "Like commingling property or sharing incomes, having a child is a cultural act of joining, a statement of commitment to a union, a demonstration of family solidarity." She discovered considerable evidence that a remarried couple's mutual child can enrich the stepfamily experience for most members. While not without blemish, most remarried couples and stepsiblings view an "ours" child as value added and contributing a vibrancy to the family unit after an initial period of adjustment.

However, some stepchildren balk at sharing toys, belongings, or family assets with a new bundle of joy. It's also natural for teenagers and young adults to feel some resentment if they're told they can't get help financing a car or attend a preferred college because the family has added one or more mutual children. Being aware of the challenges and preparing for them is essential to making a smooth transition. Of course, it's never a good idea to look to the mutual child to salvage a difficult marriage or as a way to compete with an ex-spouse who may have added one or more to their tribe.

KEEPING YOUR RELATIONSHIP WITH YOUR SPOUSE SPECIAL AND SEPARATE FROM THE KIDS

According to Patricia L. Papernow, when stepcouples find small moments of caring for each other in the midst of their struggles, this will serve to minimize tension, stress, and emotional distress for all family members. This can be accomplished when couples understand the value of stepparents having separate relationships with their partner's children and time alone with their mate.

Janna, whom you met earlier, came into a counseling session saying that she needed time away from her stepson George. She loved being a mom and stepmom but felt that many of her conversations with her husband revolved around their children, especially George, who was experiencing some challenges in school. We discussed how boundaries are important in all families, but especially stepfamilies. Over the next several sessions, Janna and her husband, Steve, decided to reassign bedrooms, putting the boys' rooms on the upper level, near each other, while theirs could be on the first floor of their home. They also discussed that they would enlist Janna's parents to babysit over an upcoming Columbus Day weekend so that they could spend two nights at a cabin and have a romantic getaway.

Janna puts it like this: "George knows that I love him, and he's finally getting it that I'm a person too, not just a stepmom who takes care of him, his dad, and little brother. I don't ever want him to feel left out or resentful that I'm stealing his dad from him, but he also needs to learn that adult relationships are separate and special. Our lives are all starting to fall into place, but it took several years of hard work and understanding each other's perspectives."

FAMILY MEETINGS

While not an original concept, a family meeting can take on new meaning in the remarried, step, and blended family. The immense effort it can take to get all family members together in one space is almost always worthwhile. But by no stretch of the imagination are these meetings easy or without conflict. The most important aspects of the family meeting are structure, flexibility, active listening, and having a method of recording or writing down all your findings.

Family meetings are useful to plan events and to hash out new roles, rules, and problems that exist between family members. For the most part, a family meeting is also a good place to be vulnerable with each other and let your feelings, thoughts, and needs be heard by other family members in a safe atmosphere. As long as stated feelings are not blameful, solutions can be reached through compromise, good listening skills, and by using rules to guide discussions.

Rules of Effective Family Meetings

- The thoughts and feelings of all family members count equally regardless of age or status. Feelings are accepted and validated and not judged to be right or wrong, reasonable or unreasonable.

- Family members are advised to write down complaints, suggestions, or grievances on a slip of paper and put them in a box. A meeting can be held when there are several slips in the box or about once a week.

- Accusations and name-calling are not allowed at meetings. The best way to avoid this is to use "I" statements rather than "you" statements, which you learned about in chapter 7.

- The problem-solving approach needs to be implemented. After brainstorming solutions, compromise is used to come up with solutions to family problems. The adults need to take the lead here because they have more experience. However, children often come up with creative solutions and feel empowered when they can share them without criticism. Once a solution has been accepted by most family members, write it down and post it in a location in your home for all to view.

- Conclude family meetings with positive feedback and encouragement so that family members will feel okay or even good about coming to meetings again. Any family member can request a family meeting with at least one day's notice given to other members.

An alternative method for holding family meetings, recommended by Bruce Feiler in *The Secrets of Happy Families,* is "What Works and What Doesn't" (see below). Regardless of what method you use, the family meeting can be beneficial for families of all ages and sizes. Even couples who do not have children (or whose children have left the nest) can profit from family meetings where they can air their concerns in a respectful environment.

What Works and What Doesn't

Some remarried couples and stepfamilies feel it's beneficial to discuss issues and make action plans based on changing circumstances. The focus needs to be on how the family is doing as a whole, rather than individual grievances. This method is an effective alternative for families when they want to build an accepting culture where all members feel validated and appreciated. Often referred to as the "two-container system," family members write down notes about what is working and what is not, deposit them in one of two containers or boxes, and take turns reading them out loud. The first box contains notes on things that aren't going well and can benefit from problem-solving strategies. The second box contains notes on what's going well. This is a good time to show appreciation for others and feel good about your role or contribution to the well-being of others as you work together to form a new family.

The following action steps need to be followed at family meetings. Regardless of which type of family meeting you choose to have, be sure to include everyone who wants to attend and have meetings in a comfortable location when most family members are available.

Four Action Steps for Effective Family Meetings

1. Use active listening by reflecting to others what you hear and asking for clarification when you are unsure. If there's a lot of conflict between family members, it's a good idea to take a twenty-minute break or schedule a smaller meeting where a subset of members can more easily feel validated and work toward a compromise.

2. Remember to take turns and give everyone an equal chance to speak without interruption.

3. Suggest that all family members turn off electronic devices during the meeting.

4. Ask one person to volunteer to take notes and to write down the agenda for the next meeting. Post it in a prominent place in your home. All members need to have choices regarding the day and time of the meeting. It's important to meet on a regular basis to assess how things are going and to set a time limit.

Most of all, have fun and enjoy your time together! Remember that your goal is to create positive stepfamily memories that will endure the test of time.

It took me a while to get over my resentment when Tom lied to me about giving his daughter a credit card to use. Even though he didn't mean to hurt me, I felt betrayed that they had conversations about our money and left me out. **DANIELLE, AGE 48**

10

Say You're Sorry and Mean It

the capacity to seek and grant forgiveness is one of the most significant factors contributing to marital satisfaction and a lifetime of love. However, many people take offenses too personally when their partner rejects or insults them, or says or does something hurtful. They focus too much on their pain and can sometimes get trapped in it for years.

Forgiving someone is a way of letting go of old baggage so that you can heal and move forward with your life. It benefits both the person who forgives and the offender because it can allow both people to let go of past resentments. Forgiving someone doesn't mean you are letting someone walk all over you or that you're excusing or minimizing what happened. Rather, it gives you the strength to stand up for yourself and what you want. It means that you agree to give up the struggle and you are ready to move forward with goodwill.

Forgiveness can be especially important in remarriages, with their increased relational complexity. Remarried couples who apologize to each other when appropriate and grant forgiveness can rid themselves of the toxic hurt and shame that prevents them from being emotionally connected and intimate. For instance, Danielle and Tom, whom you met previously, have been stressed with issues with Tom's daughter

Carrie, 23, throughout their nine-year remarriage. Carrie has never accepted Danielle into her heart, and she can be rude and disrespectful to her, even in front of family members. In fact, Carrie often went months without visiting Tom and Danielle and then would show up unannounced and ask for money or a favor. While Carrie's insolent behavior has often tested Danielle's patience, Danielle is working on acceptance and trying to forgive Tom for being permissive while raising Carrie as a single parent for many years.

Danielle puts it like this: "For a long time, I felt resentful because Tom had trouble standing up to his grown daughter who insulted me and was horrendous. He also gave her a credit card to use with his name and social security number on the account without telling me. Then one day Tom gave me a sincere apology. He said he was sorry for not setting limits when Carrie said mean things to me. He feels awful that she charged over $5,000 on the credit card. After I read our credit report and discovered it, Tom apologized. He didn't make excuses, and he seemed to understand my pain. Of course, I forgave him—he's the love of my life, and we all make mistakes, and I've made my share of them."

Many remarried couples stubbornly hold on to the belief that they have nothing to apologize for, especially if their hurtful behavior or words were not intentional. Some people believe that forgiveness requires that they forget about a transgression or that they must accept, condone, or excuse an offense in order to forgive. Other people believe that forgiving someone is a sign of weakness, and they might fear that forgiving the offender could give the offender permission to hurt them again. Given these negative beliefs, it's no wonder that some couples are reluctant to work toward forgiveness.

Unfortunately, many remarried couples have the same arguments over and over again because pride prevents them from owning their mistakes or they don't know how to communicate in a way that promotes forgiveness. However, if they learn how to apologize and grant forgiveness the right way, they'll be able to let go of big and small transgressions and move on from negative emotional events. For instance, when Danielle discovered Tom's financial infidelity, she felt intensely mistrustful and betrayed, and this caused her to go into a tailspin. For a few years she took his offenses personally and believed that he didn't respect her intelligence and didn't see her as an equal in their marriage.

Through attending counseling sessions, Tom got in touch with the reasons why financial infidelity can destroy a marriage and understood the seriousness of his actions. As a result, he apologized and promised to practice full disclosure of finances with Danielle. Tom's willingness to make amends and apologize allowed Danielle to forgive him and rebuild trust in him over time. He was specific about what he had done that was hurtful to Danielle and talked about how he would make amends. Without Tom taking responsibility for his actions, this couple told me that they would have certainly split up years ago. While Danielle occasionally feels mistrustful of Tom's behavior around Carrie, she's working on trying not to overreact and to adopt a forgiving mind-set.

With the support of a seasoned therapist, Danielle was able to gain insight and be more understanding about how Carrie's protest of her marriage to Tom was a delayed reaction to the loss of her mother at a young age. In fact, Danielle realized that Carrie didn't want her dad to get remarried because it meant that he would not belong to her anymore. By marrying Danielle, Tom was calling an end to their twenty-year mourning period. There was no easy way to replace Carrie's mother after her death. However, through the process of gaining more awareness and empathy, Danielle was able to take Carrie's and Tom's offenses less personally and show empathy to Carrie. She began to see Tom as a grieving father who had done his best to raise Carrie as a single dad, which allowed her to decide to forgive both of them. As Danielle stepped out of the role of a victim, she regained some of her personal power and could begin to live in the present rather than dwelling on the past.

FORGIVENESS IS A CHOICE

Forgiving someone is a conscious and deliberate process that helps us heal from and let go of feelings such as anger, grief, and sadness. When you truly forgive your partner and others, you're free to move on to live a life of joy and love. In fact, researcher Frank D. Fincham, of the renowned Family Institute, discovered that apologizing to your spouse and asking for forgiveness are crucial ingredients to a healthy relationship. Apologizing to your partner when appropriate will validate their feelings, clear the air, and allow you both to move on from mistakes.

Deborah and Stephen, both in their late forties, dated during high school and ran into each other at a high school reunion thirty years later. Stephen still lived in the small Vermont town where he had been raising his daughter, Alicia, 15, for over ten years, after her mother moved out. Stephen was delighted to reconnect with Deborah at their reunion and eager to make up for lost time. Deborah had been divorced for nine years and had an 18-year-old son, Nathan. She was pursuing a career as an internet entrepreneur and enjoying single life after returning to her hometown to spend time with her aging mother. But when she reconnected with Stephen, it felt like old times, and she was swept off her feet by her dynamic former flame who was now a successful small business owner and loving father. They both felt a strong and instant attraction and were inseparable after their first date, getting engaged less than a month later.

Alicia, however, didn't share her dad's enthusiasm for Deborah and Nathan and did everything within her power to sabotage Stephen and Deborah's relationship, including sneaking into their bedroom during a birthday party for her dad and stealing some of Deborah's jewelry. She also made insulting comments to Nathan, who was highly vulnerable because he had been bullied at his middle school due to his diagnosis of epilepsy. After a few years of walking on eggshells with Alicia and feeling horrible about the strain in their relationship, Deborah became more accepting of Alicia's loyalty conflicts, anger, and resentment toward her and stopped taking her rude comments and behavior personally.

Deborah puts it like this: "I get the fact that Alicia loves her dad, is possessive of him, and sees me as a threat. But it's important to me that he let her know that our marriage is strong and I'm not going anywhere. And I will not allow her to make fun of Nathan just because she resents me. For a while it seemed Stephen was afraid of losing her love and approval, and I felt hurt and left out. But once he realized that we were letting Alicia's anger and jealousy come between us, he said he was sorry for not setting limits on her behavior. Steve was sincere, and so I forgive him. I believe he was doing the best he could."

FORGIVENESS IS AN INTENTIONAL PROCESS

Practicing forgiveness involves changing your mind-set, and it's a process rather than a single act. It involves making a deliberate decision to apologize to and forgive your partner. It can be particularly challenging for remarried couples to adopt this perspective because baggage from the past often contributes to intense reactions to breeches of trust or hurtful actions in the present. It's important for both members of the couple to recognize that comments or questions from your spouse or stepchildren may trigger unfinished business from prior relationships.

As authors Gay and Kathlyn Hendricks point out, most of us arrive at our adult relationships with a backlog of ancient hurts, fears, and angers. They explain that we often forget the source of our wounds, so it appears that our current partner is inflicting them. As we saw in chapter 3, past relationships cast a large shadow over present ones, and it's common to blame our partner for our emotional pain because we don't understand that it's actually being in love that causes issues to emerge.

Add to this hurdle that you might feel vulnerable if you were let down or rejected in your first marriage, and this might cause you to fear that you'll repeat the same toxic pattern. This can occur beyond your awareness, and you might begin questioning your partner's intentions or become guarded and unwilling to open up about your thoughts and feelings, making daily communication a challenge. Becoming more attentive to your triggers can lessen this tendency to project negative feelings or intentions onto your partner and pave the way toward a healthy pattern of communicating where you truly listen and share, rather than becoming defensive or argumentative.

For instance, during the early years of my second marriage, some of Craig's questions about our finances triggered defensiveness on my part, because money was a hot-button issue in my first marriage. This led to ongoing tension and conflict, emotional distance, and feelings of mutual dissatisfaction. Over time, we realized that if we were going to sustain a happy remarriage, we needed to make a commitment to both apologizing and granting forgiveness to each other so that we could recover more easily from daily disappointments.

WHY APOLOGIES ARE SO IMPORTANT

Often people equate apologizing with weakness, and it's widely believed that if you apologize to someone, you're making yourself too vulnerable. However, apologizing can also be seen as a strength because it shows you are able to show goodwill toward your partner—forgiveness promotes love and understanding. Studies demonstrate the importance of forgiving someone so you can let go of your baggage, heal from past wounds, and enjoy a better quality of life. Apologizing and practicing forgiveness are about giving yourself and your partner the kind of future that you and they deserve.

In *The Science of Trust*, John Gottman explains that couples who are emotionally attuned can fully process and move on from negative emotional events, forgive, and ultimately create a stronger relationship. In other words, couples who are able to give sincere apologies to each other can rid themselves of the toxic hurt and shame that holds them back from feeling connected and emotionally attuned with their partner.

WHEN PEOPLE ARE RELUCTANT TO FORGIVE

Asking for or granting forgiveness may feel impossible or detrimental to your marriage at times. You might be worried that your partner will hold a grudge or you will not be able to get past the hurt you caused each other. Likewise, you may be a person who apologizes too quickly or insincerely, or accepts your partner's apology easily without really understanding or processing it fully.

Perhaps it's because intimate relationships bring the possibility of love and closeness that we're confronted with wounds from our past. Some people even create a narrative for their life that focuses on suffering, shame, and blame. However, with self-awareness and learning effective ways to cope with intense reactions to triggers, we can begin to trust ourselves and our partner enough to attain the safety needed to heal raw spots from the past.

SOME APOLOGIES ARE HARD TO ACCEPT

In some cases, apologies are hard to accept. Perhaps you don't believe the offender is sincere, or maybe you're just not ready to move on due to the intense pain you are experiencing. For instance, Danielle and Deborah each felt intensely hurt and betrayed when their stepdaughters' behaviors were disrespectful and destructive. In their situations, each had to work hard at not taking their stepdaughter's behaviors personally and feeling resentful. They needed to understand that it's common for a stepdaughter to feel rivalry with a stepmother and to try not to take their stepdaughters' behaviors to heart. Rather than pointing fingers in an effort to identify who was at fault, it was important for both of these stepmothers to accept the apologies of their spouses, even if their stepdaughters were unwilling to apologize.

When both Tom and Stephen were able to confess to the words or behavior that had caused Danielle and Deborah pain, it went a long way toward strengthening their marriages. We have to set aside the scorekeeping—the who is right or wrong—if it's a matter of your being "right" at the expense of causing pain to your spouse.

DON'T TAKE THINGS TOO PERSONALLY

While it's natural to feel hurt when a significant other has betrayed us or done something wrong, taking their actions personally can prolong the process of healing and cause undue misery and grief. My first experience with taking things too personally in my second marriage was when my husband, Craig, chose to visit his parents, who lived four hours away in Maine, at a time when I was unable to accompany him (and our children) for the entire vacation. While I understood that it was important for him to join his siblings for the first two weeks of August, the college class that I taught every summer (for twenty years) started the second week of August, which meant I'd have to cut my trip short.

As a result, for more than fifteen years I had to take the bus home from Maine in the middle of our family's two-week vacation. In my mind, Craig was putting his family before me, and I felt resentment. On the other hand, his perspective was that meeting at his family's house on the lake the first two weeks of August was a longstanding tradition that was sacred and couldn't be broken. It wasn't that he was trying to leave me out; rather, he was upholding a family ritual that had been in place for more than sixty years.

What I realized eventually was that by taking Craig's actions personally, I was giving up my personal power and allowing myself to feel left out. After this realization came to me, and our finances improved, I also decided that I didn't really need to teach the summer class and that taking time with Craig and his family could become a meaningful tradition for all of us, including our three children. In the end, I discovered that the benefits of taking the summer off from teaching and going to Craig's family home outweighed the benefit of teaching the summer class.

You might recall that as Danielle stepped out of the role of victim and stopped blaming her husband, Tom, and her stepdaughter Carrie for her unhappiness, she regained some of her personal power and could live life fully in the present. When we met for coffee about three months after our first interview, she told me that she requested the meeting because she wanted to tell me that she felt as if a weight had been lifted off her shoulders. Danielle reported that she felt happier in her remarriage now that she had stopped dwelling on the past. While she and Carrie still had moments of intense tension, and she still felt triggered when she heard Tom talk to her about money, she no longer felt the rage she had previously experienced after finding out about Tom helping out Carrie financially and not disclosing the details to her.

Danielle discovered that taking things personally made her feel worse and slowed down the healing process with the two most important people in her life, Tom and Carrie. The last time we spoke, Danielle informed me that Carrie now had a two-year-old daughter and that their relationship continues to improve. Because she is a single mom, Carrie often reaches out to Danielle for help with babysitting, and Danielle is happy to oblige—she loves children and it makes her feel good to offer assistance, since Carrie's mom died when she was a toddler. Letting go of her grievances toward Tom and Carrie allows her to feel empowered in her marriage, and in her role as a stepmother to Carrie and grandmother to her young daughter.

WHAT IS A GRIEVANCE STORY?

Forgiveness can be described as being in a peaceful state where you're living in the present moment and able to be more understanding. A grievance is exactly the opposite. By definition, a grievance is a real or imagined wrong or other cause for complaint or protest, especially of unfair treatment. It usually happens when you feel resentment over something because you believe you have been treated unjustly. A grievance story can happen when you're not able to forgive another person, and it often places you in the role of a victim.

One of the main problems of holding on to a grievance story is that it places blame on the other person, thus causing you to lose your personal power. For instance, when Leo and Janette, whom you met earlier, agreed to meet with me to discuss raising three children (now adults) in a stepfamily, Janette asked Leo if it was okay for her to discuss their separation several years before. He agreed, and she went on to describe a difficult time in their remarriage when her biological son, David, was experiencing a crisis and Janette blamed Leo, who she felt was judgmental and harsh toward his stepson. As a result, Leo moved out of their home for six months and they contemplated divorce.

Janette reflects, "I just couldn't let go of the fact that Leo seemed to be treating David differently than his own children, and I identified too strongly with David's anger when they argued. I was shocked when Leo moved out and accused him of wanting another woman because I am insecure about having put on some weight over the past few years. But by having a grievance toward Leo, I was letting my resentment drive him away, and I was taking things much too personally. I didn't realize that I was becoming such a victim until my daughter pointed it out to me. Then when David called Leo and told him he wanted him to move home so we could all be a family again, it seemed important to forgive Leo for moving out."

According to psychologist Fred Luskin, a renowned expert on forgiveness, a grievance emerges when two factors coincide. Typically, the first is that something happens in our lives that we didn't want to have happen. Then we deal with this problem by thinking about it too much, or what Luskin refers to as renting too much space in our minds. Another way to look at this dilemma, says Luskin, is to ask ourselves how we can feel hurt and not end up with a smoldering grievance. Every person in this world has been hurt or mistreated. Some people talk about their pain and dwell on it, and others talk about it and then let it go.

In my own second marriage I had a grievance story that lasted several years and was about my husband, Craig, maintaining a friendship with a former girlfriend, even though I knew that he was never unfaithful and was completely honest, informing me about their phone conversations. Sadly this grievance lasted for a few years, even after they stopped communicating. Finally, through my own awareness of the negative impact this grievance was having on our marriage, I let go of it and felt less anguish and resentment toward Craig.

WHEN TO FORGIVE YOUR PARTNER

When we feel betrayed or rejected, it's perfectly normal to feel a pain similar to a physical injury or wound. We might feel a deep sense of loss and we need to go through the stages of loss and grief in order to accept it and move on. Forgiving our partner too soon may deny us the ability to experience the anger needed for change and reconciliation.

Take Laura and Kevin, whom you met earlier. They are an engaging couple in their early forties who are raising five children in a blended family. When they argued in the early years of their remarriage, it was usually about the fact that Kevin kept secrets from Laura about his business dealings and subsequent bankruptcy. Laura hadn't known on her wedding day that she had inherited over $100,000 of debt from Kevin's first marriage because the restaurant he had with his wife before her death went into bankruptcy due to mismanagement and some bad business decisions made when his marriage was struggling. Due to her intense feelings of emotional pain after being betrayed, Laura needed time to heal, and this is a process that can't be rushed.

Laura reflects, "I felt betrayed when I found out Kevin had so much debt. I think it would have been easier to handle if he'd been open about it from the time we first started dating seriously. I know he was embarrassed, and we were both caught up in trying to start over, but it still hurts me."

OFFER A SINCERE APOLOGY

When remarried couples withhold information and/or keep secrets related to financial or sexual infidelity, the hurt can run deep. Partners need to flesh out the present and past in their efforts to be transparent when confessing wrongdoing and asking for an apology. If your partner is unwilling to apologize after betraying you or causing you hurt or anguish, this will stunt or block your ability to get over it and move on to acceptance. Not all apologies will be the same, but most will contain some of the same elements that you will learn later in this chapter.

For the most part, the healing power of a sincere apology is immediate, according to psychologist Harriet Lerner. She explains that when you are offered a genuine apology, you feel relieved and soothed. There is relief in knowing that your pain is acknowledged by your partner, and they care enough about you to be vulnerable and offer words of love and healing. Your anger and resentment toward them might even feel as if they're melting away on the spot. Often a sincere apology offers immediate understanding, peace, and more harmony. On the other hand, failure to listen well and apologize can lead to the loss of a relationship.

Likewise, when you apologize to your partner, you'll feel almost immediate relief and gratitude if they accept it. When I apologized to Craig for keeping secrets about borrowing money from my mom to pay for my kids' college tuition and not telling him, he didn't accept my apology immediately—he needed to hear it more than once. When I was able to apologize sincerely without offering excuses, Craig was better able to forgive me and move on. My apology was heartfelt and sincere when I stated, "I'm sorry for keeping a secret. I was worried about having enough money to pay for our kids' college tuition and should have had more trust in you. It won't happen again, and I will work on my trust issues."

WHY DO I NEED TO FORGIVE?

Forgiving your partner and yourself is infinitely terrifying yet necessary for achieving a healthy relationship. It's about being willing to acknowledge that you're capable of being wounded and able to risk exposing yourself. It also means that you're stepping out of the role of a victim and taking charge of your life. By apologizing and granting forgiveness to each other, you can reconcile after both small and large transgressions and regain the love and trust you once enjoyed.

The healing power of a good apology is profound and well illustrated by Janette and Leo's story. When Janette was able to let go of her grievance toward Leo for moving out and listen to his side of the story, they were able to heal the wound that had been festering for years regarding Leo's harsh treatment toward her son, David. It turns out that Leo was unaware that Janette had such intense feelings about the way he reacted to David's frequent job changes, and he offered her a sincere apology for this and for moving out in anger. By Leo being specific about his hurtful behavior and the impact it had on Janette, as well as promising to work toward repairing any damage done, Janette was able to move on from her grievance story and reopen her heart to Leo after he returned home.

The importance of practicing forgiveness takes on new meaning in a remarriage because apologizing to your partner and granting forgiveness can allow you to heal old wounds and be free to love again. In my case, I held a grudge against my ex-husband for a few years for his part in our divorce. I was unable to forgive him because I felt vulnerable and feared being hurt again. But once I understood that it takes courage to forgive someone who you believe wronged you, and that it is not about accepting, condoning, or excusing their behavior, I was free to forgive my ex and myself for the pain we caused each other during our marriage. By letting go of my grievance story and practicing forgiveness, I was fully available to fall deeply in love with Craig and find happiness in my remarriage.

WHAT IF I CAN'T FORGIVE?

Many experts believe that forgiveness is a critical aspect of recovering from interpersonal pain, but acceptance is a worthy option in cases where you are not ready to forgive. In her groundbreaking book *How Can I Forgive You?* clinical psychologist Janis Abrahms Spring explains that acceptance is a responsible, authentic choice for dealing with an interpersonal injury when the offender won't engage in the healing process by apologizing.

While Abrahms Spring encourages readers to muster up the courage to forgive others who have wronged them, she also says that forgiveness that isn't genuine is "cheap"—and not worth much. Cheap forgiveness happens when you are so desperate to preserve your marriage that you're willing to accept crumbs and forgive your spouse, even when they offend you and ignore your pain. Abrahms Spring explains that cheap forgiveness is a quick and easy pardon without taking the time to process the emotions or come to terms with the injury. She describes cheap forgiveness as dysfunctional because it creates an illusion of closeness between the offender and the person who is injured.

Instead, Abrahms Spring suggests that acceptance is an authentic alternative to cheap forgiveness and genuine forgiveness. It's a viable option when an offender is unwilling to make good or engage in the healing process, or the injured person is too wounded to forgive. She suggests that while genuine forgiveness is a worthwhile goal, acceptance is the middle ground between unforgivable hurt and cheap forgiveness. It can help you to stop dwelling on an injury and give your partner a chance to work toward genuine forgiveness if they choose to rise to the challenge.

There are many reasons why people have difficulty letting go of the past and reversing the painful consequences of their former life, writes Fred Luskin in his acclaimed book *Forgive for Good*. He points out that people may take on the pain of others' mistakes because they take their offenses personally. Luskin believes that individuals heal best when they react as if the injury happened to a close friend. He posits that when people create a grievance story that focuses on their own suffering and assigns blame, their suffering is magnified.

Luskin writes, "Forgiveness is not a focus on what happened in the past and neither is it remaining upset or holding on to grudges. You may have been hurt in the past, but you are upset today. Both forgiveness and grievances are experiences that you have in the present." If your partner's betrayal has been ongoing for a long period and they apologize, it's more likely that it will take more time for you to heal from these wounds. Don't judge yourself harshly if you don't accept their apology immediately and if you need to hear it more than once over an extended period. Some wounds are profound and may even feel like the pain that's similar to a physical injury. Forgiving your partner too soon may deny you the ability to experience the anger needed for change and reconciliation. However, if you hold a grudge and are unable to forgive your partner, it can lead to ongoing resentment.

WHEN RESENTMENT LEADS TO EMOTIONAL DISTANCE

Jeremy, 45, whom you met earlier, has felt anger and resentment toward Susan, 44, ever since he found out about her secret savings account. Susan apologized and accepted responsibility for her actions, but Jeremy was unwilling to forgive her for several months, and their emotional and sexual intimacy suffered. Jeremy was shutting down emotionally and actually slept on the couch for two months. He also told Susan repeatedly that he was unsure about his commitment to their marriage. The problem with holding on to resentment toward your partner is that it often leads to withdrawal and a lack of vulnerability. Bottling up feelings and ignoring upsetting emotions also doesn't help get at the root of what causes them. Over time, this can erode trust. In Jeremy's case, he'd been bottling up feelings of anger and resentment for some time, and he had lost trust in Susan's intentions.

Susan reflects, "Jeremy was giving me the cold shoulder and I felt his anger. He just couldn't seem to get over his feelings of resentment toward me. During our marriage, we've gotten over many hurdles, including adjusting to crazy work schedules and difficult exes. But this issue seemed too big. We both felt hurt for some time and uncertain about our future together."

In an effort to protect himself, Jeremy was unwilling to engage in repair attempts with Susan quickly. This couple was stuck in a negative pattern of interaction, and Susan wasn't acting with goodwill toward Jeremy—an essential element of a successful remarriage. However, after their second couples counseling session, Susan apologized to Jeremy in a sincere way for keeping secrets about money, and his positive feelings and goodwill toward her began to restore slowly.

Susan continues, "Jeremy finally got over his anger about me deceiving him by having a secret account. I think he realized that I feel insecure about money and didn't trust that he would approve of me saving some of my earnings. But when I explained to him how sorry I am and that I promise to never do it again, it made a big difference and we've started to get back on track emotionally and sexually. Jeremy stopped withholding sex because he was no longer holding a grudge and forgave me."

Gradually Jeremy was willing to put his relationship with Susan first, before his own needs, and accept her apology even though he didn't approve of her actions. Jeremy was wise to extend trust to Susan and not automatically assume the worst. In time, they were able to rebuild trust by taking responsibility for their own reactions and changing their mistrustful mind-sets by giving each other the benefit of the doubt. Jeremy realized that due to Susan's past, she needed more control over her income. So they came up with a budget that allowed her to continue saving some of her earnings. Jeremy also stopped taking Susan's actions personally, so he felt less angry and hurt.

For instance, when Jeremy began thinking like a forgiving person, he was able to adopt a perspective that assumes it's possible that Susan simply made an error in judgment by not telling him about her secret savings account. Jeremy also realized that Susan wasn't hurting him intentionally. Rather, she believed she couldn't be completely open and honest with him because he expressed concern about her spending in the past and she feared losing him.

When Susan was able to confess her wrongdoing and ask Jeremy to forgive her, this had a positive effect on his ability to regain trust in her and a healing effect on their remarriage. Susan promised not to keep financial secrets from Jeremy, and he realized he could grant her forgiveness but not condone her behavior. In order to accept her apology, Jeremy had to let go of his self-righteousness that was causing him to want vindication or some sort of justice. He realized that Susan's happiness, and ultimately his own, were more important than being right. As a result, he could deal with his wounded trust and hurt feelings more effectively and get back to feeling loving toward Susan.

Psychologist Susan David, author of *Emotional Agility*, explains what happens when couples don't practice forgiveness. She says, "That same need to have the rightness of your cause validated, or your unjust treatment confirmed, can steal years from your life when you let it persist." She reminds us that in many families and many countries of the world, feuds have endured for so long that no one can actually remember the original misunderstanding. She continues, "Ironically this merely prolongs the injustice, because you're depriving yourself of other good things that you value, such as the warm connection of family or friends."

Truth be told, many mistakes are not intentional, so it is best not to make them into something they're not. Listen to your partner's side of the story and avoid blaming or criticizing them when you confront them with your concerns. One of the biggest problems with ongoing resentment in remarriage is that it often leads to withdrawal and poor communication. And if you are often bottling up feelings of anger, sadness, or disappointment, this can lead to feelings of resentment.

Five Tips to Let Go of Resentment Toward Your Partner

1. **Write down three ways your hurt feelings have impacted (or are still impacting) your life.** Gain awareness of the emotions you experience about your past hurt. Talking to a close friend or therapist can help facilitate this process.

2. **Find a way to dislodge yourself from negative emotions.** Examples include therapy, yoga, improving your physical health, and practicing expressing thoughts, feelings, and wishes in a respectful way. Resentment can build when people sweep things under the rug, so be vulnerable and don't bury negative feelings.

3. **Take small steps to let go of grudges or grievances.** Repair the damage by finding ways to soothe hurt feelings. This might include writing a letter to the person who injured you—even if you don't mail it. Your letter might read something like "I release you from the pain you caused me when we used to argue."

4. **Don't let wounds fester.** Challenge your beliefs and self-defeating thoughts about holding on to hurt feelings. Processing what happened briefly will allow you to let resentments go so you can move on to a healthier relationship. Keep the big picture in mind.

5. **Accept that people do the best they can and attempt to be more understanding.** This doesn't mean that you condone the hurtful actions of others. You simply come to a more realistic view of your past. As you take stock, you will realize that all people operate out of the same basic drives, including self-interest.

THE WRONG WAY TO APOLOGIZE

You may stubbornly hold on to the belief that you have nothing to apologize for—especially if your hurtful behavior or words were not intentional. Meanwhile, your partner may be suffering and you are preventing healing and reconciliation from taking place. When Jenna and Kurt, whom you met earlier, would argue about her tendency to feel left out, their fights would get intense and harsh words would be exchanged. For a few years, they didn't understand the importance of repairing hurt feelings and so apologies weren't part of their dialogue. One day, when Kurt was heading out to work and they were arguing, Jenna accused him of ignoring her, and she yelled some obscenities. She waited two days to apologize, and when she did, she said, "I'm sorry you overreacted to my comments," which came across as insincere and made Kurt feel angrier. As a result, he carried around resentment for several days, clammed up, and refused to discuss their marriage or his stepson with her.

In this situation, Jenna's apology didn't have the effect she was looking for and perhaps made matters worse. If you do apologize to your partner, be sure to do it in a way that doesn't include excuses for your actions or words. Not all apologies will be the same, but most will contain some important elements. It's not about proving a point; if you want your relationship to flourish, you simply need to come to a more compassionate and realistic view of your marriage. When you acknowledge your flaws—the things that make you human—you can be vulnerable with your partner rather than allowing your fear of rejection or failure to overwhelm you. According to Harriet Lerner, there are five ways you can ruin an apology. The following ways have been adapted from her book *Why Won't You Apologize?*

Five Ways to Ruin an Apology

1. **Tagging a "but" onto it.** When people add a disclaimer to the end of the apology, such as "I'm sorry I yelled at you when I came home from work and dinner wasn't made, but I had a really bad day," this definitely waters down your apology and comes across as an excuse.

2. **Saying "I'm sorry you feel this way."** This phrase weakens your apology and comes across as insincere. A genuine apology keeps the focus on your actions rather than the other person's response. It holds you accountable and is more easily accepted by the person who feels hurt.

3. **Forcing an unwanted apology.** When your partner has shut down and let you know through their actions or words that they are not interested in hearing another word from you, back off and give it another try when they appear receptive. In other words, don't try to force an apology on your mate. Give them time to recover.

4. **Offering an overstated or manipulative apology.** Saying something like "Can you ever forgive me for being a horrible person?" or "My greatest fear is losing you, can you ever forgive me?" is overkill. It's out of proportion and comes across as manipulative. Manipulative apologies often include an "if," such as "I'm sorry if you took what I said the wrong way."

5. **Demanding forgiveness.** It takes time for most people to process hurt feelings and to be receptive to accepting a sincere apology with open arms. Asking yourself how you would feel if you

were walking in your partner's shoes will enhance your empathy and willingness to give them time to be open to listening to a genuine apology.

HOW DO I APOLOGIZE?

Practicing forgiveness allows you to turn the corner from feeling like a victim to having a more empowered remarriage. Experts believe that apologizing and forgiving your partner can allow you to break the cycle of pain, move on with your life, and embrace a healthier relationship. However, forgiveness takes time and has a lot to do with letting go of those things you have no control over. Perhaps the first step is being able to offer your partner a sincere apology—that is, saying you're sorry and meaning it.

In my remarriage, practicing forgiveness has never been easy because we both tend to be self-righteous and have difficulty letting go of trying to prove we're "right." However, as we learn more about each other and accept our imperfections, we see the beauty and value of adopting forgiveness as part of our daily practice of having a fulfilling marriage.

Seven Effective Ways to Apologize to Your Partner

1. **Identify two reasons you feel sorry for the hurt that your behavior or words caused your partner.** Gaining awareness of the emotions you experience about your own past hurt can help you feel empathy for your partner. Ask yourself, "Why did I feel the need to behave in a way that caused my partner pain or upset? Was my behavior intentional?"

2. **Accept responsibility for your hurtful actions or words and the damage you caused.** Acknowledge that you messed up by saying something like "I take responsibility for my actions and I'm sorry that they hurt you." One person's ability to do this can change the dynamic of the relationship and help you recover and heal as a couple.

3. **Use the words "I am sorry" and "I was wrong" when you apologize, and make it personal.** Your apology will more likely be heard and accepted if you use these words. Be specific about exactly what you did to hurt, humiliate, or embarrass your partner. For example, "I'm sorry for hurting you and violating your trust. I was wrong when I embarrassed you in front of your friend and I am sorry for my unkind words."

4. **Explain to your partner how you plan to repair the situation (if this is possible).** For example, if you said something to hurt your mother-in-law's feelings, you might offer to apologize to her over lunch or by writing her a note.

5. **Describe what you said or did in specific terms without making excuses or blaming your mate or someone else.** Using "I" statements rather than "you" statements can help you avoid the blame monster. For instance, you might say "I'm sorry for yelling at you when dinner wasn't ready at our usual time. I'm very sorry for treating you this way." This is more effective than saying, "You promised to have dinner ready at 6:00 p.m. and it aggravated me when you didn't keep your promise. I was hungry, and you weren't being thoughtful."

6. **Ask your partner to grant you forgiveness.** Be specific about your actions and words that need to be forgiven. Be sure to do so when the setting is conducive to a private conversation and there aren't any distractions (TV, cell phones, children in the room, etc.).

7. **Don't let wounds poison your love for your spouse.** Be vulnerable and don't let your pride cause you to hold on to being "right." Discussing what happened with your spouse and taking responsibility for your actions will allow you to let go of resentment, so you can improve the quality of your relationship.

Heartfelt apologies are an essential ingredient of a strong, healthy second marriage. Accepting that you and your mate do the best you can will help you be more understanding. When you acknowledge your flaws, it means that you can be vulnerable with your partner rather than allowing your fear of rejection or failure to overwhelm you or lead to a grievance story.

Granting your partner forgiveness is not letting them off the hook. It doesn't mean you approve of their actions. But by showing compassion toward your partner when you feel they've wronged you, you let go of your anger, bitterness, and resentment. In doing so, you give them less power over you. You are letting your partner know your relationship matters and you're giving them the benefit of the doubt. And by asking for forgiveness, you show that you're aware when your actions or words have been hurtful and you're able to be vulnerable enough to give a genuine apology.

Tara and Conner's story, which is woven throughout the pages of this book, demonstrates the ongoing challenges and joys of remarriage, as well as the power of forgiveness. Raising three children in a stepfamily and pursuing demanding careers, they've overcome many hurdles and successfully mastered the art of apologizing and granting forgiveness in their ten years of remarriage. During our last meeting, Conner said it best when he commented on his greatest triumph as a husband, stepfather, and father to their mutual son, Michael, age 3.

Conner puts it like this: "It's not that we don't argue, but we're no longer trying to change each other. I think Tara and I have had a stronger marriage since we've accepted each other, and we try to move beyond petty issues. I guess, for me, it's accepting that no one is perfect and that I've made errors being a stepdad and husband, but that doesn't mean I should stop trying. We do our best to remember we both have a past that affects us, but we are living in the here and now."

Tara and Conner's story is a reminder of a lesson that I learned throughout the writing of this book: the greatest gift you can give your partner is to love them enough to apologize and grant them forgiveness. A healthy, long-lasting remarriage is within your reach if you can risk being vulnerable, because it's the price you pay for intimacy. Being generous with saying you're sorry will allow you and your partner to move beyond daily setbacks and overcome the corrosive effects of past relationships and everyday hurts and disappointments.

Following the action steps below will guide you in your journey toward "unlearning" toxic patterns of relating and moving on to a place of love and healing in your remarriage!

Four Action Steps to Practice Forgiveness

1. Accept that you and your partner will make mistakes, and it is a given that you will need to recover from them by apologizing and granting forgiveness.

2. Let go of any preconceived notions that someone has to be to blame for a miscommunication, argument, or a setback in your family or marriage.

3. Show your partner by word and deed that you're willing to learn from your mistakes and that you're interested in being vulnerable and sharing your thoughts, feelings, and desires without judgment, disrespect, or malice.

4. Practice both offering an apology and accepting one from your partner. It may feel unnatural if you aren't accustomed to it, but you'll feel more comfortable over time.

Apologizing and granting forgiveness are about giving yourself and your partner the kind of future you and they deserve, unhampered by hurt and recycled anger. It's about choosing to live a life wherein others don't have power over you and you're not dominated by unresolved anger, bitterness, and resentment. Conflict isn't a bad thing in relationships, and differences don't have to lead to a breakup. Successful remarried couples remember to give each other the benefit of the doubt and learn effective ways to repair hurt feelings as they heal the wounds of the past in the present.

As the stories of the remarried couples in this book have shown you, if you want a better marriage, start by accepting your partner for who they are, listen with a generous heart, and communicate your own needs in a loving, respectful way. Instead of trying to change them, be the change you want to see in your relationship. Be sure to remain open to accepting your partner's influence as you grow stronger in your commitment to cherish each other daily. And always remember that by having the wisdom to say you're sorry and mean it, you'll be paving the way for a happy remarriage that endures the test of time!

Acknowledgments

Writing this book would not have been possible without the support of so many people. First, I want to express gratitude to my husband, Craig, who gave me another chance at happiness when he proposed to me over two decades ago. His confidence in my ability to write a guidebook for other remarried couples never wavered, even as he gently nudged me to unplug after a long day of interviewing couples and drafting their stories.

I am deeply grateful to all of the remarried couples who shared their experiences with me. Their voices form the heart of this book and are testimonies to their courage and vision for a better marriage the second time around.

The Remarriage Manual would never have existed without the steadfast support of my agent, Jacqueline Flynn, of Joelle Delbourgo Associates, who inspired me to write it during long conversations when I shared the joys and challenges of my own remarriage. I'm forever grateful for her patience and belief in my dream of inspiring other remarried couples to find lasting love.

Thanks to Joelle Delbourgo, who sent me many encouraging emails and took the time to share dozens of my articles on social media. I'm grateful for her faith in me over the last decade.

And thanks to Caroline Pincus, my thoughtful and talented editor at Sounds True, who patiently encouraged me to revise the manuscript to its current state.

I appreciate my dear friends Betsy Dees, Dale Rheault, Barbara Lamagna, Janet Oakley, and Kathy Leisge, who kept me going with their freshly brewed mugs of coffee and encouraging words during the writing of this book.

I am grateful to James Emond, reference librarian, who gave me countless hours of support while researching *The Remarriage Manual* at Bristol Community College.

Thanks to all of my friends at the Portsmouth Free Public Library, who provided a comfortable space and support during the three years that it took to write *The Remarriage Manual*. Special gratitude to Sue Rousseau, reference librarian, for her kindness, wisdom, and technical support.

And thanks to my colleague and mentor Roger Clark, PhD, professor of sociology at Rhode Island College, who sparked my passion for research and believed in my ability to write my first book, *Daughters of Divorce*. I am deeply grateful for his kindness and confidence in my research and writing skills.

Most importantly, I am grateful for the love and support of my family. Thanks again to Craig for never giving up on me and holding me tight through the book-writing process. And thanks to my three talented and loving children, Sean, Tracy, and Catherine, for being steadfast in your love and belief in me!

Notes

Introduction: An Opportunity to Start Fresh

3   **"and combining, existing families and complex relationship histories"** "Stepfamily Fact Sheet," National Stepfamily Resource Center," accessed June 9, 2019, www.stepfamilies.info/stepfamily-fact-sheet.php.

3   **"and demanding remarriage is"** Patricia L. Papernow, *Surviving and Thriving in Stepfamily Relationships* (New York: Routledge, 2013), 14–24.

Chapter One   Build a Culture of Appreciation, Respect, and Tolerance

9   **"not bound by traditions or outdated models"** Harville Hendrix and Helen LaKelly Hunt, *Making Marriage Simple: 10 Relationship-Saving Truths* (New York: Harmony, 2013), 50.

15   **"even decide to have a mutual child"** Susan D. Stewart, *Brave New Stepfamilies: Diverse Paths Toward Stepfamily Living* (Thousand Oaks, CA: Sage Publications, 2007), 52–64.

18   **"and support each other goes up"** Amanda Lenhart and Maeve Duggins, "Couples, the Internet, and Social Media," Pew Research Center, February 11, 2014, www.pewinternet.org/2014/02/11/couples-the-internet-and-social-media.

20   **"in your relationships with family members"** Lori Cluff Schade et al., "Using Technology to Connect in Romantic Relationships: Effects on Attachment, Relationship Satisfaction, and Stability in Emerging Adults," *Journal of Couple & Relationship Therapy: Innovations in Clinical and Educational Interventions* 12, no. 4 (2013): 313–38.

23   **"with thoughtful remarks"** John Gottman, *Why Marriages Succeed or Fail: And How You Can Make Yours Last* (New York: Fireside, 1994), 206.

Chapter Two   Make Your Remarriage a Top Priority

31   **"and adding children to the mix"** Ted L. Huston et al., "The Connubial Crucible: Newlywed Years as Predictors of Mar*ital Delight, Distress, and Divorce,"* *Journal of Personality and Social Psychology* 80, no. 2 (February 200): 237–52.

32   **"go through tough times together"** John M. Gottman and Joan DeClaire, *The Relationship Cure: A 5-Step Guide to Strengthening Your Marriage, Family, and Friendships* (New York: Harmony, 2001), 22.

34   **"both socially competent and self-reliant"** Diana Baumrind, "Current Patterns of Parental Authority," *Developmental Psychology* 4, no. 1, part 2 (January 1971): 1–103.

34   **"nourish this important couple relationship"** Emily Visher and John S. Visher, *How to Win as a Step-Family*, 2nd ed. (Levittown, PA: Brunner/Mazel, 1982), 77.

36   **"such as buying an expensive gift"** Saeideh Heshmati et al., "What Does It Mean to Feel Loved: Cultural Consensus and Individual Differences in Felt Love," *Journal of Social and Personal Relationships* 3, no. 1 (2019): 214–43.

36   **"your marriage on a daily basis"** E. Mavis Hetherington and John Kelly, *For Better or for Worse: Divorce Reconsidered* (New York: W. W. Norton, 2002), 1–16.

36   **"on a regular, planned basis"** William J. Doherty, *The Intentional Family: Simple Rituals to Strengthen Family Ties* (New York: Quill, 2002), 12–14, 168–87.

37   "satisfying to everyone" Doherty, *Intentional Family*, 12–14, 168–87.

37   "couples who have children spend together" Eli J. Finkel, *The All-or-Nothing Marriage: How the Best Marriages Work* (New York: Dutton, 2017), 22–27.

40   "brings couples closer" Charlotte Reissman, Arthur Aron, and Merlynn R. Bergen, "Shared Activities and Marital Satisfaction: Causal Direction and Self-Expansion Versus Boredom," *Journal of Social and Personal Relationships* 10, no. 2 (1993): 243–54.

41   "ups and downs of remarried life" Doherty, *Intentional Family*, 187.

41   "stress-reducing conversation with your partner" John M. Gottman and Nan Silver, *The Seven Principles that Make Marriage Work: A Practical Guide from the Country's Foremost Relationship Expert* (New York: Three Rivers Press, 1999), 87.

42   "to help you both feel connected" Gottman and Silver, *Seven Principles that Make Marriage Work*, 246–53.

44   "repairing friendship, love, and trust" Gottman and Silver, *Seven Principles of Making Marriage Work*, 87.

44   "hallmarks of a great sex life" Chrisanna Northrup, Pepper Schwartz, and James Witte, *The Normal Bar: The Surprising Secrets of Happy Couples and What They Reveal about Creating a New Normal in Your Relationship* (New York: Harmony, 2013), 35–70, 176–97.

44   "your sense of relationship satisfaction" Julianne Holt-Lunstad, Wendy A. Birmingham, and Kathleen C. Light, "Influence of a 'Warm Touch' Support Enhancement Intervention Among Married Couples on Ambulatory Blood Pressure, Oxytocin, Alpha Amylase, and Cortisol," *Psychosomatic Medicine* 70, no. 9 (November–December 2008): 976–85.

45   "who weren't sexually intimate" Andrea Meltzer et al., "Quantifying the Sexual Afterglow: The Lingering Benefits of Sex and Their Implications for Pair-Bonded Relationships," *Psychological Science* 28, no. 5 (May 1, 2017): 587–98.

51   "to find long-lasting love" John M. Gottman and Julie Schwartz Gottman, *The Science of Couples and Family Therapy: Behind the Scenes of the Love Lab* (New York: W. W. Norton, 2018), 144–76.

Chapter Three   Ditch the Baggage from Your First Marriage

61   **"takes insight and great courage"** Sigmund Freud, *A General Introduction to Psychoanalysis* (New York: Renaissance Classics, 2002), 213–24.

62   **"each of you gets your needs met"** Harville Hendrix and Helen LaKelly Hunt, *Making Marriage Simple: 10 Relationship-Saving Truths* (New York: Harmony, 2013), 20.

64   **"to make sense of the change"** Sue Johnson, *Hold Me Tight: Your Guide to the Most Successful Approach to Building Loving Relationships* (London: Piatkus, 2008), 105.

69   **"if it's intense, it's your own"** Mona Barbera, *Bring Yourself to Love: How Couples Can Turn Disconnection Into Intimacy* (Boston: Dos Monos Press, 2008), 80.

69   **"tangled up with your partner"** Barbera, *Bring Yourself to Love*, xxiv.

70   **"remarriage you need to thrive"** Patricia L. Papernow, *Surviving and Thriving in Stepfamily Relationships* (New York: Routledge, 2013), 13.

Chapter Four   Don't Keep Secrets about Money

74   **"lives intermingle over time"** Patricia Schiff Estess, *Money Advice for Your Successful Remarriage: Handling Delicate Financial Issues Intelligently and Lovingly* (New York: ASJA Press, 2001), 95–117.

74   **"reason why couples divorce"** Lawrence H. Gagnon and Marilyn Coleman, "Preparing for Remarriage: Anticipating the Issues, Seeking Solutions," *Family Relations: Interdisciplinary Journal of Applied Family Science* 38, no. 1 (January 1989): 28–33.

76   **"have committed financial infidelity"** "Celebrate Relationships, but Beware of Financial Infidelity," National Endowment for Financial Education, February 14, 2018, www.nefe.org/press-room/polls/2018/celebrate-relationships-but-beware-of-financial-infideltiy.aspx

82   **"toward financial harmony"** Mary Hunt, *Debt-Proof Your Marriage: How to Manage Your Money Together* (Grand Rapids, MI: Revell, 2016), 50.

86   **"foundation of a strong marriage"** Schiff Estess, *Money Advice for Your Successful Remarriage*, 39–59.

87   **"argue about money regularly"** The Fidelity Investments Couples & Money Study (formerly known as the Couples Retirement Study) analyzed retirement and financial expectations and preparedness among 1,662 couples. This biennial study was launched in 2007 and this data was fielded in April 2018. A couples guide and fact sheet can be found at www.fidelity.com/bin-public/060_www_fidelity_com/documents/pr/couples-fact-sheet.pdf.

87   **"financial success in your remarriage"** Hunt, *Debt-Proof Your Marriage*, 141–70.

89   **"used for beverages, snacks, etc."** Schiff Estess, *Money Advice for Your Successful Remarriage*, 81–94.

89   **"for your remarried family"** Hunt, *Debt-Proof Your Marriage*, 97–102.

89   **"two-pot economic system"** Barbara Fishman, "The Economic Behavior of Stepfamilies," *Family Relations: Interdisciplinary Journal of Applied Family Science* 32, no. 3 (July 1983): 359–66.

90   **"their financial management styles"** Kay Pasley, Eric Sandras, and Mary Ellen Edmondson, "The Effects of Financial Management Strategies on Quality of Family Life in Remarriage," *Journal of Family and Economic Issues* 15, no. 1 (Spring 1994): 53–70.

90   **"avoid dealing with these issues"** Chelsea L. Garneau, Brian Higginbotham, and Francesca Adler-Baeder, "Remarriage Beliefs as Predictors of Marital Quality and Positive Interaction in Stepcouples: An Actor-Partner Interdependence Model," *Family Process* 54, no. 4 (December 2015): 730–45.

94   **"competing for resources"** Anne C. Bernstein, *Yours, Mine, and Ours: How Families Change When Remarried Parents Have a Child Together* (New York: W.W. Norton & Co., 1989), 293-298.

96   **"furniture, and family mementos"** Schiff Estess, *Money Advice for Your Successful Remarriage*, 81–94, 121–29.

97   **"a couple and find happiness"** John M. Gottman and Julie Schwartz Gottman, *The Science of Couples and Family Therapy: Behind the Scenes of the Love Lab* (New York: W. W. Norton, 2018), 144–59.

Chapter Five   Don't Let Mistrust Stop You from Being Vulnerable and Intimate

103   **"infidelity and betrayal"** Sue Johnson, *Hold Me Tight: Your Guide to the Most Successful Approach to Building Loving Relationships* (London: Piatkus, 2008), 29–30.

103   **"not getting your needs met"** Johnson, *Hold me Tight*, 29–38.

104   **"things don't work out"** Brené Brown, *Daring Greatly: How the Courage to Be Vulnerable Transforms the Way We Live, Love, Parent, and Lead* (New York: Gotham Books, 2012), 34.

104   **"feeling is a weakness"** Brown, *Daring Greatly*, 33.

106   **"the primal panic mode"** Johnson, *Hold Me Tight*, 129–31.

108   **"erodes trust in a relationship"** Brown, *Daring Greatly*, 52.

110   **"turn toward each other"** John M. Gottman, *The Science of Trust: Emotional Attunement for Couples* (New York: W. W. Norton, 2011), 30.

110   **"way to deepen intimacy"** Gottman, *Science of Trust*, 197–201.

Chapter Six   Get Sexy and Fall in Love All Over Again

122   **"he or she behaves"** Andrew G. Marshall, *I Love You But I'm Not In Love with You* (Deerfield Beach, FL: Health Communications, 2007), 13.

122   **"by elation and passion"** Dorothy Tennov, *Love and Limerence: The Experience of Being in Love* (Lanham, MD: Scarborough House, 1998), 16.

122   **"not accepting each other's differences"** Marshall, *I Love You*, 3–22.

124   **"we will examine it closely"** Harriet Lerner, *Marriage Rules: A Manual for the Married and the Coupled Up* (New York: Gotham Books, 2012), 72.

124   **"three 'demon dialogues'"** Sue Johnson, *Hold Me Tight: Your Guide to the Most Successful Approach to Building Loving Relationships* (London: Piatkus, 2008), 31.

124   **"four or five years"** John M. Gottman and Julie Schwartz Gottman, *The Science of Couples and Family Therapy: Behind the Scenes of the Love Lab* (New York: W. W. Norton, 2018), 144–59.

124 **"second marriage or subsequent intimate relationships"**
Gottman and Gottman, *Science of Couples and Family Therapy*, 144–59.

125 **"and another being the distancer"** Laurie J. Watson, *Wanting Sex Again: How to Rediscover Your Desire and Heal a Sexless Marriage* (New York: Berkley Books, 2012), 6.

126 **"their marriage is doomed to fail"** John M. Gottman and Nan Silver, *Why Marriages Succeed or Fail: And How to Make Yours Last* (New York: Simon and Schuster,1994), 68–103.

126 **"walk in their partner's shoes"** Watson, *Wanting Sex Again*, 46–49.

128 **"turning toward each other"** Chrisanna Northrup, Pepper Schwartz, and James Witte, *The Normal Bar: The Surprising Secrets of Happy Couples and What They Reveal about Creating a New Normal in Your Relationship* (New York: Harmony, 2013), 35–70.

129 **"desire a satisfying sex life"** Northrup, Schwartz, and Witte, *Normal Bar*, 35–91.

129 **"does not last forever"** Michele Weiner Davis, *The Sex-Starved Marriage: Boosting Your Marriage Libido* (New York: Simon and Schuster, 2003), 3–17.

133 **"affectionate touch as well"** Julianne Holt-Lunstad, Wendy A. Birmingham, and Kathleen C. Light, "Influence of a 'Warm Touch' Support Enhancement Intervention Among Married Couples on Ambulatory Blood Pressure, Oxytocin, Alpha Amylase, and Cortisol," *Psychosomatic Medicine* 70, no. 9 (November–December 2008): 976–85.

135 **"start running (distance)"** David Schnarch, *Passionate Marriage: Keeping Love and Intimacy Alive in Intimate Relationships* (New York: W. W. Norton, 2009), 322–53.

Chapter Seven   Don't Make a Big Deal about Nothing . . . But Do Deal with Important Issues

138 **"or a failure of love"** Deborah Tannen, *That's Not What I Meant: How Conversational Style Makes or Breaks a Relationship* (New York: Ballantine, 1986), 113–14.

138 **"context of a loving remarriage"** Tannen, *That's Not What I Meant*, 113.

140   "**information we hear**" Howard J. Markman, Scott M. Stanley, and Susan L. Blumberg, *Fighting for Your Marriage: The Best-Selling Marriage and Divorce Prevention Book* (San Francisco: Jossey-Bass, 2001), 91–104.

143   "**we can let go of a lot**" Harriet Lerner, *The Dance of Connection: How to Talk to Someone When You're Mad, Hurt, Scared, Frustrated, Insulted, Betrayed, or Desperate* (New York: Harper, 2001), 136–38.

144   "**a huge difference**" John M. Gottman and Julie Schwartz Gottman, *The Science of Couples and Family Therapy: Behind the Scenes of the Love Lab* (New York: W. W. Norton, 2018), 205.

145   "**how happy your marriage will be**" Markman, Stanley, and Blumberg, *Fighting for Your Marriage*, 91–104.

146   "**and avoiding or stonewalling**" John M. Gottman and Nan Silver, *Why Marriages Succeed or Fail: And How to Make Yours Last* (New York: Simon and Schuster, 1994), 68–103.

147   "**respect between partners**" Daniel B. Wile, *After the Fight: Using Your Disagreements to Build a Stronger Relationship* (New York: Guilford Press, 1993), 89–99.

149   "**you need five positive ones**" John M. Gottman, *The Science of Trust, Emotional Attunement for Couples* (New York: W. W. Norton, 2011), 15–17.

152   "**couples feel more connected**" Gottman and Silver, *Seven Principles for Making Marriage Work*, 87–92.

Chapter Eight   Manage the Flames of Conflict

157   "**conflict from escalating**" John M. Gottman and Nan Silver, *The Seven Principles for Making Marriage Work: A Practical Guide from the Country's Foremost Relationship Expert* (New York: Three Rivers Press, 1999), 22–23.

157   "**way to avoid resentment**" Gottman and Silver, *Seven Principles for Making Marriage Work*, 2–24.

159   "**damage to your marriage**" Howard J. Markman, Scott M. Stanley, and Susan L. Blumberg, *Fighting for Your Marriage: The Best-Selling Marriage and Divorce Prevention Book* (San Francisco: Jossey-Bass, 2001), 138–51.

159   **"withdrawal and avoidance"** Markman, Stanley, and Blumberg, *Fighting for Your Marriage*, 43–66.

161   **"couples have repair skills"** John M. Gottman and Julie Schwartz Gottman, *The Science of Couples and Family Therapy: Behind the Scenes of the Love Lab* (New York: W. W. Norton, 2018), 151.

162   **"who can't reciprocate"** Ross Rosenberg, *The Human Magnet Syndrome: Why We Love People Who Hurt Us* (Eau Claire, WI: PESI, 2013), 3–23.

163   **"main causes of divorce"** John M. Gottman and Nan Silver, *Why Marriages Succeed or Fail: and How to Make Yours Last* (New York: Simon and Schuster, 1994), 13–31.

164   **"withdraw or distance"** Paul Schrodt, Paul L. Witt, and Jenna R. Shimkowski, "A Meta-Analytical Review of the Demand/Withdraw Pattern of Interaction and Its Associations with Individual, Relational, and Communicative Outcomes," *Communication Monographs* 81, no. 1 (2014): 28

164   **"any successful relationship"** Harriet Lerner, *Marriage Rules: A Manual for the Married and Coupled Up* (New York: Gotham Books, 2012), 95.

166   **"safety and goodwill"** Daniel B. Wile, *After the Fight: Using Your Disagreements to Build a Stronger Relationship* (New York: Guilford Press, 1993) 167–98.

Chapter Nine   Embrace Your Role as a Stepparent and Create Positive Stepfamily Memories

179   **"reconciling the two"** Karen Horney, *Neurosis and Human Growth: The Struggle Toward Self-Realization* (New York: W. W. Norton, 1991), 64–85.

182   **"much of a payoff"** E. Mavis Hetherington and John Kelly, *For Better or for Worse: Divorce Reconsidered* (New York: W. W. Norton, 2002), 193.

184   **"when their dads remarried"** Constance Ahrons, *We're Still Family: What Grown Children Have to Say about Their Parents' Divorce* (New York: HarperCollins, 2004), 134.

184   "adolescents residing in stepfamilies" Valarie King, Lisa M. Boyd, and Maggie L. Thorsen, "Adolescents' Perceptions of Family Belonging in Stepfamilies," *Journal of Marriage and Family* 77, no. 3 (June 2015): 761–74.

186   "well-established stepfamilies" Patricia L. Papernow, *Surviving and Thriving in Stepfamily Relationships* (New York: Routledge, 2013), 27–42.

193   "a child between them" Kay Pasley and Michelle Lee, "Stress and Coping Within the Context of Stepfamily Life," in *Families and Change: Families Coping with Stressful Events and Transitions*, 4th ed., ed. Sharon J. Price, Christine A. Price, and Patrick C. McKenry (London: Sage, 2010), 235–61.

193   "a younger half sibling" Lawrence H. Ganong and Marilyn Coleman, "Do Mutual Children Cement Bonds in Stepfamilies?" *Journal of Marriage and the Family* 50, no. 3 (August 1988): 687–98.

193   "of family solidarity" Anne C. Bernstein, *Yours, Mine, and Ours: How Families Change When Remarried Parents Have a Child Together* (New York: W. W. Norton, 1989), 23.

193   "initial period of adjustment" Bernstein, *Yours, Mine, and Ours*, 34–36.

195   "all family members" Papernow, *Surviving and Thriving*, 34.

196   "and What Doesn't" Bruce Feiler, *The Secrets of Happy Families* (London: Piatkus, 2013), 14–32.

Chapter Ten   Say You're Sorry and Mean It

201   "move on from mistakes" Frank D. Fincham, Julie Hall, and Steven R.H. Beach, "Forgiveness in Marriage: Current Status and Future Directions," *Family Relations: Interdisciplinary Journal for Applied Family Science* 55, no. 4 (October 2006): 415–27.

203   "is inflicting them" Gay Hendricks and Kathlyn Hendricks, *Conscious Loving: The Journey to Co-Commitment* (New York: Bantam, 1990), 42–43.

204   "a stronger relationship" John M. Gottman, *The Science of Trust: Emotional Attunement for Couples* (New York: W. W. Norton, 2011), 27–28.

208   **"then let it go"** Fred Luskin, *Forgive for Good: A Proven Prescription for Health and Happiness* (New York: HarperOne, 2002), 33–44.

209   **"feel relieved and soothed"** Harriet Lerner, *Why Won't You Apologize? Healing Big Betrayals and Everyday Hurts* (New York: Touchstone, 2017), 2.

211   **"process by apologizing"** Janis Abrahms Spring, *How Can I Forgive You? The Courage to Forgive, the Freedom Not To* (New York: Perennial, 2004), 4–5.

211   **"who is injured"** Abrahms Spring, *How Can I Forgive You?* 15–35.

211   **"rise to the challenge"** Abrahms Spring, *How Can I Forgive You?* 54–115.

211   **"suffering is magnified"** Luskin, *Forgive for Good*, 201.

211   **"have in the present"** Luskin, *Forgive for Good*, 111.

214   **"you let it persist"** Susan David, *Emotional Agility: Get Unstuck, Embrace Change, and Thrive in Work and Life* (New York: Avery, 2016), 38–39.

214   **"family or friends"** David, *Emotional Agility*, 38–39.

217   **"listening to a genuine apology"** Lerner, *Why Won't You Apologize?* 13–24.

Recommended Reading List

Berger, Marcia Naomi. *Marriage Meetings for Lasting Love: 30 Minutes a Week to the Relationship You've Always Wanted.* Novato, CA: New World Library, 2014.

Coleman, Joshua. *The Marriage Makeover: Finding Happiness in Imperfect Harmony.* New York: St. Martin's Griffin, 2003.

Gottman, John M., and Julie Schwartz Gottman. *8 Dates: Essential Conversations for a Lifetime of Love.* New York: Workman, 2019.

Gottman, John M., and Nan Silver. *The Seven Principles for Making Marriage Work: A Practical Guide from the Country's Foremost Relationship Expert.* New York: Three Rivers Press, 1999.

Hendrix, Harville, and Helen LaKelly Hunt. *Making Marriage Simple: 10 Relationship Saving Truths.* New York: Harmony, 2013.

Hunt, Mary. *Debt-Proof Your Marriage: How to Manage Your Money Together.* Grand Rapids, MI: Revell, 2016.

Johnson, Sue. *Hold Me Tight: Your Guide to the Most Successful Approach to Building Loving Relationships.* London: Piatkus, 2008.

Lerner, Harriet. *Marriage Rules: A Manual for the Married and the Coupled Up*. New York: Gotham Books, 2012.

Schiff Estess, Patricia. *Money Advice for Your Successful Remarriage*. New York: ASJA Press, 2001.

Watson, Laurie J. *Wanting Sex Again: How to Rediscover Your Desire and Heal a Sexless Marriage*. New York: Berkley Books, 2012.

Weiner Davis, Michele. *The Sex-Starved Marriage: Boosting Your Marriage Libido*. New York: Simon and Schuster, 2003.

Index

About the Author

erry Gaspard, MSW, LICSW, is a licensed therapist with over thirty years of clinical experience specializing in children, individuals, couples, families, divorce, and remarriage, as well as an author, nonfiction writer, and college instructor. She is a popular speaker who frequently offers commentary on divorce, marriage, remarriage, and relationship issues. Two of Terry's research studies on adult children of divorce have been published in the *Journal of Divorce and Remarriage*. Her book *Daughters of Divorce: Overcome the Legacy of Your Parents' Breakup and Enjoy a Happy, Long-Lasting Relationship* was published by Sourcebooks in 2016. She is the owner of movingpastdivorce.com and a regular contributor to the *Gottman Relationship Blog*, Patheos.com, marriage.com, thegoodmenproject. com, divorcedmoms.com, and divorcemagazine.com.

About Sounds True

Sounds True is a multimedia publisher whose mission is to inspire and support personal transformation and spiritual awakening. Founded in 1985 and located in Boulder, Colorado, we work with many of the leading spiritual teachers, thinkers, healers, and visionary artists of our time. We strive with every title to preserve the essential "living wisdom" of the author or artist. It is our goal to create products that not only provide information to a reader or listener but also embody the quality of a wisdom transmission.

For those seeking genuine transformation, Sounds True is your trusted partner. At SoundsTrue.com you will find a wealth of free resources to support your journey, including exclusive weekly audio interviews, free downloads, interactive learning tools, and other special savings on all our titles.

To learn more, please visit SoundsTrue.com/freegifts or call us toll-free at 800.333.9185.

In loving memory of Beth Skelley, book designer extraordinaire.
Her spirit lives on in our books and in our hearts.

sounds true
WAKING UP THE WORLD